Mapping the Wessex Novel

Also available from Continuum

London Narratives, Lawrence Phillips
Wessex, Barbara Yorke

Mapping the Wessex Novel

Landscape, History and the Parochial in
British Literature, 1870–1940

Andrew Radford

continuum

Continuum International Publishing Group

The Tower Building	80 Maiden Lane
11 York Road	Suite 704
London SE1 7NX	New York NY 10038

www.continuumbooks.com

First published 2010
Paperback edition first published 2012

British Library Cataloguing-in-Publication Data
A catalogue record for this book is available from the British Library.

ISBN: 978-0-8264-3968-0 (hardcover)
   978-1-4411-3159-1 (paperback)

Library of Congress Cataloging-in-Publication Data
Radford, Andrew D., 1972-
  Mapping the Wessex novel : landscape, history and the parochial in British literature, 1870–1940 / Andrew Radford.
     p. cm.
  Includes bibliographical references and index.
  ISBN 978-1-4411-3159-1 (pbk. : alk. paper) – ISBN 978-1-4411-4833-9 (ebook pdf) – ISBN 978-1-4411-0093-1 (ebook ePub) 1. English fiction—19th century–History and criticism. 2. English fiction—20th century–History and criticism. 3. Wessex (England)—In literature. 4. Landscapes in literature. 5. Local history in literature. 6. Regionalism in literature. I. Title.

  PR868.W47R33 2012
  823'.8099427–dc23

                                                           2011039974

Typeset by Newgen Imaging Systems Pvt Ltd, Chennai, India
Printed and bound in Great Britain

For Lily

Contents

Acknowledgements

Many of the chapters in this book were delivered as seminar papers or at university conferences. I am grateful to the organizers of such events and to those who listened and responded, in particular at the universities of York and Swansea. I am indebted to the British Academy for helping me start and develop this project. Completing the book would not have been possible without the support of colleagues, friends and family. In particular, I would like to thank Roger Ebbatson, Brian Donnelly, Anthony Leyland, Phillip Mallett, Mark Sandy, Ve-Yin Tee and Rhian Williams for generous feedback, information or advice regarding the work-in-progress. I also benefited greatly from the encouragement of Steve Beaumont.

An early draft of Chapter 5 appeared under the following title and I am most grateful to the editors for permission to reproduce the revised material here: 'Excavating a Secret History: Mary Butts and the Return of the Nativist', *Connotations*, vol. 17, no. 1 (2007/2008), 80–108.

List of Abbreviations

The following short-form designations are employed for frequently cited texts.

AL	*After London*
AR	*Ashe of Rings*
AWM	*Armed with Madness*
CC	*The Crystal Cabinet: My Childhood at Salterns*
DFT	*Death of Felicity Taverner*
FFMC	*Far from the Madding Crowd*
GR	*A Glastonbury Romance*
JO	*Jude the Obscure*
Journals	*The Journals of Mary Butts*
MC	*Maiden Castle*
RN	*The Return of the Native*
SH	*The Story of My Heart*
T	'A Tryst at an Ancient Earthwork'
TBS	*Tom Brown's Schooldays*
TMOC	*The Mayor of Casterbridge*
TSWH	*The Scouring of the White Horse*

Chapter 1

Introduction

What Makes a 'West-Country Man'?

O Young England! Young England! You who are born in these racing railroad times, when there's a Great Exhibition, or some monster sight, every year [. . .] why don't you know more of your own birth-places? [. . .] You're all in the ends of the earth, it seems to me [. . .] you don't know your own lanes and woods and fields [. . .] And as for the country legends, the stories of the old gable-ended farmhouses [. . .] they're gone out of date altogether. [. . .]

[. . .] If you will go gadding over half Europe now every holidays, I can't help it. I was born and bred a west-country man, thank God! A Wessex man, a citizen of the noblest Saxon kingdom of Wessex, a regular 'Angular Saxon', the very soul of me *adscriptus glebae* [attached to the soil]. There's nothing like the old country-side for me, and no music like the twang of the real old Saxon tongue, as one gets it fresh from the veritable chaw in the White Horse Vale.

(*TBS* p. 6)

In this impassioned aside, the narrator of Thomas Hughes's 1857 novel *Tom Brown's Schooldays* hails the talismanic appeal of the moniker 'Wessex' and proudly declares himself to be a 'west-country man'. 'Wessex', as one of the kingdoms of Britain's 'Anglo-Saxon heptarchy' (Rogers, 2001, p. 219), operates here as a unit of geographical inspection and a lens through which to ponder the cultural politics of place. For Hughes, the term certifies selfhood, bolsters a communal zeal that never goes 'out of date' (*TBS* p. 6) and hallows 'verities felt lacking in national patrimonies' (Lowenthal, 1997, p. 81). He sees himself as the blithe ambassador of a redemptive, ennobling rustic archive rich in moral precept; not as an inescapably fallible, biased chronicler prone to hedging, hunch and sketchy surmise. Hughes cleaves to supposedly timeless 'traditions'; where other formal 'faith' has become half-hearted, halting and tame, he signals instead ritual devotion to local legacies by reminding his pampered boy readers of plangent 'songs' and vivid 'country legends' (*TBS* pp. 6–7). Hughes, like the keen field archaeologist O. G. S. Crawford half a century later, was conscious that 'the large open area' of Wessex was in prehistoric times 'thickly populated' and 'the centre of gravity of England, to which all roads led' (Crawford, 1921, p. 158). Hughes signals the steady accrual of archaeological data that is passed on through generations not only as visible, concrete vestiges like the powdering of flint flakes and potsherds; but also as a subliminal heritage that is far from austerely impersonal: an agglomeration of benign ancestral echoes, elemental harmonies, fanciful patterns and native auras. For twenty-first century readers whose investment in space and place has been radically reconfigured (or disfigured) by the hectic global circulations of uprooted communities, texts, raw materials and consumer goods, the adjectival form of 'parish' (*TBS* p. 6) is laden with pejorative semantic associations; it often foments bellicose xenophobia, separatist enmity or queasy partisan extremes; retooling folk jamborees and nature conservation into 'an agent' of spitefully petty provincialism (Lowenthal, 1997, p. 63).

When Hardy averred in old age 'that it is better for a writer to know a little bit of the world remarkably well than to know a great part of the world remarkably little' (qtd. in Rowley, 2006, p. 230), he was not espousing a grimly policed boundedness in which an embattled enclave forswears any hint of creative flexibility or 'large views' (*TBS* p. 7). Hughes and Hardy variously chafe against and productively complicate this notion of 'life lived long and quietly in one place' (*GR* p. 547) as if it were the quintessence of dreary finitude. Each shows that the parochialism of Wessex engenders not patronizing pity for the socially retrograde but rather piquant and enticing conditions of possibility. In Mary Butts's novel *Armed with Madness* (1928), 'stretches of very insular behaviour' often provoke 'flashes of illumination, exercises of the senses' (*AWM* p. 6) which confront, process and even corrode hegemonic social, sexual and political discourse. In response to the cultural tensions fostered by rapid material change, John Cowper Powys's *A Glastonbury Romance* (1933) crafts an intensely lyrical feeling of umbilical attachment to the open, undulating grassland, steep-sided valleys and granite moors as 'the secret of the mystic value of the commonplace' (*GR* p. 508). On a cursory reading, this definition of what Mary Butts labels 'local enthusiasms' (*AR* p. 145) merely ordains miniscule fractions, the mundane and the quotidian in a district whose agricultural terraces have been 'made and marked by time' (Hauser, 2007, p. 194). Yet it also exalts a 'narrow aperture' (*GR* p. 969) through which to gauge the outdoor footprints of long-lost prehistoric tribes, as well as fiercely contested ideologies of Englishness (Peltz and Myrone, 1999, pp. 1–13).

In Hughes's novel the 'Wessex soil' is charged with 'far-horizoned meanings' (*GR* p. 821) which throw into bolder relief a cluster of discursive tensions between sober empiricism and ecstatic trance; the cloying cuteness of tourist kitsch and deep, durable institutions; the bustling metropolitan hub and the secluded rural periphery; the seemingly dishevelled present of 'town-tuned nerves' (*AR* p. 137) and the more structured hierarchies of bygone ages. Hughes retools this terrain as part of a wider aesthetic and archaeological campaign to make the humble topography of his barrow-haunted 'birth-place' key to 'the formation' of unswerving national fealty (Corbett, Holt and Russell, 2002, p. ix).

That *Tom Brown's Schooldays* went into at least 70 editions while it remained in copyright implies that Hughes's commitment to the 'noblest Saxon kingdom of Wessex' appealed to a sizeable and sympathetic audience (Young, 2008, p. 7). He is not interested merely in repackaging 'heritage' (*TBS* p. 10); nor does he finesse a hackneyed paean to those 'quiet' and 'dogged' indigenes whose contribution to the 'greatness' of the 'British nation' (*TBS* p. 1) is undervalued. His vehement appeal to 'Young England' manages a swiftly evolving social actuality, and grapples with some intractable quandaries in the history of nostalgia (Young, 2008, pp. 7–9). Could the scattered settlements of Hughes's natal region and the sacramental rhythms of the agricultural year be vehicles of social amelioration as well as traditional worth? Was it possible to verify the respective rights of leisured landowners, tenant farmers, labourers and arriviste-ramblers over the Wessex terrain?

Hughes targets a callow crowd of bourgeois 'boy readers' (*TBS* p. 15) who 'go gadding over' Europe for 'long vacations', taking advantage of improved mobility, to view paintings 'at Dresden and the Louvre' (*TBS* p. 6). He implicitly measures the dead hand of the picturesque and the vapid, inauthentic fad for sightseeing tours abroad against his own fervent sense of local pride in 'these racing railroad times', whose ceaseless flux has brought 'large-scale disruption' to both 'the social fabric and the physical landscape' (Rode, 2006, p. 2). This position, however, is seamed with barely acknowledged contradictions. Advancements in transport technologies and cheap railway tickets permitted more people from poorer backgrounds to savour the visual stimulus of antiquarian excursions. Hughes's reference to the 'railroad times' carries a special inflection given that 1857, the year in which his novel was published, marked the official opening of the Wiltshire, Somerset and Weymouth Railway. By enjoining decentred and displaced 'young cosmopolites', 'belonging to all counties and no countries' (*TBS* p. 7) to appreciate a plentiful archaeological bequest on their doorstep, Hughes seeks to combat the debilitating ennui that he views as a byword for metropolitan modernity. He assigns cultural prestige not to the well-heeled connoisseur's visual pleasure but to the land-labourer's immersion in austere and 'mysterious' chalk 'downs' (*TBS* p. 9). That this hinterland harbours a diffuse, animate and expansive power reflects his sense that a 'proper society' should have 'more affinity' with skills-based, practical and pre-industrial values (Moore-Colyer, 2002, p. 199).

Hughes concedes the aesthetic and practical benefits of foreign travel to 'the present generation' (*TBS* p. 2). Yet he also shows a profound concern with the perils of dislocation from those 'straggling [. . .] old-fashioned villages' (*TBS* p. 8) that epitomize the nearly extinguished virtues of a yeoman past, and where, according to an 1880 commentator, 'the rude old simple heathenism' is 'thinly disguised, and all this, perchance, within hearing of the steam whistle of our modern world' ([Anon.], 'Old Rural Songs and customs', 1880b, p. 245). In his disappointment with the lacklustre, shapeless uniformity of suburban villas, Hughes espouses a politically conservative vision of a return to a quasi-feudal social fabric. According to this paradigm, patrician and free-holding peasants agree to a cooperative partnership in a mutual interchange of commercial initiatives. He describes in particular the 'Saxon' bequest of 'a land of large rich pastures' (*TBS* p. 7), such as that found in his native Uffington, in what is today southwest Oxfordshire. In *Tom Brown's Schooldays* 'out-of-the-way corners' (*TBS* p. 8) becomes 'a microcosm of potential nationhood' (Sanders, *TBS*, p. xxii), in which a corporate organism in the 'social scheme' is 'grounded in the materiality of human life' and the 'artifactual' (Walker and Schiffer, 2006, p. 67).

Instead of being swayed by the gaudy splendour of 'some monster sight' (*TBS* p. 6), Hughes adjures his affluent yet stranded audience to cherish the ingenuous, easygoing camaraderie personified by the rustic sons of his natal region, who are 'bounded' (*TBS* p. 7) by the soil (*adscriptus glebae*), like serfs in a feudal hierarchy (Young, 2008, p. 8). Filiations of memory and custom operate as a much-needed antidote to the haste of the modern machine age, especially the 'iron chariots' of the 'Great Western Railway' (*TBS* p. 5), whose owners approach the barrow-studded locale with a view to speedy acquisition and territorial conquest, rather than obeying the dictates of canny restraint and reciprocity.

Hughes also renders the 'shadowy lanes' and 'footpaths' which move in meandering curves across the country; these tracks promulgate associations of communal comfort between 'the country folk' (*TBS* p. 7), as well as offering a chance to put oneself in 'the perceptual position of ancient wayfarers' (Hauser, 2007, p. 275). *Tom Brown's Schooldays* fashions Wessex as a locus of countless 'routes' – a vibrant mythology of road-lore implying a once flourishing system of trade – as well as ethnic 'roots': subjective impressions, inspired guesswork and cartographic images are all firmly embedded in sheltered 'nooks' (*TBS* p. 8) which trigger a refreshed sense of regional togetherness. Hughes singles out the 'old Roman' Ridgeway, whose origin, according to Richard Jefferies's *Wild Life in a Southern County* (1879) 'goes back into the dimmest antiquity' (p. 52) and operates as a device for intervolving numberless generations, fixing fractured social links and releasing dormant energies. That this key upland track of prehistoric Wessex, running 'for many a long, long mile across the downs' (Jefferies, 1879, p. 52) resembles a 'ruled line' (*TBS* pp. 10–11) in Hughes's territorial frame implies the 'paradoxical ability' of this road 'both to fulfil and to frustrate desire' (Rode, 2006, p. 21) – carrying the whiff of adventure, enticing destinations as well as cheerless restrictions. Hughes signifies that this now largely overgrown but broad causeway encrypts myriad interpersonal engagements, from the most archaic patterns of barter among flint merchants, to the sorties of Roman legionaries and the journeys of thirteenth-century pilgrims. Such 'transactions' have been partially 'ruled out' though by an invading army, whose imperial bureaucracy, with its network of cultural power, patronage and privilege has left indelible signatures on the terrain (Mitchell, 1994, p. 1; Rode, 2006, pp. 1–10). The 'ruled line', in addition to implying how the Roman soldiers 'straightened out' by subjugation the older sinuous tracks, also intimates the narrative connections that lend *Tom Brown's Schooldays* its distinctive momentum.

In Hardy's *The Return of the Native* (1878), treading the old tracks, imaged as interlacing threads of communication, carries with it associations of traversing time and space; revisiting an earlier mindset in which 'feeling[s] go beyond their register' (*RN* p. 263). This notion anticipates Hilaire Belloc's *The Old Road* (1904), R. Hippisley Cox's *The Green Roads of England* (1914) and especially Donald Maxwell's *The Enchanted Road* (1927), all of which represent the 'track' as one of those 'primal things which move us', the 'most imperative and the first of our necessities' (Belloc, 1904, pp. 3–4; Hauser 2007, p. 273). H. J. Massingham magnified this concept in his ethnographic survey of the Wessex 'green roads' in *Downland Man* (1926):

> The track ways join hands with the more ancient of the earthworks, the circles with the barrows [. . .] These are all the leaves, scattered, foxed, torn and barely decipherable, of a single volume, part of a set wrinkled deep in time, written in a foreign language, but very history. And when we have put the leaves together and then the volumes, and read them from first page to last, we shall know many things at last of which we now possess hardly a glimmer, and that knowledge is going to burst the safe and studious walls of the archaeological hermitage and throw its beams upon the world as it is to-day. (Massingham, 1926, p. 62)

Like Hughes, Massingham wears 'the grandiose robes of the prophet' (Massingham, 1926, p. 62), positioning himself as a translator of runic symbols embedded in the wider and deeper heritage of fosses, ramparts and other memorials left by the occupants of pre-Roman Britain.

For John Cowper Powys, the road which carries John Crow across Salisbury Plain in *A Glastonbury Romance*, 'seemed full of human memories. There was not a signpost or a milestone on that wayside but had gathered to itself' some 'encounter of heart-struck lovers' (*GR* pp. 76–77). Similarly, Hughes's 'birth-place', which 'teems with Saxon names and memories' (*TBS* p. 15), is the composite outcome of historical courses, revealing arcane 'biographies' whose 'accretions of meaning' (Thomas, 1996, pp. 78–79) not only limn the 'legends' synonymous with them, but also invite additional 'home-spun' tales (*TBS* p. 1) to them. Hughes's buoyant account posits that a dedication to the 'vague old stories that haunt' this Wessex hinterland (*TBS* p. 5), uncovered, arranged and catalogued by both professional ethnographers and amateur antiquarians, comprises a vital facet of Victorian culture. Far from an effete and sterile exercise in garnering musty 'relics of bygone times' (*TBS* p. 5), Hughes contends that a return *to* the native, 'peeling away multiple layers of past meaning' (Rode, 2006, p. 20) is an attempted resuscitation of the 'Angular' Saxon's extrovert virility, a 'stalwart' trait (*TBS* p. 2) he opines is sadly lacking in his era of brash technological advance, characterized by the 1851 'Great Exhibition' (*TBS* p. 6). Instead Hughes reappraises the seasonal survivals of 'high days', 'holidays and bonfire nights' (*TBS* p. 15), as well as a more natural 'museum' of imperilled artefacts: the 'noblest Saxon Kingdom of Wessex', which boasts the greatest concentration of prehistoric landmarks in Britain, including cromlechs, earth-works, ancient roads, stone-circles and dyked embankments. He draws attention to one spatial site in particular: the 'White Horse Vale' (*TBS* p. 5) which also resonates through Richard Jefferies's 'A Strange Story' (1866), written for the *North Wilts Herald* when he was only 18 years old; as well as his 1880 novel *Greene Ferne Farm*, partially set in the terrain between White Horse Hill and the Marlborough Downs.

The 384-feet long White Horse of Uffington is a chalk figure on the edge of the Berkshire Downs, overlooking the Vale of the White Horse, and was most probably created in the Late Bronze Age, at some point between 1400 and 600 B.C. (Schwyzer, 1999, pp. 42–46). From the twelfth century to the present day, the wonder of the Horse has had less to do with its great antiquity or the resourcefulness of its makers than with 'its stubborn and remarkable survival' (Schwyzer, 1999, p. 45). This 'great Saxon white horse', 'carved out on the northern side of the chalk hill' (*TBS* p. 11) is, according to Hughes, 'sacred ground for Englishmen' (*TBS* p. 10); a site traditionally assumed to commemorate the 'true' son of Wessex King Alfred, and his victory over the 'Danes' at 'Ashdown' (*TBS* p. 10). Hughes adroitly weaves the tale of Alfred and the White Horse into the imaginative fabric of his opening gambit. Of especial note to Hughes is the fact that the endurance of the 'White Horse' has relied upon the ritual rehearsal of communal memory. He describes the periodic weeding and cleaning of the gigantic image, traditionally termed 'scouring', an 'immemorial custom' (*TSWH* p. vii) without which it would have quickly vanished beneath the lush vegetation of White Horse Hill – a fate that overtakes the graven figure in Richard Jefferies's bleak dystopian fable *After London* (1885). According to the *OED*, scouring could refer to the specific act of cleaning out a furrow, trench, ditch or water channel, cut into the earth (Schwyzer, 1999, pp. 42–45). The Berkshire custom of 'scouring' the 'rude colossal figure' (*TSWH* p. x), which has taken place at least once every generation for almost three millennia according to Philip Schwyzer, is quite literally an act of making Wessex novel again: the White Horse is not only a subject of 'antiquarian history'; it adumbrates an intricate chronicle of myriad beginnings, ruptured roots and rancorous blood-feuds across time (Schwyzer, 1999, pp. 45–50).

I propose that literary representations of Wessex can themselves be construed in varying degrees as deliberate acts of 'scouring'; not just a sedulous sifting of local annals but also making them afresh. By installing himself as 'chronicler to the White Horse', Thomas Hughes converts it into something audacious and startling: in the words of the 1859 *Eclectic Review*, he infuses it with 'a rustic relish [. . .] quite inimitable – tersely, strongly Saxon' ([Anon.], 'Scouring', 1859, p. 111). 'Coming down to comparatively modern times', Hughes remarks, 'it is curious that so little notice should have been taken of the White Horse by our antiquaries' (*TSWH* p. 308). What might represent a neglected or occluded history is refurbished so as to project a triumphant regional and national narrative that repeatedly connects sober self-awareness to what Hughes terms 'intense local attachment, love for every stone and turf of the country where' he was 'born and bred' (*TSWH* pp. vii–viii). This undertaking transcends the dedicated antiquarian's fussy reconstruction as 'creation', according to Vernon Lee:

> Is not what we think of as the Past – what we discuss, describe, and so often passionately love – a mere creation of our own? Not merely in its details, but in what is far more important, in its essential, emotional, and imaginative quality and value? Perhaps some day psychology may discover that we have a craving, like that which produces music or architecture, for a special state of nerves [. . .], obtainable by a special human product called the Past – the Past which has never been the Present. (Lee, 1904, pp. 196–97)

In her 1904 essay 'Puzzles of the Past' Lee posits that instead of carrying frozen fragments across the waves of time, the 'Past' is a sumptuous 'product' of canny aesthetic fashioning coupled with the scope and depth of 'emotional' affinity. Hughes concedes in *The Scouring of the White Horse* that he 'has no knowledge whatsoever of the Anglo-Saxon tongue, or of Saxon and other antiquities' (*TSWH* p. x). Yet it is his adroit merging of literary invention and keen affiliation with landmarks of local topography – his sincere 'love' for a 'quiet corner' of the region of his 'birth' (*TSWH* p. x) – that fuels Hughes's imaginative archaeology. He strives to broker a more rewarding link between Wessex and its inhabitants given that the relationship between these remote hamlets and the historical locale is mutually defining. This effort 'to let no old custom, which has a meaning, however rude, die out, if it can be kept alive' (*TSWH* p. xii) has been construed as a frantic salvaging of the mental and physical heirlooms of his ancestors. But it is more accurate to call this project a restless seeking out of ancestral imprints which offer fructifying possibilities for his art.

Scouring the Regional Past

Hughes's concept of regional belonging and his portrayal of the 'West Country' as a locus of genuine, densely layered and active cultural vitality have profound implications for the writers addressed in this book – Thomas Hardy, Richard Jefferies, John Cowper Powys and Mary Butts – all of whom share an enthralled fascination with material history, especially that of archaeology. 'Rub the map and civilization as we know it disappears. The Bronze Age appears' (p. 56), according to Graham Swift's novel *Out of this World* (1988). My chosen authors 'map' myriad districts of Wessex while being aware of their own status as natives embroiled in complex histories of self-imposed exile and anxious return, radical estrangement and empathy (Birch, 1981, pp. 348–58). Between 1805 and 1874, the first series of Ordnance Survey maps was produced; by the end of the nineteenth century, an extensively revised second series was 'widely available' (Stout, 2008, p. 178). Hughes acclaims the pedagogical and recreational utility of the state-sponsored 'surveys for the Ordnance Map of Berkshire'; this cartographic landscape, recording the exact location of 'Roman camp', 'cairn' and 'cromlech' (*TBS* p. 9), offered a framework for the nascent science of archaeology and consolidated 'a semi-mystical blending of race and place' (Daniels, 1998, p. 118). Dud No-Man, Powys's novelist-hero of *Maiden Castle* (1936), strolling into the parlour of his friend Mrs Dearth, notices 'a warm fire [. . .] and, covering almost the entire wall opposite the fire, an enormous map of the county of Dorset, printed in Dorchester in the early days of Queen Victoria' (*MC* p. 98). An image that recurs in their work is of Wessex as a seemingly measureless geographical palimpsest: a patiently worked, scarred and scored surface on which manifold generations have stamped their aesthetic impressions and mystical insights for posterity. Lionel Johnson treats Hardy's Wessex in 1894 as a 'living palimpsest' built up over centuries of pertinacious human effort and prior to that, aeons of geology, 'stratified by the successive passages of historic time':

> There are barrows, camps, rings all over the district, of which the learned cannot determine the origin and date: one race may have succeeded to its predecessor's works, and changed them for its own needs, until the mounds, raised by human hands, have come to look like human work. That is an inverse symbol of the immaterial results of ancient history, upon this tract and people: get past confused traces, blended and crossed, of historic ancestry, and you reach the primitive pagan stock. (Qtd. in Clarke, 1993, p. 382)

The 'scouring' of this natural document of palpable and chronological humanity in selected regional novels – implying a thorough search as well as purifying of dusty genealogies and other physical artefacts – signifies an abiding concern with fantasies of an authentic, essential and recoverable social identity.

Above all, 'scouring' manifests an obsessive regard for the august or wistful associations of a mythologized point of inception; for the numinous site where commencement and commandment blurs, and from which cultural cachet springs. So the narratives in this study evoke a 'heavily stratified archaeological dig' (Moses, 1995, p. 33), to disinter those 'archives' which delineate procedure and precedence (Steedman, 2002, pp. 4–5). From the 1850s onwards, disciples of the nascent sciences of humankind – anthropology, archaeology, palaeontology and geology – were privileging south-central England as a copious reserve of what E. B. Tylor designated as 'survivals' – the residual remains of long-forgotten cultures. Hardy's correspondence and fiction chart how topics of national history move from being a source of recondite squabbling among dilettante dabblers to a focus for newly exploding populations and new social classes. The popularity of the 'study of antiquity' went far beyond that 'class of persons loving the past, because it affected to hate the present and despair of the future' (Swayne, 1880, p. 3). Hardy illustrates a more mainstream culture devoted to the imaginative reconstruction of distant epochs, through the publication of historical romances (such as Elfride Swancourt's Arthurian romp in *A Pair of Blue Eyes* [1873]); painting and sculpture; interior design and architectural fads such as Gothic restoration; opulent theatrical entertainments and popular exhibitions; as well as organized visits to museums, art galleries, medieval castles and ruined monasteries. Thomas Hughes's sly dig at his youthful readers who go 'gadding' overseas mirrors a burgeoning leisure industry and the appealing prospect of cheaper European excursions for those keen to inspect newly excavated sites and learn more about the cultures that occupied them (Pearson, 2006a, pp. ix–xix). Hardy, like those authors influenced by his regional writing, transforms Wessex into a stage upon which to test numerous narratives of attachment between the recent and the remote.

Many current surveys of nineteenth-century British earth science too quickly assume that excavators sought to distance themselves from and quarantine the distorted or discoloured evidences of barbaric beginnings. Inquiry into regional tradition and lore may sometimes decree a perceived separateness from that history, and a need to laud as well as memorialize the gulf. Yet also manifest is an undaunted quest for ghostly 'conversations'; imaginative empathy animates the defunct and quickens the sense of association between 'then' and 'now'. So Wessex becomes a 'laboratory' for prosecuting experiments in the 'institution of heritage' (Lowenthal, 1997, p. 4). This notion preoccupies Hardy, though he is acutely aware of how this enterprise can descend into socially regressive nostalgia or the glorifying of genealogies that Peter Widdowson's *Hardy in History* impugns, so that the landscape becomes 'England's prime anachronism – a vast museumized ruin' (Lowenthal, 1994, p. 24). Hardy, like the other Wessex novelists featured here, deploys 'imaginative archaeology' to render an infinitely stratified conception of place; running through each chapter is a sense of the modern moment emerging from and declaring itself in relation to the littered layers of past human experience which herald it.

Imaginative Archaeology

Hardy's multifaceted conception of 'Wessex' was formulated at a time when 'Schliemannism' and spectacular 'spade-lore' were undermining the cultural kudos of traditional classical research. Although G. C. Swayne argued in 1880 that philology could still claim a prestigious position among the inductive

sciences, its hypotheses were often derided as woolly, 'ungrounded fancies'
([Anon.], 'On the Influence of Archaeology', 1850, p. 162) when set against
the raw data gleaned from uncovered artefacts. With 'a new audacity', prompted
by an aggrieved sense of how the genetic study of archaic institutions had been
stultified by the continuing commitment to translation studies and aesthetic
appreciation, the archaeologist was 'dropping a sounding-line into the oceanic
depths of the remote past, and dredging up' striking 'evidences of the life and
labour of prehistoric man' (Swayne, 1880, p. 3). For outspoken champions of
linguistic scholarship and conventional narrative history such as Robert Tyrrell
in the 1888 *Fortnightly Review*, empiricist archaeological techniques were a most
unwelcome innovation:

> She [grammar] is invaded on every side by archaeology, anthropology,
> epigraphy, and dilettantism. It is more blessed to gush than to construe [. . .]
> the absence of the trammels of grammar lightens the burden of the editor's
> erudition, and enables him more easily to find or overlook in the text
> whatever suits his purpose. (Tyrell, 1888, p. 48)

Tyrrell's grumble mirrors the degree to which Schliemann's archaeological
forays in Greece and at the site of Troy in the 1860s and 1870s had become a
'galvanizing force' in a Victorian milieu defined by the unchecked growth
of industrial capitalism and the emergence of large urban centres (Pearson,
2006a, p. x). Newspaper and middlebrow magazine editors devised breezy,
eye-catching methods to expound, visualize and publicize how Schliemann
came and 'hewed about this hill with his pickaxe, brought up the "Burnt City"
from its weird sleep of 3,000 years, laid bare the heroic graves at Mykene, and
made the vast pre-historic palace of the birthplace of Herakles, in Argolis, rise
from its hiding-ground' (Blind, 1885, p. 143). For these cultural commentators,
the past of uncovered vestiges was amenable to multifarious, even contradictory
interpretations: it vouchsafed an inspiriting glimpse of human ingenuity through
the ages; it was also a sober 'warning' about the dangers of degeneration (Pearson,
2006a, p. x). That Wessex writers shared this fascination with literary 'excavation'
would have met with Oscar Wilde's full approbation. In 'The Truth of Masks:
A Note on Illusion' (1891) he invites his readers to extract a telling lesson from
how archaeology became, in 'the age of Shakespeare', one of 'its special
characteristics':

> The curious objects that were being constantly brought to light by excavations
> were not left to moulder in a museum, for the contemplation of a callous
> curator, and the *ennui* of policemen bored by the absence of crime. They
> were used as motives for the production of a new art, which was not to be
> beautiful merely, but also strange. [. . .] And indeed archaeology is only really
> delightful when transfused into some form of art [. . .] Art, and art only, can
> make archaeology beautiful [. . .] For archaeology, being a science, is neither

good nor bad, but a fact simply. Its value depends entirely on how it is used, and only an artist can use it. We look to the archaeologist for the materials, to the artist for the method. (Wilde, 1994, p. 1162)

Through the magnifying lens of Wilde's aesthetic historicism, archaeology is rescued from the joyless and stolid realm of 'priggish pedantry'. It was 'not a mere science for the antiquarian; it was a means by which they could thrust the dry dust of antiquity into the very breath and beauty of life, and fill with the new wine of romanticism forms that else had been old and outworn' (Wilde, 1994, p. 1162). While late-Victorian middlebrow magazines continued to report archaeology either as a uniquely compelling cultural phenomenon or as an evolving professional institution, Wilde repackages it as a resplendent fund of intriguing literary tropes, open to the visionary artist who wishes, through wild surmise and speculation, to make the ancient past move 'as a pageant before our eyes, without obliging us to have recourse to a dictionary or an encyclopaedia for the perfection of our enjoyment' (Wilde, 1994, p. 1160). This thesis augurs Mary Butts's notion in 1929 that the artist should, with impudent brio, 'take over' the 'anthropologist's material' (*Journals* p. 324). How else, Butts enquires, can the suffocating silences of geological time be evoked in concrete human terms except through the creative writer's rich repertoire of literary effects? Wilde asserts that he is better equipped to piece together and exploit the shattered fragments of a defunct past than those archaeologists and ethnographers who expound a stagnant ideal of calmly rational spectatorship that discounts how all conclusions are brittle fictions governed by cultural standpoint. Aesthetic representation by contrast refuses to reify 'the dry dust of antiquity' (Wilde, 1994, p. 1162); rather it reconnects with historical happenings in surprising ways, affirming affective relations with revenants who touch the contours of the modern moment with spectral fingertips.

Wilde avers that in the most plodding 'archaeological novel' the findings of scientific excavation are apparent only as a surfeit of 'strange and obsolete terms': the 'services of laborious scholars' are not sufficiently transfigured by the aspiring author's fierce originality of vision (Wilde, 1994, p. 1163). O. G. S. Crawford, in his 'Editorial Notes' to the first edition of his journal *Antiquity*, defined archaeology as 'a branch of science [. . .] founded upon the observation' and painstaking collection of 'facts' (1927, p. 1). Wilde spurns Crawford's disciplinary yoke so as to craft a more daring and resonantly innovative cross-pollination of archaeological method and aesthetic technique (Hodder, 1996, p. 3). Shakespeare, in Wilde's estimation, scours 'the facts of the antiquarian and converts them into dramatic and picturesque effects' (Wilde, 1994, p. 1168). Wilde puckishly 'translates' archaeology into an exuberant thought-adventure that prioritizes haphazard, arbitrary and miscellaneous subjective impressions so often silenced in worthy forensic analysis.

Wilde's thesis adumbrates myriad possibilities for a discussion of how Hardy, Jefferies, Powys and Mary Butts each 'exhume' Wessex in the creative patterns of their fiction. Literary depictions of excavation from Thomas Hardy's *The Return of the Native* (1878) to John Cowper Powys's *Maiden Castle* (1936) exploits the necromantic metaphor of salvaging, resurrecting or communing with the megalithic dead. What unifies all the 'West Country' novelists in this study is a sustained engagement with emerging archaeological and anthropological accounts of the cultural past so as to underscore the '[d]iscovery of a new value, a different way of apprehending everything' (*AWM* p. 9), grounded in what the classical scholar Jane Ellen Harrison termed 'autochthony' – the mystical potency of place.

In the 1895 Preface to *Far from the Madding Crowd* Hardy believed that he was 'correct in stating that, until the existence of this contemporaneous Wessex in place of the usual counties was announced in the present stories [. . .] it had never been heard of in fiction and current speech' (qtd. in Haslam, 2009, pp. 165–74). It was in fact his friend and mentor William Barnes who first deployed this term in his antiquarian researches. What is striking however is Hardy's sure sense of rescuing a defunct designation from oblivion: he gives Wessex 'a fictitious significance as the existing name of the district once included in that extinct kingdom [. . .] Finding that the area of a single county did not afford a canvas large enough for this purpose' he '*disinterred* an old one' (*FFMC* p. 6; my italics).

In my next chapter, Hardy's concept of uncovering the 'extinct' denomination of 'Wessex' offers a critical platform on which to gauge his status as a cultural embalmer in *The Return of the Native* (1878) and *The Mayor of Casterbridge* (1886). These two novels show Hardy participating in and contributing to an antiquarian culture of signal depth and diversity. He develops a textured archaeological vision based on his own intermittent fieldwork, coupled with his assiduous reading of the excavatory sciences. Moreover, his imaginative project wittily exploits the semantic ambiguities of the term 'curiosity', which variously specifies a pleasing pastime, a fascinated yet unresolved musing, or a cluster of complex cultural codes and practices. Hardy also scrupulously historicizes 'curiosity' and lends it 'anthropomorphic' shape in a figure of droll, self-regarding eccentricity – the amateur antiquarian narrator (Bann, 1999, p. xxi). For this personage Wessex itself epitomizes a copious storehouse of 'curiosities': archaic and rare objects, peculiar habits or mysterious monuments. For Raymond Williams, the authentic 'Hardy country' is 'that border country [. . .] between custom and education, between work and ideas, between love of place and experience of change' (Williams, 1971, pp. 98–99). Yet this region is more precisely a place where Hardy probes the very basis of late-Victorian ethnography through a persistent pose of epistemological doubt, apprehension and unease.

In *The Return of the Native* does Hardy present Wessex as a locus of reinvigorated regional identity? His concern with a bounded locality makes a more trenchant point about evolutionary anxieties, the eidetic recall of traumatic events and the hazards of a narrow nativism. Hardy is often perceived both by his legion devotees and by detractors as the laureate of a legacy of loss by abrasion, territorial conquest and the casual brutalities of oppression. However, *The Return of the Native* and *The Mayor of Casterbridge* variously express an enigmatically ambivalent attitude towards the imperilled prehistoric residues that clutter the region. Hardy's approach to the work of recovering, preserving and restoring ancient artefacts is more deeply vexed than Oscar Wilde's for instance, who turns to the ancient world as a receptacle that contains a 'buried spirit of progress' that 'in vain [. . .] the middle ages strove to guard' (Wilde, 1994, pp. 1161). Wilde implies here that the resurgence and veneration of antiquity in post-medieval Europe may even supply desperately needed social and cultural correctives to a fractured late-Victorian milieu. Hardy, however, cannot underscore the buoyant optimism of this view.

Chapter 3 canvasses Richard Jefferies's trenchant contributions to the literature of English husbandry and economic geography in the second half of the nineteenth century. I begin with Jefferies's *The Story of My Heart* (1883), focusing on its conceptual and cultural definitions of place. Initial critical reaction to this metaphysical quest narrative was muted, and apart from a percipient recent reading by Simon Grimble (2004), this text has attracted very little sustained scholarly commentary. What studies there are tend to belittle 'a passive, onanistic, version of the Romantic sublime' (Hapgood, 2003, p. 68). The bulk of Jefferies's journalism documents what many consider 'the birthplace of English field archaeology': the chalk downs of north Wiltshire and west Berkshire, and that terrain of the White Horse Vale, which lies between his birthplace of Coate, near Swindon and White Horse Hill (Grinsell, 1940, p. 216). This expanse was 'home, not just of the finest monuments, but to the first and best archaeologists' Richard Colt Hoare (Stout, 2008, pp. 140–41). *The Story of My Heart* implies that between the ages of 17 and 27 Jefferies was keenly alert to issues of local history and topography. In his early antiquarian opus *The History of Swindon and its Environs* Jefferies charts the area surrounding his natal home with a rapt regard analogous to that of contemporary ethnographers and missionaries who were mapping the most remote regions of empire (Grinsell, 1940, p. 217).

As Rolf Gardiner would later describe it in the 1920s, the Wiltshire soil encourages walkers 'to discard the nervous titter of the waking mind and yield to the inherent forces of the spirit incarnate in the earth' (Gardiner, 1943, p. 19). This longing for open-air epiphany, glimpsing 'a borderland of the miraculous' (*GR* p. 1171) through what Jeremy Hooker calls 'ditch vision' (Hooker, 1996, p. 4) – a capacity to divulge the numinous in the rurally local – is central to *The Story of My Heart*. However, Jefferies does not straightforwardly anchor such vision in the notion of disinterment as reincarnation. That Jefferies is frequently situated, along with Gilbert White, William Cobbett and W. H. Hudson within the cosy category of 'country writer', leaches the threat of his dissident difference which is such an exceptional signature of his rural sociology. Jefferies renders the Wiltshire countryside as a wilderness, not so much in terms of panoramic scale or magisterial vistas, but as a realm whose dolmens, cairns and tumuli attest an unruly and tortured past reminiscent of Hardy's *The Mayor of Casterbridge*. However, in Jefferies's dystopian fable *After London* (1885) that 'wilderness' which offered the suddenness of surprise in the spiritual auto-biography, becomes an altogether more sinister phenomenon, stripped of any cathartic, purgative or restorative connotations.

After London evokes a condition of bucolic Wessex that prompts comparison with the cataclysm depicted at the close of John Cowper Powys's *A Glastonbury Romance*: 'the waters of the sea had swept so far inland, mingling with the waters of the land, that the configuration of the country had completely changed' (*GR* p. 1116). Chapter 4 concentrates on Powys, who situated six narratives in Dorset and nearby Somerset, and, indeed, referred to four of them as his 'Wessex Novels'.[1] *A Glastonbury Romance* and *Maiden Castle* deliberately refashion the regional writing of Hardy and Jefferies. Like Clym Yeobright, John Crow in *A Glastonbury Romance* and Dud No-man of *Maiden Castle*, return to a locale which has left an ineffaceable imprint on their sense of self. However, their attempts to recapture a primeval rapport with this expanse, or to craft a successful and fulfilling niche within it, end in biting disillusionment. This failure underscores the potential risks, as well as enticements of allowing the borderline between diurnal actuality and aesthetic experiment to collapse. Dud succumbs to the view that Hardy's protagonists actually traverse the Dorchester streets through which he roams in search of the next fleeting frisson. When Dud measures his own behaviour in purchasing a 'wife' against Michael Henchard's in selling his in a fit of drunken fury, he makes a comparison as if he and the First Citizen of Hardy's narrative 'had an identical ontological status' (Moran, 1990, p. 189).

My analysis of Powys's fiction also takes its cue from Richard Maxwell's seminal 1990 essay 'The Lie of the Land' which gauges *A Glastonbury Romance* in terms of its obsession with earth worship, and the falsehoods and mystical conditions to which such reverence gives rise. The critic John Bayley exploits these ideas to fix Powys as a largely undemanding and inoffensive 'domestic' novelist who seeks escapist solace by charting the relaxed rhythms of 'a small historic town' (Bayley, 1985, p. 9). Similarly, Vernon Young in 'The Immense Inane' (1986) interprets Powys's portrayal of interpersonal and anthropological relationships as a panicked rejection of 'the world' in which he lived: he 'retreated throughout our mid-century, first to Dorsetshire' then 'to that utopia resorted to by writers who are intimidated out of thought by the mounting contradictions of their time' (Young, 1986, p. 255).

Both commentators fail to discern that an intricate and shifting elemental perception is extracted from the 'parochial' in Powys's 1930s novels, under-pinned by archaeological discoveries. So the west-country town of Glastonbury, like the largest hill-fort in the British Isles which *Maiden Castle* celebrates, is rendered as 'enchanted soil where the Eternal once sank down' (*GR* p. 1063). *Maiden Castle* is very much concerned with the 'mounting contradictions' of the time as it assiduously traces and dramatizes the extensive digs that Mortimer Wheeler undertook in this area between 1934 and 1938; and which became according to Adam Stout, 'one of the most famous British archaeological excavations of the twentieth century' (Stout, 2008, p. 217). W. J. Keith was one of the first Powys scholars to delineate this vivid archaeological background to *Maiden Castle,* and my own discussion develops some of Keith's core findings. In his Dorset diary Powys wrote, 'Why does Maiden Castle thrill me so? Only because of the other horizons? Or is there another reason? A supernatural one?' (Krissdöttir and Peers, 1998, p. 152) Powys's narrative measures Wheeler's 'scientific' archaeology against a gnomic 'supernatural' creed, which greatly complicates the conventional perception of Powys as 'a naïf out of his time' (Maxwell, 1990, p. 193).

The oracular, uncompromising and politically disruptive pastoral fiction of Mary Butts constitutes Chapter 5. Bryher [Annie Winifred Ellerman] wryly remarked in a brief memorial to her friend in 1937: 'dull' was the verdict of 'one reviewer' after reading Butts's literary depictions of the west country (Bryher, 1937, p. 160). 'Dull' or comfortingly predictable are not words that immediately spring to mind given how Butts transmutes the endangered prehistoric residues of her homeland into witnesses that certify her own ancestral virtues. Like Powys's *A Glastonbury Romance* (1933), Butts's *Taverner Novels – Armed with Madness* (1928) and *Death of Felicity Taverner* (1932) – are abstruse narratives of 'West Country Grail-questing' that attest a multilayered archaeological and ecological saga (Baldick, 2004, p. 231).

According to the narrator of *A Glastonbury Romance* the 'books say that [King] Arthur saw the Grail in five different shapes; and that what the fifth shape was has never been revealed' (*GR* pp.1169–70). *Armed with Madness* toys with the idea that this 'fifth shape' may be a 'jade cup' fished from the bottom of a stagnant well. Whereas *A Glastonbury Romance* seems to its critics a chaotically 'sprawling, and overfreighted work' (Baldick, 2004, p. 231), the verbal texture of *Armed with Madness* betrays lapidary grace and a fondness for taut, telegraphese syntax. Like her more renowned literary precursor Hardy, Butts envisaged herself poised at a cultural crossroads: responsive to the nervous antipathies of metropolitan modernity, yet impelled by a solemn historical duty to recall and reanimate arcane and occult lore. According to Butts, her native place, which 'no man, not Hardy even, has found full words for' (*CC* p. 63), engenders 'a fresh "spiritual" adventure [. . .] a re-statement & a development of our old experience in the field which gave us our religions' (*Journals* p. 341). This 'old experience' Butts avers, is not only inscrutable to the interwar open-air movement but also beyond the ken of many professional archaeologists and ethnographers such as Mortimer Wheeler, who had sought strenuously to uncover and calibrate the megalithic districts of Wessex.

Though Lawrence Rainey lauds *Armed with Madness* as a provocatively transgressive 'masterpiece of Modernist prose' (Rainey, 1998, p. 14), Mary Butts was, until the publication of Patrick Wright's influential study *On Living in an*

Old Country (1985), a misconstrued figure who had 'slipped through the net of literary histories of the period' (Blondel, 1997, p. xv; Garrity, 2008). However, thanks largely to the pioneering research of Wright, Ian Patterson, David Matless and especially Jane Garrity, Mary Butts's former role as the wan apparition of a forgotten modernism has been amply 'fleshed out' (Matless, 2008, pp. 335–57).[2] Nathalie Blondel, a 'world authority on Butts' (Scott, 2004, p. 189), has diligently traced her affiliations with Jean Cocteau, Ford Madox Ford, John Rodker, Wyndham Lewis, H. D., Ezra Pound, and their avant-garde coteries during the period from 1914 to 1922 (Blondel, 1997, pp. 5–50).

Born in 1890, Butts grew up in Parkstone on the edge of Poole, Dorset. She eventually settled in Sennen Cove, near Land's End in Cornwall, a 'whole district thick with folklore' (Manning-Sanders, 1949, pp. 40–41). Here she lived from 1930 until her untimely death in 1937. The American novelist Glenway Wescott, referred to her as 'English to the core' (Wescott, 1923, p. 282), a remark that implies the key importance of *how* one should reside in the 'farthest corner' of an island nation (Manning-Sanders, 1949, p. 39). Butts's typical heroine, such as Vanna in the eco-feminist and pacifist novel *Ashe of Rings*, demonstrates the '[n]ecessity for a new experience of reality after the failure of religion' (*Journals* p. 242). She is a custodian of the inherited privileges of the 'truly English', and resembles Butts's re-imagining of Cleopatra as a 'priestess [. . .] a woman of the ruling caste in a lost civilisation: an athlete: trained in certain lost rites' (*Journals* p. 272).

Butts's genetically ordained and venturesome protagonists locate the 'yardstick for all conduct' (*Journals* p. 89) in 'ancient mysteries' (*AWM* p. 138) that radiate from tangible survivals such as 'green hill' tumuli (*DFT* p. 210). Here, among the 'limitless downs', are adumbrated exotic enigmas and elaborate patterns of 'obscure initiation' (*AR* p. 15) that cannot be crystallized by the shared national grammar of suburban picturesque. Like Richard Jefferies, Butts is drawn to the 'earthworks and trees' as much more than 'a place to picnic in and archeologise about' because it exists 'real by itself, without any reference to us' (*AR* p. 169). While Butts's imaginative excavations reinvent 'Hardy's country' (*AWM* p. 13) as a 'temenos' of 'race' (*AR* p. 39), she adopts a position of recalcitrant resistance to any stress on the collective enjoyment of the countryside, such as the hiking which 'reached epidemic proportions by the early 1930s, with the railway companies running special "excursion" trains most weekends' (Stout, 2008, p. 180). She inveighs against the rambling and cycling clubs and what youth movement leader Rolf Gardiner termed 'experiments in community'. Gardiner's 'Wessex Camps' in 1934–1936 were 'part of a determined effort to restore that landscape to a new and conscious vigour, and to build up a regional centre of rural example and civic inspiration' (Gardiner, 1972, p. 101). The 'trespassers' and 'semi-Bohemians' who aggravate Jefferies's sturdy field detective in *The Gamekeeper at Home* (1978, p. 102) also exercise Mary Butts, for whom 'coarsely mischievous intruders' (Jefferies, 1978, p. 108) become a signal source of 'eugenic impatience'

(*AR* p. 24), even existential dread. Indeed, Patrick Wright pinpoints class '[e]xclusion', reinforced by bias and mystification, along with ethnic 'anathema', as concepts 'active' at the very foundation of Butts's 'sacred geography' (Wright, 1985, p. 124). For Butts, the complex culture underlying the open-air movement, with its 'week-end tramps with an ordnance map, or a cottage shared with friends' (Butts, 1998a, p. 283) was nothing more than trivializing dilettantism against which she affirms patrician, pre-industrial teachings immune to correction.

Key to Butts's self-serving, exclusionary and origin-obsessed rendering of Wessex is the groundbreaking research inaugurated by the Cambridge Ritualists, such as James George Frazer's *The Golden Bough* which Butts deemed 'one of those great works of science whose business is the fertilization of minds to come' (Butts, 'The Past Lives Again', 1934c, p. 44). She also avows a lifelong fascination with Jane Ellen Harrison's comparative anthropology, which Butts construes as analogous to her own enterprise – to vaunt matrilineal legacies as an urgent, fructifying presence in the 'scent-charged air' (*DFT* p. 205), instead of a distant and rightly forgotten developmental phase in the story of civilization. In a recent essay on D. H. Lawrence's fiction, Hugh Stevens poses a question that resonates through Mary Butts's idiosyncratic vision of regional topography: 'Can fiction be modernist when it aims to help us to recapture a pre-modern, or even "primitive", relationship with nature and with our own bodies, and dissolve boundaries between the self and the world?' (Stevens, 2007, pp. 137–38). These boundaries between self and the world have often served as 'one of our litmus tests of modernism' (de Lange et al., 2008, p. xi). Butts responds by showing that a modern culture cannot survive, let alone thrive, unless it recaptures the isolate individual's multiplied perception of an 'equivocal' Wessex very much 'off the regulation road' (*AWM* p. 12).

Chapter 2

Hardy's Heathens

Coining Wessex

Barry Cunliffe's 1993 study of the tribal kingdom of Wessex methodically documents the region's 'high degree of physical coherence', and the concentration of prehistoric residues dominating its 'sweeping landscapes':

> Thomas Hardy, responsible for reintroducing the word [Wessex] into everyday use, used it with delightful vagueness though to him the Dorset focus was all-important. 'Wessex' has an undoubted charm about it due in no small part to Hardy's lively imagination. With its connotations of sweeping landscapes – the seed bed of our deeply rooted British culture – it has come to stand for stability, tradition and reliability [. . .] Advertising copy-writers have much to thank Hardy for. Indeed so persuasive is the term that it has been used in this series of regional histories in place of the somewhat less emotive 'Central South England' [. . .]
>
> For us, then, Wessex means the counties of Somerset, Avon, Dorset, Wiltshire, Hampshire and Berkshire. (Cunliffe, 1993, p. 1)

That an astute archaeological survey should hail a late-Victorian novelist of 'Wessex' mirrors Hardy's capability to fashion his literary milieu into a 'bellwether' of 'urgent Western accommodations' to a shifting sense of 'cosmic and cultural location' (Kort, 2004, p. 25). Cunliffe construes Hardy as an author peculiarly concerned with questions of cultural persistence, as well as the existential implications of 'com[ing] home' (*RN* p. 173). What if the archaeologically rich terrain of Egdon Heath, with its 'stone arrow-heads used by the old tribes' and 'faceted crystals from the hollows of flints' (*RN* p. 340), discloses the 'seed-bed' of a robust body politic? This notion would be scornfully dismissed by the condescending outsider in *The Return of the Native* who muses: 'in what other state than heathen could people rich or poor exist, who were doomed to abide in such a world's-end as Egdon?' (*RN* p. 407). But for Cunliffe, Hardy's 'lively imagination' conjures a parochial narrative in which to confront and process vivid myths of national belonging; an account of 'archaeological endeavour in Wessex would be a microcosm of the cultural and scientific evolution of the nation' (Cunliffe, 1993, p. xvi).

Cunliffe's buoyant interpretation prioritizes the 'undoubted charm' of this literary 'Wessex', and so fails fully to register that the traditional beliefs, legends and customs current among the rural peasantry in the fiction becomes a site of deep unease for Hardy. His regionalism 'eulogizes', according to Michael Valdez Moses, 'a society whose distinctive features are gradually being effaced by the homogenizing influence of modernity' (Moses, 1995, p. 31). But Hardy's sustained enquiry into social phenomena is not impelled by cloying sentimentality for 'traditional values' or 'the poetry of existence' (*RN* p. 74); nor does it betray 'a romantic effort to clothe' the 'culture of the rural masses with the authentic values of antiquity' (Hodgen, 1936, p. 47). As Cathy Lynn Preston contends, his work both participates in and enables, 'while simultaneously contesting', such modes of 'pastoral representation and appropriation' (Preston, 1995, p. 44). Indeed, Hardy is quick to underscore those incidences in his fiction where characters succumb to a delusional, fruitless or 'tragically desiccated nostalgia' (Moore, 1990, p. 126). The ailing John South's primitive paranoia concerning his 'totem-elm' in *The Woodlanders* (1888) not only leads to his 'debilitation and death', but also becomes a 'perverse source of suffering for his two dependents' Marty South and Giles Winterborne (Moore, 1990, p. 118).[1] This scene of neurasthenic torment in the sheltered recesses evokes 'evil fires that burn just a very little way beneath the thin and crumbling crust of our boasted modern civilisation' (Summers, 1927, pp. 184–85).

Many other 'residuary bequests of former generations' ([Anon.], 'History and Biography', 1871b, p. 271) are exposed as 'diseased' and morbid, such as the sinister occult practices in 'The Withered Arm' and Susan Nunsuch's 'ghastly invention of superstition, calculated to bring powerlessness, atrophy and annihilation on any human being against whom it was directed' (*RN* p. 359). As J. S. Udal remarked in his 1892 essay 'Witchcraft in Dorset': 'There is no part of England [. . .] more prone to belief in the supernatural [. . .] than the West; and, of the western counties, none more so than Dorset' where 'the belief in witchcraft still ekes out a flickering existence' (Udal, 1892, pp. 35, 38). These habits and ideas, falling beyond E. B. Tylor's cosy category of 'fond and foolish customs' (Tylor, 1871, I, p. 94) do little to support Cunliffe's sanguine sense of the 'reliability' and 'stability' of Wessex folk-culture; rather they throw into sharper relief Tylor's disabused perception of cultural inertia. Indeed, as Arthur Mitchell reflected nearly a decade after the publication of Tylor's *Primitive Culture* (1871), 'there is no intrinsic tendency in human societies [. . .] to pass ever on and ever up to something better and higher and nobler' (Mitchell, 1881, p. 228).

So to claim that the goal of Hardy's imaginative excavations and discoveries was analogous to William Barnes's – to safeguard the mental as well as physical heirlooms of his antecedents, without 'the smallest reference' to 'any of the social sins and vices of peasant life' (Cambridge, 1887, p. xxi) – is problematic. Francis Turner Palgrave opined in the *National Review* that 'mere animal coarseness, sordid want, cunning and meanness triumphant, these are excluded [from Barnes's poetry]; in this sense he idealizes the reality of life' (Palgrave, 1887, p. 820). That Cunliffe proposes 'advertising copy-writers' owe a signal debt to the Wessex Novels is striking, and pays lavish tribute to a canny young author ready to position himself in a crowded literary marketplace as the purveyor of a compelling literary 'brand', whose unifying 'territorial definition' braids together myriad Tylorian survivals, episodes and personages (Zeitler, 2006).

This literary 'brand', so often construed as synonymous with static serenity or yearning for imaginative and interpersonal connection, ill accords with the jarring experience of reading those Wessex novels in which folklore remnants feature prominently, such as *The Return of the Native* and *The Mayor of Casterbridge*. In the former narrative, Egdon Heath itself is imagined as bypassed by the modern world; this cultural survival is a hinterland of disenchanting strangeness: 'To many persons this Egdon was a place which had slipped out of its century, generations ago, to intrude as an uncouth object into this. It was an obsolete thing, and few cared to study it' (*RN* p. 176). But Hardy's indefatigable antiquarian narrator does 'study it' closely; exhuming the skeleton of native stock and finding in fossilized debris numerous instances of ethnographic significance. His view of the tribal indigenes in *The Return of the Native* mixes an amused awe for their tenacious resilience with a conviction that among their rapidly dwindling numbers are dogged exponents of ignorant sentimentality and insular atavisms. To be driven back into 'the old paths' (*RN* p. 260) in this novel frequently implies a reversion to vindictive prejudice, and not the fine principles of unvarnished dignity or 'reliability' which may be, in Cunliffe's opinion, 'the seed-bed of our deeply rooted British culture'. This 'seed-bed' may point up glaring evolutionary gaps, brutish interludes or a congeries of divergent yet intersecting bequests. Hardy utilizes moments of archaeological and ethnographic resonance to canvass, often with cagey provisionality, the degree to which landmarks actually meld the strata of the unrecorded past with the social and cultural formation of modernity (Zeitler, 2006). In this regard *The Return of the Native* emerges as a crucial early work.

Reading the Face of Egdon

When we speak of the face of the earth, the face of the waters, quoting that ancient imaginative expression, we probably refer to an extent or expanse of space rather than the suggestion of a featured mask. But in describing some comparatively small localised area of land and sea, it is perhaps possible to think of it in a more literal sense as, in fact, something like a countenance. [. . .]

As I see it, there appears a gigantic face composed of massive and unusual features: at once harsh and tender, alarming yet kind, seeming susceptible to moods but, in secret, overcast by a noble melancholy – or, simply, the burden of its extraordinary inheritance. Indeed, the past is always evident in that face. And it is not always the farthest past which is most assertive. There are certain places, at certain times, where the record of some drama can start into life as a scar glows with sudden memory. Such places, at such times, are inseparable from the deeds associated with them: the wreckings of the Chesil Bank, the vile robberies of Cranborne Chase, the murder at Corfe, or the sadism of the Bloody Assize.

(Nash, 1936, p. 9)

The artist and photographer Paul Nash's *Shell Guide to Dorset* (1936) is dedicated to 'all those courageous enemies of "development" to whom we owe what is left of England'. His account of this region, like Edmund Blunden's *The Face of England: In a Series of Occasional Sketches* (1932) is couched in terms that make a detailed comparison with the 'gigantic face' of Hardy's Egdon, whose 'folds' and 'wrinkles' have been affected by the vicissitudes of English history, irresistible. Nash's tone of hushed reverence raises questions which reverberate powerfully through Hardy's novel, which gauges how 'the burden' of the heath's 'extraordinary inheritance' regulates, or even contaminates, its present inhabitants. Could Egdon's animistic potencies convert a 'real perusing man' with lofty 'scholastic plans' (*RN* p. 250) such as the genteel diamond merchant Clym Yeobright, into a pitiless 'barbarian' (*RN* p. 84)? Does the 'furzy wilderness' of 'Bruaria' – as Egdon is designated in 'Domesday' – imply not an 'obscure, obsolete, superseded' force (*RN* p. 5), but rather a volatile 'subterranean heat' (*RN* p. 61), a 'mysterious emanation' (*RN* p. 143) inciting 'instincts towards social nonconformity' (*RN* p. 67), even a 'wildness' in those who make a meagre living off this 'singularly colossal' expanse?

Gazing into Mrs Yeobright's face, Johnny Nunsuch feels like 'one examining some strange old manuscript, the key to whose characters is undiscoverable' (*RN* p. 290). Like Hardy, Nash is unusually attuned to the face of Dorset as furrowed and scarred by the blemishes of a messy, disordered past – a 'lawless state' (*RN* p. 56) which may yet 'assert' itself in frightening or unexpected ways on these 'thinly populated slopes' (*RN* p. 69). The heath's 'lonely face' not only implies 'tragical possibilities' (*RN* p. 5) then but also Nash's darker 'deeds' and hectic 'drama', encompassing natural 'disaster' (*RN* p. 5), depredation and atavistic cruelty. As Hardy's antiquarian narrator notes, the terrain boasts a 'subtle beauty' yet it is also a 'home of strange phantoms' and 'spectral visitants' (*RN* p. 74): the thorn bushes on this expanse 'had a ghastly habit after dark of putting on the shapes of jumping madmen, sprawling giants, and hideous cripples' (*RN* p. 69); 'disconnected tufts of furze' stand upon 'stems along the top, like impaled heads about a city wall' (*RN* p. 54). This latter grisly image presages Humphrey's pointed reference to French revolutionary ferment, in which 'the king's head was cut off years ago' (*RN* p. 106), as well as Saint George, who 'cut[s] off' the 'Saracen's head' (*RN* p. 139) in the mummers' play.

Egdon Heath, a 'tract of country unaltered from that sinister condition which made Caesar anxious every year to get clear of its glooms before the autumnal equinox' (*RN* p. 50), epitomizes a testing ground in which primal layers are excavated, to gauge the 'lower stage[s]' (*RN* p. 60) of humanity, such as the 'reddleman' Diggory Venn, 'one of a class rapidly becoming extinct in Wessex, filling at present in the rural world the place which, during the last century, the dodo occupied in the world of animals' (*RN* p. 7). Diggory is a living breathing 'survival' – an 'interesting, and nearly perished link between obsolete forms of life and those which generally prevail' (*RN* p. 8) – in the bizarre natural museum which is Egdon. At the end of the first chapter Hardy evokes the terrain as a complex confluence of ancient residues and modern energies. The antiquarian narrator's responsiveness to Rainbarrow, the collective name for the three peripheral tumuli rising above the heath, seems 'so strong' as to initiate the very 'process of narration' (Lothe, 2007, 15):

> [E]verything around had been there from prehistoric times as unaltered as the stars overhead [giving] ballast to the mind adrift on change [. . .] The great inviolate place had an ancient permanence [. . .] With the exception of an aged highway, and a still more aged barrow [. . .] themselves almost crystallised to natural products by long continuance – even – Egdon's trifling irregularities were not caused by pickaxe, plough, or spade, but remained as the very finger-touches of the last geological change. (*RN* p. 6)

This narrator is less interested in the glib fixities of nostalgic reminiscence as in the heath's shifting, 'liminal space' (Marzec, 2007, p. 115) and its association with 'twilight' identities (*RN* p. 3), given that Egdon's 'pastoral isolation has been disrupted by the introduction of the railway' (Kort, 2004, p. 32). That the antiquarian narrator's attention lingers on a 'bossy projection of earth' called Rainbarrow and the hoary 'highway' (*RN* p. 6), indicates Hardy's slyly sardonic awareness that the modern world's discovery of ancient civilization through excavation was being chronicled extensively in the pages of middlebrow general interest weeklies such as *The Illustrated London News* (Sinnema, 1998). Magniloquent reports from these journals reminded readers of the heady events which had defined a century of unprecedented archaeological discovery; locating the buried cities of Herculaneum (from 1711) and of Pompeii (from 1748); Napoleon's invasion and scouring of Egypt in 1798–1799; the plundering of the Parthenon marbles from Greece in 1806; to Austen Henry Layard's Assyrian digs at Nineveh in the 1840s. In each instance, journalists had gleefully tied images of reckless adventure and exotic glamour to archaeological modes and methods.

Hardy, as if alert to this colourful conception of the 'spectacular find', such as the dynastic talismans which entranced moneyed Englishmen making the Grand Tour (Cunnington, 1975, p. xiii), offers instead Egdon's modest topography and its 'ferment of stagnation' (*RN* p. 105), whose barrows may yield little more than 'a few pieces of tile, and brick of the thin Roman kind, with some fragments of iridescent glass' (Hardy, *Public Voice*, 2001, p. 193). However, as Daniel Wilson stressed, from such seemingly drab remains as splinters of Romano-British pottery 'garnered in the grave' (Wilson, 1863, I, pp. 20–21), we find 'a new and vivid account of daily life from early times, to lay beside the traditional verbal accounts of heroic exploits of leaders' (Vaughan, 1998, p. 61). Unlike Egypt, 'that poor, ransacked country of shoddy bric-a-brac' (Crawford, 1921, p. 41), the heath's chipped flint arrowheads and other 'archaeological wealth' ([Anon.], 'Archaeological Institute', 1865, p. 199) exude an understated grace; the barrows seem 'perfect as at the time of their erection' (*RN* p. 3) and attract further symbolic observance to them, conditioning the very heath-folk who shelter, converse and make merry on or before them. This is why in *Contrasts* (1836), Augustus Pugin proclaimed, 'There is no need of visiting the distant shores of Greece and Egypt to make discoveries in art. England abounds in hidden and unknown antiquities of surpassing interest' (Pugin, 1969, pp. 17–18). The 1864 *Temple Bar* reinforced this patriotic and archaeological fervour:

> People are miserable in these days if they cannot *do* the Alps, the Pyramids, the Great Wall of China [. . .] Heaven forfend that I should underrate [. . .] the most wondrous relics of historic greatness! But, after all, which of us knows this England of ours thoroughly? On highway and byway there are perpetual novelties for us, if only we keep our eyes open. The temptation is great to plunge into a foreign country, to breathe an untried atmosphere, to mingle with an entirely different race. Yet I do believe there is half as much pleasure thus to be obtained as by exploring Old England. ([Anon.], 'Through Berks', 1864b, p. 52)

For this contributor, as for Pugin and Hardy, 'Old England' is accessible through its venerable settlement sites, defensive earthworks and round barrows; the copious material 'archive' of home underscores how the numinous emerges in and through the lumpish routines of daily labour.

Hardy's amateur fieldwork attests a lively awareness of his era's archaeological and antiquarian undertakings. The Dorset Natural History and Antiquarian Field Club, founded in 1875, started to publish annual *Proceedings* in 1877, to which Hardy occasionally contributed. However, in his Wessex Novels he puckishly debunks the strictly inductive methods of documenting the 'fragments of olden times' (Gomme, 1880, p. vii), whose advocates insisted that this material legacy was detached from, and quantitatively different to, current pursuits, conditions, rituals and trends. By the 1870s however, the 'father of scientific archaeology' (Bowden, 1991, p. 154) General Augustus Lane Pitt-Rivers, with a sprawling estate on the borders of Wiltshire and Dorset, started to canvass intricate connections between 'artefacts' and their 'stratigraphic context', thus finessing 'new standards of excavation technique' (Bettey, 1994, p. 127) and publishing his findings in the colossal four-volume *Excavations in Cranborne Chase* (1887–1898). For the Hardy whose imagination was inquisitive about time Pitt-Rivers's concept of a more thorough archaeology was discouraging.

Hardy's own capacity for visionary hallucination deliberately derails any scholarly attempts to identify a straightforward 'scientific theory' in it. This reflects an understandable nervousness that his amateur testimony would not be deemed a sufficiently weighty and wise contribution to archaeological journals whose editors sought to give the emergent science a more stringent and 'professional' perspective. Before archaeology 'can take its place among the exact sciences', opined one contributor to the *Quarterly Review*, it 'must certainly be based on a much more minute observation of individual instances' ([Anon.], 'Prehistoric Times', 1870a, p. 436).

But in *The Return of the Native*, Hardy queries ethnographic assumptions, practices and incidents so as to prioritize his own fleeting and fugitive subject-ive impressions. His temperamental bias and artistic tactic of imaginative archaeology is diverse, freewheeling and haphazard; a zestful and mischievous riposte to the site-centred and artefact-obsessed methods of contemporary excavators. The folklorist George Laurence Gomme, in *The Village Community* (1890), seemed to endorse this broadening of remit and restless ranging across myriad epochs:

> If we want to get at the true origin of what is now found on English soil as heirlooms of the past, we must take into our purview not one particular period, or one particular area; we must consider *all the remains of the past* and pick out from the whole group the evidence we seek for. (Gomme, 1890, p. 2; my italics)

In *The Return of the Native*, Hardy fuses both the pertinacity of a Pitt-Rivers, and the jovial dilettantism of the enlightened yet untrained enthusiast, such as the parish clergyman John Hutchins (1698–1773) whose systematic attempt to delineate Dorset's topography, vernacular buildings and practical crafts espoused the virtues of 'delving and poking about in odd corners' to 'unearth the riches of antiquity' (Buckman, 1877, pp. ix–x).

However, Hardy was certainly alert to the type of hapless and wilfully eccentric amateur antiquarian that cultural commentators such as Walter Pater deplored: Parson Swancourt in *A Pair of Blue Eyes* (1873) is one grotesquely comic example from the early fiction. In a region dominated by sizeable estates, Swancourt curries favour with the local gentry through a slavish interest in descent of land, ecclesiastical patronage, genealogy, armorial bearings and manorial history. Hardy construes his own antiquarian passion in a very different light, holding in delicate equipoise a regard for historical continuities as well as deep fractures, sudden dislocations and radical otherness. This encourages Hardy to adopt a bifocal perspective on the heath's prehistoric vestiges: a sense of droll or piquant incongruity 'animates' the 'rusty implements of a bygone barbarous epoch' (*RN* p. 196) as they are disinterred.

The signal weakness of Victorian earth science, as Hardy viewed it, was that its high-minded rational procedures of 'keen observation' (*RN* p. 132), cautious comparison, measured inference, and generalization evacuated archaeological traces and Brand's 'popular opinions' not only of energizing 'incongruity' but also of any capacity to have emboldened the cultures of which they were once the bedrock. Instead, Hardy wonders about the possibility of a mystical connection between living communities and the material terrain, whose 'fine broad roads' (Dunkin, 1871, p. 146) as well as long and round barrows, are both rendered by and composed of it. Charles Warne partially endorsed this perception in his antiquarian survey *Ancient Dorset* which was published the same year as Hardy's *Under the Greenwood Tree* in 1872. Warne paid full tribute to the county of Dorset first of all 'from an archaeological point of view' because it 'stands pre-eminent for the number, variety, and importance of its ancient remains, many of them existing in a perfect state of preservation. Its earthworks claim a place amongst the finest of the kind in Britain' (Warne, 1872, p. i). Just as old wives' tales for E. B. Tylor are atrophied, 'shifted, or mutilated' yet still 'carry their history plainly stamped upon them' (Tylor, 1871, I, p. 17), so for Hardy, field monuments – including Egdon's weather-worn 'Druidical stone' (*RN* p. 188) – evince a compelling temporal formation and enthralling accretions of meaning that have crusted around a particular spot, becoming entrenched in the immediacy of felt sensations, or, as *The Trumpet-Major* and *The Dynasts* variously reveal, inscribed into the magisterial 'annals' of (inter)national affairs.

In *The Return of the Native* Hardy imaginatively summons, through a persistent focus on Rainbarrow, the myriad pasts which infuse this curious corner of Wessex, and indeed a particular conception of 'Celtic identity' (Henderson, 1911, pp. 1–2). Rainbarrow's centrality becomes even more pronounced when the narrator delineates the 'custom[s] of the country' which the villagers enact upon it. That 'the instincts of merry England' linger on the heath, according to this narrator, with 'exceptional vitality' (*RN* p. 389–90) is troubling, as the first pagan practice in the novel reveals: the 5th November bonfire-lighting: 'It was as if these men and boys had suddenly dived into past ages and fetched therefrom an hour and deed which had before been familiar with this spot' (*RN* p. 15). Druidic ceremonials, Celtic funeral pyres, Saxon rites and Viking festival fires: this ostensibly 'long, unbroken chain of human experience' (Rogers, 2001, p. 219) has been staged upon Rainbarrow.

The bonfire-lighting productively underscores the gulf between 'history' and 'heritage' in Hardy's narrative. The local *historian* assesses with painstaking precision those bygone times which have become utterly remote from and alien to contemporary experience. The *purveyor* of heritage by contrast posits that forsaken or forgotten fragments bespeak an urgent presence, an informing and beneficent spirit whose role is to enrich the modern moment and shape the future. Hardy's antiquarian narrator may laud and campaign for a heritage epitomized by the tangible grandeur of Rainbarrow. But it is doubtful whether the Egdon 'men and boys' possess, or would wish to acquire, such knowledge of art objects, institutions, tribal rituals and sacred traditions. 'It was as if' implies more the narrator's hope, rather than confident expectation, that these Egdonites of assorted ages consciously 'connect with' the sedimented layers of prehistoric and early historic periods. How they act on the summit is socially codified and inculcated – an issue of prosaic and unglamorous habit. Yet the fantasy of 'unbroken' continuity is an idea which John Cowper Powys's anti-hero Dud No-Man seizes upon in *Maiden Castle*:

> 'It isn't just sensation that I live for [. . .] It's something that has behind it more than you think – the feelings of our race for thousands of years. For instance, this morning, warm though it was, I lit a fire in the grate to celebrate Midsummer's Eve. What are all your electrical apparatuses compared with a fire that I light with my own hands? It isn't only a sensual pleasure; it's a religion, it's an ecstasy of life'. (*MC* p. 338)

However, Hardy makes us doubt whether the Egdon 'men and boys' appreciate the 'religion', the 'ecstasy of life' which would enable fuller integration into a knowable community. The Egdonites seem more comfortable in the realm of the typical and the vernacular; indeed their very delight in the humdrum over the numinous and reverberant actually hastens the attrition of historical memory. This episode makes apparent that the ancient burial mounds which emboss the Egdon terrain have outlasted spiritual utility; they are converted into emblems of popular purpose, and still afford the practical benefit of 'cover' for illicit 'trysters' such as Wildeve and Eustacia, who meet 'in the little ditch encircling the barrow – the original excavation from which it had been thrown up' (*RN* p. 78).

Bonfire-lighting reveals 'how slowly the relics of Paganism disappear among country people', yet despite the raucous ebullience of Grandfer Cantle and his aged cronies the custom implies merely the stasis of stale conventions. Hardy invokes and contributes to, while simultaneously complicating, Robert Hunt's promotion of a primitive, dark, and wild-west country:

> Those wild dreams which swayed with irresistible force the skin-clad Briton [. . .] have not yet entirely lost their power where even the National and British Schools are busy with the people, and Mechanics' Institutions are diffusing the truth of science. In the infancy of the race, terror was the moving power: in the maturity of the people, the dark shadow still sometimes rises, like a spectre, partially eclipsing the mild radiance of that Christian truth which shines upon the land. (Hunt, 1865, p. 25)

That this illiterate crowd has 'imbibed much of what was dark' in the heath's tone signifies that any multiplied consciousness of their milieu or subliminal sensation of correspondence is of a diluted, debased kind. While the heath may boast prodigious 'fertility' to the regional 'historian' (*RN* p. 14), these native sons of its soil ponder the lamentable 'breakdown' (*RN* p. 16) and 'barrenness' (*RN* p. 14) which mar matrimonial dreams, professional agendas and in the case of the simpleton Christian Cantle, healthy human development. Christian is after all designated throughout by a process of negation or grievous lack: he is 'the man no woman will marry' (*RN* p. 23), a 'slack-twisted [. . .] fool', a 'wether' or eunuch (*RN* p. 24). These images of emaciation, deferral and decay connote what the folklorist Robert Hunt called in 1865 the 'constantly repressing influences of Christian teaching' (Hunt, 1865, p. 25). For W. Y. Evans-Wentz in 1911, the west-country Celts 'had already combined in their own mystical way the spiritual message of primitive Christianity with the pure nature-worship of their ancestors'. However 'in later times new theological doctrines were super-imposed on this mysticism of Celtic Christianity, the Sacred Fires were buried in ashes, and the Light and Beauty of the pagan world obscured in sackcloth' (Evans-Wentz, 1911, p. 12). In the grotesquely comic figure of Christian Cantle we view this effacement of a 'pagan world' and a stifling of the 'Sacred Fires'.

Signatures in the Soil

If Hardy shows the Egdon bonfire-lighting as a ritual which fails to uncover a revivified pagan potency, this does not prevent the episode itself from echoing throughout the text as an enticing yet involuted cipher. This is because Hardy becomes obsessed by how a personal disposition emerges out of a venerable process of writing the self into the furzy expanse his protagonists traverse – a hinterland whose hollows, valleys and rifts are so rich in tenacious tradition. Nativity, as Hardy implies in the opening chapter, becomes at least as much an issue of long residence in a remote rural parish – a 'land of the *living* dead' (Massingham, 1988, p. 53) – as it is of birth. And so the sense of cold, estranging desolation imbuing *Jude the Obscure* is intimately enmeshed with the relentless (and reckless) erasure of the minute specificities of provincial life.

> The fresh harrow-lines seemed to stretch like the channellings in a piece of new corduroy, lending a meanly utilitarian air to the expanse, taking away its gradations, and depriving it of all history beyond that of the few recent months, though to every clod and stone there really attached associations enough and to spare – echoes of songs from ancient harvest-days, of spoken words, and of sturdy deeds. Every inch of ground had been the site, first or last of energy, gaiety, horse-play, bickerings, weariness [. . .] in that ancient cornfield many a man had made love-promises to a woman at whose voice he trembled by the next seed-time after fulfilling them in the church adjoining. (*JO* pp. 8–9)

Translating the 'harrow-lines' should be part of the steady unveiling of the con-figuration of regional 'history'. The runic clues embedded in 'clod and stone' require great 'patience to discover, knowledge to decipher, insight, sometimes amounting to genius, to interpret. But the writing is there, all else awaits the competence of the reader' (Randall, 1934, p. 5). But what if only the most recent 'page' is discerned, given that the turf-script has been 'harrowed' or 'plundered' in the archaic sense? The lineaments of this 'ancient cornfield' are literally constituted by what has occurred there over generations ('sturdy deeds', 'horse-play', 'love-promises'). However, this 'expanse' is stripped of epistemo-logical plenitude (ditties from 'ancient harvest-days', vernacular 'words' of philological import, vestiges of pagan fertility rites and local legends) by the prosaic procedures that invest it with human resonance: tilling the earth. Terms such as 'inch of ground' and 'site' imply that the deep concave of this cheerless field, rather than offering a soothing sense of barely changing permanence and durability – how 'the remote past presses on the present, moulding our lives, forming the everyday scene' (Nicholson, 1951, p. 383) – has become instead an exhausted mine of ethnographic ore. As George Laurence Gomme noted in his 1883 article on 'Primitive Agricultural Implements', the enclosure of common grazing land and clearance of forests by private landowners led to the fortuitous unearthing of artefacts in tumuli and cairns, which were either razed to make way for ploughing, or were ransacked for stone to construct the enclosing field walls. Richard Jefferies's *Wild Life in a Southern County* (1879) targets the ploughman 'who eagerly tears away the earth, and moves the stone to find a thin jar, as he thinks – in fact, a funeral urn [. . .] He is imbued with the idea of finding hidden treasure, and breaks the urn to pieces to discover – nothing' (p. 56). The rapacious farmer and road man blithely destroy what once offered to an antiquarian sensibility the elegiac or uncanny recognition of origins from which modern culture had become divorced.

In *The Return of the Native*, the incapacity of the current Egdonites to react emphatically to the heath's remotely sombre gaze by adding their signatures to the palimpsest of the turf's cultural continuity deprives them and us of their 'evidence': it becomes a 'missing page in the history of the country' ([Anon.], 'Excavations in Bokerly Dyke', 1893a, p. 73). Robert Hunt's *Popular Romances of the West of England* (1865) explained that 'our Celtic ancestors – in the very darkness of their ignorance – were taught, through their fears, a Pantheistic religion' and that 'in the maturity of the people, the dark shadow still some-times rises, like a spectre, partially eclipsing the mild radiance of that Christian truth which shines upon the land' (Hunt, 1865, pp. xiii). Does that 'dark shadow' impinge upon the consciousness of 'an imaginative stranger'? There is a hint of this Gothic effect when '[Eustacia] sighed bitterly, and ceased to stand erect, gradually crouching down under the umbrella as if she were drawn into the barrow by a hand from beneath' (*RN* p. 358). The barrow seems to come alive with the memory of those now mouldering within it, revivifying the layers of Egdon's past, right back to 'the ancient world of the carboniferous period, when the forms of plants were few, and of the fern kind' (*RN* pp. 205–206).

If Grandfer Cantle and his aged companions do not quite possess the fecund-ating 'imagination' to envisage the original makers of Egdon's archaeological sites, then that 'moment of vision' falls to the self-consciously 'modern' Clym Yeobright, in whose 'face could be dimly seen the typical countenance of the future' (*RN* p. 170). In an 1869 article for the *Saturday Review* on 'The Survival of Instincts' the contributor averred:

> Few things are more curious than the way in which old creeds, supposed long ago to be dead and buried, and satisfactorily forgotten, every now and then crop up to assert their continued vitality. [. . .] Even amongst people who pass themselves off very successfully as contemporary mortals we find these curi-ous resurrections of extinct superstitions which suggest that their believers are rather the inhabitants of a past epoch, who by some accident have not heard of their own death, than real living and moving moderns. ([Anon.], 'Survival of instincts', 1869c, p. 536)

Perhaps, Hardy implies, the 'modernity' that Clym embodies is a condition in which the mind is haunted by impulses it cannot fully comprehend, let alone regulate; impulses which adumbrate a primal and perennial connection to the apparently 'obsolete' energies emanating from Egdon's sandy terrain. Clym might be a link between 'the fundamental animism of the lower races' and 'the higher regions of civilisation' (Tylor, 1871, I, p. 78). Clym's face can be scruti-nized as a 'page' (*RN* p. 138), a document of ethnographic resonance whose worry-lines reveal a bizarre conflation of the animistic and the super-subtle.

Clym's visage, like that of the heath he loves, is grazed with ancestral imprints. He had been 'so inwoven with the heath in his boyhood that hardly anybody could look upon it without thinking of him' (*RN* p. 170). This once prosperous merchant in the 'nick-nack trade' wishes to 'raise the class at the expense of individuals [. . .] What was more, he was ready at once to be the first unit sacrificed' (*RN* p. 174). The suggestion here is that Clym views himself not simply as a humanitarian 'prophet' (*RN* p. 175) but rather as a willing victim of a primitive blood-sacrifice. When the socially ambitious Mrs Yeobright accuses her son of planning 'to go backward in the world' by his 'own free choice' (*RN* p. 177) she indicates the repercussions of a mortifying loss of caste, genteel respectability and 'good name'. But Hardy mischievously exploits the myriad evolutionary associations of this slide *backwards* and *downwards* into a lower 'stratum' (*RN* p. 111) of anachronistic barbarism. Egdon's uncovered 'riches' impact upon the modern moment in ways that complicate any stable sense of human 'destiny' (*RN* p. 191); as well as generating insecurities about the past's tangible proximity to the present, such as when Clym attends a 'barrow' opening on the 'heath'.

'Man's attempted explanation of natural phenomena is begotten, in the early periods', according to George Laurence Gomme, of 'fear and of a deeply rooted notion that between man and nature there existed the most intimate relationship' (Gomme, *Handbook of Folklore*, 1890, p. 8). Christian Cantle personifies this nagging 'fear': he avers that the archaeological 'operation' – with its associations of a gruesome surgical incision into the numinous 'body' of herb-scented turf – shows scant cultural reverence for regional heritage. Indeed, digging a 'hole' violates, or even severs an essential link between the milieu and those entombed within it:

> 'They have dug a hole; and they found things like flower-pots upside down, Miss'ess Yeobright: and inside these be real charnel bones. They have carried 'em off to men's houses; but I shouldn't like to sleep where they will bide. Dead folks have been known to come and claim their own. Mr Yeobright had got one pot of the bones, and was going to bring 'em home – real skellington bones – but 'twas ordered otherwise. You'll be relieved to hear that he gave away his, pot and all, on second thoughts; and a blessed thing for ye, Mis'ess Yeobright, considering the wind o' nights.'
> 'Gave it away?'
> 'Yes. To Miss Vye. She has a cannibal taste for such churchyard furniture seemingly'. (*RN* p. 191)

However much these 'urns' may resemble cheery 'flower-pots' – and the window-sill of Eustacia Vye's parlour displays 'a pair of ancient British urns' (*RN* p. 121) – there is little of the cosily domestic about them in Christian's eyes. Rather he implies that the uncovering of 'charnel bones' has profoundly unsettled a natural framework by transferring these ragged remnants from the burial site of a community's forebears into living 'men's houses'. Such imprudent, even desecrating interference – ravaging the past in the very process of revering it – could rouse angry revenants from their eternal 'sleep'; they may even seek to reclaim 'their own' and exact vengeance upon those ready to rifle 'natural' shrines. That the sacked remains of an ancient British tomb ('real skellington bones') are repackaged as a 'love-token' underscores the often bizarre conjunction of sexual appetite, gendered subjectivity, death and the archaeological 'dig' in Hardy's narrative. Mrs Yeobright is troubled and jealous that her son has presented this grotesque 'gift' not to herself but to Eustacia Vye, whose 'cannibal taste' for such 'churchyard furniture' implies that she 'feeds off' the desiccated and sinister relics. This confirms for Christian Eustacia's 'pagan' reputation as a sorceress, effectively bewitching a serious-minded young scholar away from his aggrieved mother. Eustacia's disposition simultaneously revises and subverts Cathy Lynn Preston's concept of how Hardy depicts 'the proverbial country wench' – 'trope of the female labourer's potentially corrosive sexuality coupled with its witch-like' attraction (Preston, 1995, p. 60).

In Clym's vexed attitude to his native soil can be found Hardy's own enigmatic ambivalence towards this secluded corner of Wessex. Yeobright wishes to effect the 'passing from the bucolic to the intellectual life' (*RN* p. 174) by becoming a schoolteacher to the intellectually undernourished scions of Egdon.

This connotes impatience with the 'false' doctrines of gentility to which his mother clings with desperate tenacity; yet Clym's ardent reformist rhetoric adumbrates the glib assumptions and metaphors of cultural stratification: he invites Eustacia to help him 'clear away' the 'cobwebs' of pernicious superstition and other intellectual crotchets, so inaugurating a new era of 'high class' pedagogy (*RN* p. 187). It is after all, according to Tylor, the 'office of ethnography to expose the remains of crude old culture which have passed into harmful superstition' (Tylor, 1871, II, p. 453).

Even as Clym, the earnest exponent of 'advanced' thinking, tries to goad and guide his neighbours out of primitive culture using the light of learning, he seems to grasp, and revel in, Egdon's primordial potency. Such energy flows from those 'relics of an unrecorded past' that for George Laurence Gomme epitomized the very essence of 'Folk-lore', which is 'often the only possible means of penetrating to the pre-historic past of nations, and it is certainly the only means of tracing out many of the land-marks in the mental development of man' (Gomme, 1890, pp. 2–3). In the eyes of the antiquarian narrator, there is more than a hint of the absurd in Clym's 'local peculiarity', which mingles highbrow gravitas 'chain[ing] himself [. . .] to his books' (*RN* p. 249), monastic (or masochistic) fervour, with a relish for 'wild and meagre living [. . .] and brotherliness with clowns' (*RN* p. 174). Does the narrator fix Clym here in the dilettante role of scholar-gypsy, a sentimental tourist in his own 'rural world' (*RN* p. 174), whose sandy soil and burial sites signify a gigantic necropolis? Even as the narrator debunks Clym's quixotic fancies, he shows how Egdon materializes a psychic state radically different from the young man's quiet 'studious life in Paris' (*RN* p. 174). According to Gillian Beer, '[i]n an evolutionary order it is not possible to choose to return to an earlier state'. And so Clym appears 'an invader – an alien force which disrupts and changes' (Beer, 1983, p. 254). Yet this 'alien force' visualizes the 'forgotten Celtic tribes' who once dominated the terrain: over 'the shoulder' of this countryman it seems 'peered the strikingly similar visage of the savage' (Hodgen, 1936, p. 53).

If Clym registers a 'barbarous satisfaction' in observing how the heath resists faltering endeavours at reclamation, would he feel a similar gratification in witnessing the 'lowest class' Egdonites defy his patronizing pedagogical attempt to 'cultivate' them (*RN* p. 193)? If the 'whole fabric of everyday life, in other words, is shot through with dreams, fantasies, superstitions, religious yearnings' (Thrift, 1996, p. 165), then it is Clym who comprehends this condition of the 'possible' through a willed instinctual immersion in the heath, disavowing his 'rational occupation' as schoolmaster (*RN* p. 173): '[Clym's] daily life was of a curious microscopic sort, his whole world being limited to a circuit of a few feet from his person. His familiars were creeping and winged things, and they seemed to enroll him in their band' (*RN* pp. 253–54). The irony here which Hardy exploits to the full is that in order to grasp the atavistic rhythms of the heath Clym must throw himself into the 'full swing' of modern manual 'labour' (*RN* p. 253). The narrator affirms the unencumbered, bracing and vibrant profusion of an organic milieu; yet even while he does this, Clym defaces a 'sequestered spot' (*RN* p. 195) through his gruelling work: 'where the furze grew thickest he struck the first blow in his adopted calling' (*RN* p. 253).

We 'seem to want', according to the narrator, 'the oldest and simplest human clothing where the clothing of the earth is so primitive' (*RN* p. 56). What is unclear from this much-discussed episode is whether Clym's decision to pursue a 'lowly' vocation is a half-hearted gesture of revolt against his domineering mother, or stout resistance to a peculiarly modern and oppressive notion of genteel refinement: a prohibitive and punitive culture in which, according to Tylor, men have 'learned to give poison secretly and effectually [...] have raised a corrupt literature to pestilent perfection [...] have organised a successful scheme to arrest free inquiry and proscribe free expression' (Tylor, 1871, I, p. 28).

The native, longing 'to be in some world where personal ambition was not the only recognised form of progress' (*RN* p. 195), truly returns through a drastic – and to Eustacia humiliating – expression of togetherness with the local furze-cutters, renouncing 'that rookery of pomp and vanity, Paris' where Clym had once thrived (*RN* p. 101). To Eustacia this is a lamentable 'social failure' (*RN* p. 255). 'It is an object of some importance to anthropologists', Tylor argues, 'to know where the lowest limit of human existence lies' (Tylor, 'Wild Men', 1863, pp. 21–33), and to Mrs Yeobright furze-cutting is the very nadir of 'existence' for her once diligent and dutiful son. But as Hardy demonstrates in the novel's fourth book, Clym experiences a more shattering atavistic descent into the 'abyss of undiscoverable things' (*RN* p. 324), 'com[ing] down in the world' (*RN* p. 284) to the level of a 'brute' (*RN* p. 315), when he discovers the part played by Eustacia in his mother's death on the heath. Egdon's 'imperturbable countenance [. . .] which, having defied the cataclysmal onset of centuries, reduced to insignificance by its seamed and antique features the wildest turmoil of a single man' (*RN* p. 327). This 'turmoil' is evidenced by Clym's 'inhuman language' according to his spouse.

While it may be feasible to combat the cobwebs of superstition in 'upland hamlets', it is far more challenging to 'clear cobwebs from a *wild man's* mind' (*RN* p. 331; my italics). Eustacia's description of her enraged and grief-stricken husband as a 'wild man' resonates with a grim irony, evoking the 'wild man' figure of the medieval mummers' play (traditionally portrayed clutching a tree). While Clym possesses neither the feral, inhuman aggression nor the perverse lubricity of his medieval counterpart, he speaks here with a brutal 'tongue' (*RN* p. 412) which for Eustacia is 'too relentless – there's a limit to the cruelty of savages!' (*RN* p. 334) In this instance, his wounding 'words were as the rusty implements of a bygone barbarous epoch' (*RN* p. 196). For the Duke of Argyll in 1869, 'nothing in the Natural History of Man can be more certain than that both morally, and intellectually [. . .] he can, and he often does, sink from a higher to a lower level' (Duke of Argyll, 1869, p. 156). Clym's savagery is apparent in his tacit acceptance of the provincial prejudice and paranoia that impelled

Susan Nunsuch to behave 'so barbarously to Eustacia' by condemning her as a 'witch' (*RN* p. 325), with 'a magic reputation' (*RN* p. 187). Such malign and baleful conceptions 'lurk like moles underneath the visible surface of manners' (*RN* p. 325). Clym tells Eustacia: 'Don't look at me with those eyes, as if you would *bewitch* me again. Sooner than that I'd die' (*RN* p. 332; my italics); she has 'injured him by marrying him' (*RN* p. 245); her 'charms' are more of 'a curse rather than a blessing' (*RN* p. 260); plus she casts 'a spell over' the hapless Wildeve during the 'moonlight dance' (*RN* p. 282) at East Egdon: an enchantment which 'intensifie[s]' later when he plans a 'scheme for a combined elopement' (*RN* p. 373).

In the final 'Aftercourses' section of the novel, Clym's solitary walks across Egdon imply that the locality itself casts the most potent 'spell'. Along the widower's lonely way 'the past seized upon him with its shadowy hand [. . .] His imagination would then people the spot with its ancient inhabitants: forgotten Celtic tribes trod their tracks about him, and he could almost live among them' (*RN* p. 387). Clym's 'imagination' indicates not so much a buoyant affirmation of the heath's elemental rhythms, but rather a frustrated and feckless outsider's retreat into a partially fabricated elsewhere, since the modern moment is drained of any domestic or romantic possibility. Clym now views himself as 'the mere corpse of a lover' (*RN* p. 398) and it is fitting that so much of his time is taken up with tending the graves of his mother and Eustacia. Whereas in the opening gambit a 'stranger' envisions an ancient Celt above Rainbarrow as an enabling thought-adventure offering moments of multiplied perception, here Clym lapses into solipsistic self-indulgence as he makes these mute naturalized monuments 'speak'; though this 'message' says little as to how contemporary mores might be enriched based on an archaic paradigm. The 'forgotten Celtic tribes' should signify modern man's cultural ancestors, whose rituals have been sustained and nurtured in an unbroken line. However, the representation, retrieval or reanimation of the Wessex past is here little more than the hackneyed literary trope of Gothic supernaturalism. The past's 'shadowy hand' is far from a consoling commentary on the conditions of cultural memory and Clym's metaphysical intimacy with the 'amplitude of tanned wild' around him (*RN* p. 148).

Whereas Rainbarrow functioned as an impromptu 'stage' for Grandfer Cantle's 'dance of death' at the start, the tumulus now functions as a 'pulpit' for the 'itinerant preacher' Clym. These gatherings show how the past and present overlap, but only to divulge moribund matter – the censorious moralism infusing Clym's cheerless parables – rather than to irradiate a locus of therapeutic cultural communion. Here Hardy's ethnographic enterprise resembles that of Tylor's 'anatomist', who 'carries on his studies on dead rather than on living subjects' (Tylor, 1871, I, p. 158). Clym addresses myriad spiritual 'subjects', but he fails to secure anything but a desultory 'congregation'. He cannot refresh or transmute the atavistic forces which imbue Egdon's archaeological residues. *The Mayor of Casterbridge* is even more stark in its acknowledgement that the figure who should harness the austere 'spirit of place' – Michael Henchard – is ironically the one rendered peripheral by his own fraught awareness of the strata underpinning the county town over which he presides as 'First Citizen'. Although the furmity 'hag' professes that 'the world's no memory' (*TMOC* p. 24), this is a district in which galling remembrance is sedimented into the soil. Just as Hardy felt in 1887 the numberless folds of history to lie upon him like a physical encumbrance during a visit to the Holy City of Rome in the *Life*, so Henchard suffers under a more oppressive atavistic 'weight' in Casterbridge, which is the 'pole, focus, or nerve-knot of the surrounding countryside', and where fertility is the people's most highly prized value: 'the subjects of discussion were corn [. . .] sowing and reaping, fencing and planting' (*TMOC* p. 62); and rain drifts 'like meal'.

When Hardy fuses various historical happenings in the exposition of an anthropological event, for example, the November bonfires or the mummers' play, he fosters incongruities that divulge an inscrutable mystery or a searing truth. But *The Return of the Native* reveals how the creative spirit which savours incongruity is undaunted by the fact that existing folk-rites may be little more than detritus carried along the waves of time. *The Mayor of Casterbridge* also exposes historical incongruities, yet the spirit which thrives on such gaps and fissures in the earlier novel now evinces a more sobering awareness of broken links, forgotten legacies and 'blasting disclosure[s]' (*TMOC* p. 126). The Casterbridge locale is 'untouched by the faintest sprinkle of modernism' (*TMOC* p. 29) and 'dotted with barrows, and trenched with the remains of prehistoric forts' (*TMOC* p. 18), such as 'Mai Dun, of huge dimensions and many ramparts' (*TMOC* p. 310). This is a locus of personal discovery, bringing to the 'surface buried genealogical facts, ancestral curves, dead men's traits' (*TMOC* p. 126), while also implying larger, more 'bloodshot' and traumatic regional archives; but it is for readers to reconstruct this 'vista of past enactments' (*TMOC* p. 117) by 'transporting our minds backwards' (Newton, 1850, p. 11). This 'vista' is clouded by worries about the very representability and recoverability of regional lore. According to the 1870 *Quarterly Review*

> Once an object is swept into the great dust-bin of prehistoric archaeology, we need give ourselves no further trouble about it. The cry now is, it belonged to people who have long passed away: we know nothing of their language or their religion, still less of their manners or customs; and if this be so, it is no use inquiring for what purpose the monument was erected, nor at what period: all that we are now allowed, is to worship. ([Anon.], 'Prehistoric Times', 1870a, p. 432)

Frederic Harrison extended this perception of the 'great dust-bin' of history in his 1911 *Autobiographical Memoirs*: 'To collect facts about the past, and to leave the application of this information for any one or no one to give it a philosophical meaning, is merely to encumber the future with useless rubbish' (qtd. in Freeland, 2005, p. 225). For George Henderson in *Survivals in Belief among the Celts* (1911), 'Folk-consciousness thinks in pieces: it gives small answers to great questions' (Henderson, 1911, p. 343); yet how can we place these 'pieces' in an orderly or intelligible arrangement? Here ethnographic commentators, like Hardy in *The Mayor*, oscillate nervously between construing antiquity as irretrievably lost and unknowable, or as ready to strengthen contemporary cultural and political agendas.

A History of Violence

It would be a worthy attempt to rehabilitate, on paper, the living Durnovaria of fourteen or fifteen hundred years ago [. . .] we may ask what kind of object did Dorchester then form in the summer landscape as viewed from such a point; where stood the large buildings, where the small, how did the roofs group themselves, what were the gardens like, if any, what social character had the streets, what were the customary noises, what sort of exterior was exhibited by these hybrid Romano-British people, apart from the soldiery? [. . .] These are merely the curious questions of an outsider to initiated students of the period.

(Hardy, *Public Voice*, 2001, p. 64)

So the amateur antiquarian 'outsider' Hardy concludes his thought-adventure on the Romano-British remains unearthed in the foundations of Max Gate. What would a 'living Durnovaria' have looked like when the Romans made it into 'one of their chief cities of the South' (Treves, 1906, p. 343)? Hardy's article reflects his keen enthusiasm for antiquarian ventures between 1880 and 1887. This included his joining the Society for the Protection of Ancient Buildings and The Dorset Natural History and Antiquarian Field Club, as well as his designing and constructing Max Gate. Hardy's reference to 'the customary noises' hints not at a straightforward or monolithic conception of west-country 'belonging' but rather a tortuous – and tortured – 'hybrid Romano-British' identity that *The Mayor of Casterbridge* sedulously excavates (Tandon, 2003, pp. 471–89). In his 1906 travelogue *Highways and Byways in Dorset*, Sir Frederick Treves remarked that 'there is little doubt' that the 'embryo of the town of Dorchester stood within the great ramparts of Maiden Castle, and was already a place of consequence when the Romans landed in Britain' (Treves, 1906, p. 343).

For Dud No-Man, in John Cowper Powys's re-visioning of *The Mayor* in *Maiden Castle*, the '"aura" of this old Roman-British town, with its layers upon layers of human memories, semi-historic and prehistoric, seemed to have a magical power over' his 'imagination' (*MC* p. 112). Hardy proclaims this tangled social and cultural identity, as well as the intricately stratified heritage in the novel's full title: *The Life and Death of the Mayor of Casterbridge, A Story of a Man of Character*. As Bharat Tandon observes, 'The Life and Death', with its weighty intimations of a stark 'Puritan allegory', frames a 'British derivative of the Latin major', which is joined to 'a place-name merging *castra* with the Old English *brycg*' (Tandon, 2003, pp. 472–74). On the high street of the county town Elizabeth-Jane traces the 'crusted grey stone-work remaining' from a 'remoter Casterbridge' (*TMOC* p. 60) than that announced by Roman layout.

The Mayor of Casterbridge disinters historical and philological 'relics', as Hardy searches for resonances and links across the 'ruins' of time (*TMOC* p. 127). This narrative, far from confirming the view that between the excavated 'remains' of Roman soldiers and the 'living there seemed a gulf too wide for even a spirit to pass' (*TMOC* p. 70), actually relishes the felt pressure of multifarious pasts, and how they commingle in instinctual impulses, as well as in place-names, regional argot and architectural vestiges such as the 'ruins of a Franciscan priory' (*TMOC* p. 127). Hardy gives prominence to the rubble and dust of bygone battles, especially the Roman amphitheatre of Maumbury Ring, situated on the southwest side of Dorchester. According to the 1908 *British Architect* this 'reputed amphitheatre' was 'undoubtedly the largest and the most important structure of the kind in Great Britain. It was, moreover, one of the ancient monuments of the rarest type remaining in our country; and therefore it was surprising that the place had been untouched so long by the spade of the field archaeologist' ([Anon.], 'Notes on Current Events', 1908, p. 220). The correspondent charts how by the turn of the twentieth century Maumbury had become a signal archaeological site, especially to H. St George Gray, who was conducting excavations there in the early autumn of 1908. More than two decades after completing *The Mayor of Casterbridge*, Hardy published an article on Maumbury Ring in *The Times*. Hardy, in this piece comes across as an enthralled observer, eager to query the findings with Gray, whose follow-up digs over the next few years indicated that the site was Neolithic in provenance, the Romans having taken over and adapted existing earthworks.

The 1908 *British Architect* correspondent describes Maumbury as 'elliptical in shape' – elliptical and challenging also in the subliminal resonances it transmits throughout Hardy's novel ([Anon.], 'Notes on Current Events', 1908, p. 220). Bloodthirsty spectacles such as gladiatorial combats were staged in the amphitheatre during the Roman occupation and later executions on the town gibbet, as well as more recent 'pugilistic encounters almost to the death' (*MC* p. 73). This is a venue so scarred by eruptions of historic brutality that romantic meetings can never take place there:

Casterbridge announced old Rome in every street, alley, and precinct. It looked Roman, bespoke the art of Rome, concealed dead men of Rome. It was impossible to dig more than a foot or two deep about the town fields and gardens without coming upon some tall soldier or other of the Empire, who had lain there in his silent unobtrusive rest for the space of fifteen hundred years. He was mostly found lying on his side, in an oval scoop in the chalk, like a chicken in its shell; his knees drawn up to his chest; sometimes with the remains of his spear against his arm. (*MC* pp. 70–71)

While it has been widely canvassed that *The Mayor of Casterbridge* is 'the most overtly archaeological of Hardy's novels' (Tandon, 2003, p. 472), in which his thinking shadows and enriches the nascent sciences of humankind, critics disagree about the meaning behind Hardy's pointed stress on the fictionalized 'ancient borough' (*TMOC* p. 29) as a locale replete with, and constituted of, ruined buildings and broken 'bodies': 'the detritus of all earthly things, the fine grains of nothingness into which the world is day by day being ground down by the actions of the elements and man' ([Anon.], 'Dust Ho!', 1866b, p. 645). That the excavated 'remains' of a dead Roman soldier might appear to the untutored eye 'like a chicken in its shell' is striking; hinting not at inert, moribund matter but a spectral presence in the process of *becoming*, until it emerges from its subterranean cell to impact in potentially surprising ways upon the modern moment. This concept of the underground tomb as a receptacle of esoteric energy has darker connotations; such as when Hardy gauges some of the other 'transactions' inextricably associated with the 'earthen circle' over the centuries. F. J. Harvey Darton refers to 'the scene of a peculiarly horrible execution in the eighteenth century' (Darton, 1922, p. 41) which Hardy elaborates:

> Apart from the sanguinary nature of the games originally played therein, such incidents attached to its past as these; that for scores of years the town gallows had stood at one corner; that in 1705 a woman who had murdered her husband was half strangled and then burnt there in the presence of ten thousand spectators. Tradition reports that at a certain stage of the burning her heart burst and leapt out of her body to the terror of them all, and that not one of those ten thousand people ever cared particularly for hot roast after that. (*TMOC* p. 71)

The 'woman who had murdered her husband' is Mary Channing, the last woman to be burned to death in Dorchester. At the time of her execution in 1705 she was just 19 years old. Casterbridge has been for 'centuries' an 'assize-town'; its inhabitants are therefore inured to witnessing 'sensational exits from the world' (*TMOC* p. 328). No 'exit' is more 'sensational' than the legalized murder of Mary Channing, and this fragment of salvaged time profoundly destabilizes our perception of what constitutes diurnal actuality and a fever-dream. Like Dud No-Man in *Maiden Castle*, Hardy is obsessed with this historic event; yet whereas Dud registers a 'sick disgust with all the material happenings that had ever taken place in this town of such tragic roots' (*MC* p. 24), *The Mayor*'s narrator reduces the execution to a literary conceit – an unexpected flourish of 'gallows humour'. The furmity-hag crows to Susan Henchard of doing 'business with the richest stomachs in the land' (*TMOC* p. 24); however, the 'strongest' stomach among the spectators at the public killing cannot deal with the visceral impact of Channing's burning body: 'not one of those ten thousand people ever cared particularly for hot roast after that'.

Why does the antiquarian narrator mobilize this macabre play of wit, testing the limits of 'bad taste'? He focuses primarily on the assembled crowd's atavistic 'appetite' for and 'consumption' of gory spectacle, just as the victim's 'body' is eventually reduced to the desiccated form of 'ashes', but not before her 'heart leapt out of her body'. The narrator prioritizes the gruesome materiality of the human form in acute distress; how it is 'purified' by fire, then reassembled and recorded in the annals of written 'Tradition'. Mary Channing does not 'go quietly' in this account: the narrator's antiquarian 'map' of the Roman amphitheatre intersects with the geography of the female body at its centre – its status as an autonomous, sentient entity as well as its porous vulnerability. Excavating this sight/site of horror, the narrator implies the body's propensity for sudden and sickly transformation; it becomes a target for, and final point of resistance against, the remorseless machinery of disciplinary control.

Hardy signifies that there may be little separating the butchery staged to regale Roman dignitaries nearly 2,000 years ago and the eighteenth century spectacles of public burning. *All the Year Round* elaborated this viewpoint in its 1885 survey of Dorchester's topographical oddities: 'An English holiday of [. . .] barbarous character was afforded early in the last century by the burning of one Mary Channing, just previously executed for the murder of her husband, a crime then regarded in the light of petty treason, and as worthy to be marked with extreme punishment' ([Anon.], 'Chronicles of English Counties', 1885a, p. 352). Hardy's testimony reinforces the grim irony of a supposedly humane, 'enlightened' polity which permits – even promotes – such events as retributive justice; preserving, according to Cyrus Redding in the *New Monthly Magazine*, the monstrous 'abuses of the dark ages' (Redding, 1868, p. 329).

The tragic corporeality of Mary Channing – what it discloses about our prurient predilections, our inescapable mortality as well as efforts to invest the body's material existence with transcendent humanity – continued to haunt Hardy until he was nearly 80, as indicated by an entry in his notebooks under the date 25 January 1919. This is not the typical antiquarian's delight in unravelling the tangled skeins of bygone ages but reportage itself as a mode of 'blood-sport'. The strategic omission of 'horrible' data reveals a core component of Hardy's imaginative excavations in *The Mayor of Casterbridge*: a fixation on the reappraisal of deviant, heretical or redacted historical 'reports', especially those which evince how little control women have over their own words, bodies, desires and destinies. Apparently guilty of 'extraordinary crime' (*TMOC* p. 247), Mary Channing cannot speak for herself, and Hardy repeatedly returns to how the voiceless are dispensed with. 'Telling good stories' (*TMOC* p. 40) reveals as much as it conceals about regionally based power relations and the framework of male patronage and privilege that effectively writes Mary Channing off. Yet even as she is *sentenced* and executed, she returns to haunt Hardy through a novel which depicts, and morbidly savours, a 'general drama of pain' (*TMOC* p. 335) in which human and agricultural fertility are key, whether it be the outlandish details of Channing's charred body or 'the full breasts of Diana Multimammia' (*TMOC* p. 330).

Who in this novel has the lofty authority to identify what constitutes a historical 'fact' beyond the possibility of accidental coincidence? What does the anti-quarian narrator really glean and surmise from yellowing tomes and other 'rural records' (*TMOC* p. 26)? And how are the hapless victims of regional history separated from those who can palliate it: such are the questions that reverberate through the text. As a stoical Susan Henchard grimly acknowledges at the outset, 'anything' is 'possible at the hands of Time and Chance except perhaps *fair* play' (*TMOC* p. 6; my italics). It is on the annual *fair* field of Weydon-Priors, with its 'sale by auction of a few inferior animals' (*TMOC* p. 8) where Henchard drunkenly dismantles marital and market etiquette by con-verting his own family into chattel – an act which confirms how '*pulling down* is more the nater of Weydon' (*TMOC* p. 7). As a married woman and a penniless member of a rustic underclass Susan Henchard feels the lack of 'fair play' acutely in the 'casual disfigurements that resulted from the straitened circumstances' of her life (*TMOC* p. 27).

In Hardy's various references to Mary Channing's ritual 'disfigurement' and death, the insistent focus on the present writer's 'ancestor' who handed down the data indicates that regional identity and culture should not be construed simply as an immovable trait; instead a more fluid and mercurial concept of Wessex emerges through acts of storytelling in which lingering splinters of fact have been partially concealed by an overlay of generations of fantasies – rhetorical as well as economic 'transactions' occur 'under the thin bland surface' of civic affairs (*TMOC* p. 38). These acts are not only performed by the benefi-ciaries of municipal prestige, such as the First Citizen Michael Henchard, but also by 'underworld' figures like the 'old woman haggard, wrinkled, and almost in rags' (*TMOC* p. 23) who sells furmity at Weydon-Priors Fair, itself the locus of a transgressive or oppositional past, with its 'peep-shows, toy-stands, wax-works, inspired monsters' and 'readers of Fate' (*TMOC* p. 8).

Like the 'antiquated slop' (*TMOC* p. 9) she peddles to Henchard in the gloomy tent, the hag's yarns of 'bygone times' are a heady 'witches' brew', a 'laced *concoc-tion*' (*TMOC* p. 9; my italics) of disparate, highly spiced ingredients, including primitive superstition, scurrilous rumour and a corrosively cynical folk-wisdom. This 'old flagrant female' (*TMOC* p. 193) divines the high-minded 'clergy's taste' at least as well as that of 'coarse shameless females' (*TMOC* p. 24), among whose number Mary Channing may have been included by her historic accusers. The furmity-hag's 'white-apron' (*TMOC* p. 8) connects her with the similarly garbed prostitutes of Mixen Lane – a deprived and depraved enclave within the picturesque borough of Casterbridge with its avenues of majestic trees. By contrast, the Lane's foul urban ambience and sullied symbols of crime and retribution (the gallows, gaol and hangman's cottage) underscores the close association between fecundity and mortality. When the furmity-hag reappears, accused of urinating on holy ground, she speaks back at, and debunks the chief magistrate Henchard's 'exhibition' (*TMOC* p. 10) of ostensibly civilized 'law' – a law which once demonized and dismantled Mary Channing in front of a baying mob. The furmity-hag, like the Casterbridge underclass of Mixen Lane, grasps only too well the signal part blood 'sacrifice' (*TMOC* p. 45) plays in the pursuit of individual honours, affluence and preferment, as well as in the formation of cultural memory. Although 'people at fairs change like the leaves of trees' (*TMOC* p. 23), she can recall 'every serious fight o' married parties, every murder, every manslaughter' (*TMOC* p. 24). For this caustic observer of, and participant in, regional affairs, it is 'the sly and the underhand that get on in these times!' (*TMOC* p. 24)

That Hardy coolly dissects these layers of fraught and tormented retrospect is perhaps unsurprising given that the very name of the annual fair where Henchard makes such a fateful scene – Weydon-*Priors* – advertises the furtive, backward-looking glance. The execution of Mary Channing in 1705 and Henchard's disavowal of his spouse and child in a fit of drunken fury signifies a perverse past that is always and irreconcilably opposed to the dictates of sober civic governance and propriety; as H. Calderwood remarked, '[m]en are not so completely independent that each man's acquirements are entombed with his body' (Calderwood, 1871, p. 212). The 'haunting shade' (*TMOC* p. 298) of the 'innocent' Mary Channing hovers around this stratified narrative of a self-confessed 'woman-hater' (*TMOC* p. 78) for whom human bodies disastrously lose their sanctity and become damaged 'articles' (*TMOC* p. 11) for a quick sale. 'The antiquary', according to E. B. Tylor, 'excavating but a few yards deep, may descend from the debris representing our modern life, to relics of the art and science of the Middle Ages, to signs of Norman, Saxon, Roman, Romano-British times, to traces of the higher stone age' (1871, I, p. 53). But what if the exacting process of stratigraphic observation and recording obfuscates instead of irradiates a crisp image of the past? According to Hardy, in his paper to the *Dorset Natural History and Antiquarian Field Club*, archaeologists have done little 'towards piecing together and reconstructing these evidences into an *unmutilated* whole' orchestrating 'a true picture by which the uninformed could mentally realize the ancient scene with some completeness' (Hardy, *Public Voice*, 2001, p. 64; my italics). Here are monitory intimations of physical and editorial amputation; conjuring a partial and incomplete body of archaeological evidence, a susceptible body politic at a time of seismic social upheaval, as well as Mary Channing's bruised and burning form.

Whether it is the Roman centurion's 'Empire', the British penal code of the eighteenth century, or the primitive wife-auction – all demand 'bodies', which are then converted into cash, dust or ash. Weydon-Priors fair, Mixen Lane and the Roman amphitheatre vouchsafe lurid examples of vicious 'blood sports': the savagery of a remorseless competitive fight for survival at myriad moments in time. Tylor's *Primitive Culture* is in part a chronicle of 'the most fiendish delight in bloodshed': '[f]ighting' is one of the 'outstanding engagements of the savage', announcing 'his bravery, his patience, his endurance, his industry, his defence of those depending upon him, and his provision for their wants' (Calderwood, 1871, p. 215). Casterbridge becomes an 'arena', whose most recent manifestation of discord is the rancorous trade-war between Michael Henchard and his artful Scottish assailant, Donald Farfare, which maps ominously onto fierce and epochal 'struggle' between distinct 'social regimes' (Musselwhite, 2003, pp. 50–88) down the centuries (Celtic versus Roman, Saxon versus Norman, capital versus labour). The lavish festive entertainment that Henchard arranges for the townsfolk on an 'earthwork' close to the town boasts a 'stage for boxing, wrestling, and *drawing blood generally*' (*TMOC* p. 104; my italics). Even the 'mossy gardens' that Elizabeth-Jane admires while strolling through the Casterbridge streets, contain a species called 'bloody warriors' nestling among the 'nasturtiums' and 'dahlias' (*TMOC* p. 60). But the long history of belligerent antagonism extends to a period that predates the Roman occupation, an era hinted at when Hardy evokes the 'ancient country' of Wessex as an archaeological 'dig':

> into this road they directed the horse's head, and soon were bowling across that ancient country whose surface never had been stirred to a finger's depth, save by the scratchings of rabbits, since brushed by the feet of the earliest tribes. The tumuli these had left behind, dun and shagged with heather, jutted roundly into the sky from the uplands, as though they were the full breasts of Diana Multimammia supinely extended there. (*TMOC* p. 330)

Hardy conducts a bravura philological time-voyage, 'traversing strange latitudes' (*TMOC* p. 58) of semantic ambiguity. The Latinate 'tumuli' have gathered over the centuries a patina of Old English associations ('dun and shagged with heather'). An 1866 reviewer argued that in 'Dorsetshire the bucolic mind largely prevails. There the worship of Ceres and Diana go hand in hand' ([Anon.], 'Archaic anthropology', 1866a, p. 941). The pointed reference to 'Diana Multimammia' conjures up Sir James George Frazer's vivid delineation of Diana's fertility priest – 'a dark figure with the glitter of steel at his shoulder'– warily circling his tree in the holy grove at Nemi, as part of a ritual of unceasing assassination in the seminal, multivolume *The Golden Bough* (1890–1915). Of the goddess Diana, Frazer observes, 'fire seems to have played a foremost part in her ritual. [. . .] the sacred fire would seem to have been tended by Vestal Virgins' (Frazer, 1994, p. 14).

In the eyes of the assembled crowd who demanded the most savage 'ritual' slaughter in 1705, Mary Channing was the very antithesis of 'Vestal' purity, and she becomes the victim of uncomprehending social laws in an earthwork whose sloping banks may have witnessed numerous executions with the same pitiless impassivity. To see, in Wordsworth's terms, 'Our dim ancestral past in vision clear' (Wordsworth, 1986, p. 507) is not a validation of progressive enlightenment, universal uplift or providential patterning. Like 'the monolithic circle at Stonehenge' (*TMOC* p. 231), the past at this juncture is shaped as a 'selectively remembered accretion' (Cubitt, 1998, p. 10) pointing towards the dreary repetition of error. The Roman Ring, Hardy implies, adumbrates an order based on indiscriminate acts of heedless brutality. And death here is not the exacting but precious pledge of new hope for the Casterbridge indigenes; Hardy intimates how crimes are re-enacted and compounded over the centuries in the relentless 'battle of life' (*TMOC* p. 161). According to H. Calderwod in his 1871 review of Tylor's *Primitive Culture*, a persuasive argument for progress-ive theory 'rests upon the capabilities of man as a *rational* being [. . .] it is by power of thought that they are able to bring their lower nature into subjec-tion, and raise the standard of culture for the higher nature' (p. 215). This 'subjection' of the 'lower' self is something which Michael Henchard never convincingly achieves.

Hardy's alertness to grotesque human error repeating and reverberating across time interrogates Walter Pater's notion of cultural development not as a succession of startling and innovative discoveries but as a recrudescence of 'past practices', customs and beliefs (Snyder, 2008, pp. 1–21). In *Plato and Platonism* (1893), Pater reflects that 'as in many other very original products of human genius, the seemingly new is old also, a palimpsest, a tapestry of which the actual threads have served before, or like the animal frame itself, every particle of which has already lived and died many times over' (Pater, 1893, pp. 7–8). So Donald Farfrae seems to his Casterbridge employees 'like the poet of a new school who takes his contemporaries by storm; who is not really new, but is the first to articulate what all his listeners have felt, though but dumbly till then' (*TMOC* p. 54). The unquiet spirit of bygone days, which haunts the physical fabric of the modern moment, Pater depicts in positive terms: 'in the midst of a frozen world, the buried fire of ancient art rose up from under the soil' (Pater, *Renaissance*, 1996, p. 146). Until the arrival of Michael Henchard, whose temperament is likened to 'volcanic fires' (*TMOC* p. 235), Casterbridge is in one sense 'a frozen world', surrounded by 'remote copses' and 'lonely uplands' (*TMOC* p. 264). An 1862 reviewer discussed the county of Dorset in the mid-nineteenth century as having 'an unpleasant notoriety [. . .] and a bad name, not easily shaken off, of being chronically behind the age' ([Anon.], 'Review of Hutchins', 1862b, p. 285). But it is not the 'buried fire' of 'ancient art' which erupts into the surface milieu; rather a resurgent past of 'satirical mummery' (*TMOC* p. 276), 'rough jest' (*TMOC* p. 280) and riotous 'orgie' (*TMOC* p. 288) brings with it discord, dereliction and predatory passion. This is the history dominated by bellicose 'fools' such as Henchard – 'rogues', 'wanton hussies' and 'slatterns' (*TMOC* p. 53); and this heritage is nowhere better illustrated than in the raucous skimmity-ride, an atavistic throwback which causes 'the dangerous illness and miscarriage' of Lucetta (*TMOC* p. 288) – another instance of spoiled fecundity which implies the leering mask behind High-Place Hall, whose 'chipped lips' bespeak syphilitic degeneration (*TMOC* p. 142), as well as the stark images of Mary Channing's broken body in the Roman ruin.

The gloomy grandeur of the Roman amphitheatre casts a long shadow across the world of a novel which enumerates myriad 'arenas' for unseemly and garish public entertainment, such as the 'old bull-stake' and 'cock-pit' (*TMOC* p. 141).

Casterbridge boasts not only a site of primitive struggle in the Roman Ring –
'still smooth and circular, as if used for its original purpose not so very long ago'
(*TMOC* p. 72) – but also the nearby corn-market which has become the modern
'centre and arena of the town' (*TMOC* p. 181), where the 'spectacular drama'
of Henchard and Farfrae's 'trade-antagonism' (*TMOC* p. 115) is enacted. And
so the escalation of the vendetta between Henchard and Farfrae is couched in
martial rhetoric: 'A time came when, to avoid collision with his former friend as
he might, Farfrae was compelled, in sheer self-defence, to close with Henchard
in mortal commercial combat' (*TMOC* p. 116). Although Henchard is committed to shaming his more dynamic younger adversary in this bad-tempered
contest, the 'amazing energy' (*TMOC* p. 114) for which he was once widely
venerated has now gone to seed. In defeat, Henchard had 'no wish to make
an *arena* [. . .] of a world that had become a mere painted scene to him' (*TMOC*
p. 320; my italics). However, the full significance of the Roman Ring is tied to
a point in Hardy's literary career when he could no longer illustrate such 'ruins'
as possible tokens of an austere but enriching framework, which allowed
our primeval forebears to secure a stable future for their tribes. He sees instead
'the essentially cruel heartlessness of Paganism' ([Anon.], 'Primitive man',
1874, p. 70) infusing 'recurring cycles of barbarism and civilisation' (Brewster,
1853, pp. 136–37).

Gather Ye The Fragments That Are Left

[Archaeology affords] links in that chain of continuous tradition, which connects the civilized nineteenth century with the race of the primeval world, –
which holds together this great brotherhood in bonds of attachment [. . .]
which, traversing the ruins of empires [. . .] spans the abyss of time, and transmits onward the message of the Past.

(Newton, 1850, p. 26)

For Charles Newton, one of the most eloquent proponents of the emergent
discipline of archaeology, the 'dig' uncovers a buoyant and inspiriting 'message'
of movement onwards as well as upwards. Newton's sanguine concept of steady
progress is grounded in a stable archive of 'tradition': as the modern moment
is the outcome of earlier epochs, Britain inscribes its myriad august feats into
the archaeological record as a munificent bequest to future generations. But as
Hardy demonstrates in *The Mayor of Casterbridge*, rarely do we salvage from the
soil an 'unmutilated whole'. He adumbrates an unnerving 'message'; indeed
there is scant evidence of a noble fraternity held together in 'bonds of attachment'. Although Henchard initially treats Farfrae as an admired younger sibling,
the country town becomes a clammy, claustrophobic 'stage' for fretful acrimony,
myopic one-upmanship and internecine strife. *The Mayor of Casterbridge* illustrates not so much Charles Newton's 'ruins of empires' as an empire of ruins

and dust. At Weydon-Priors Fair the young Henchard rants about the 'ruin of good men by bad wives'; his preferred 'weapon' for 'mortal commercial combat' with Farfrae fails to 'deal *ruin* at the first or second stroke' (*TMOC* p. 116; my italics). The former First Citizen is left 'unmanned' (*TMOC* pp. 250, 323) and resembles in his autistic isolation a 'dark ruin' (*TMOC* p. 326). As a pensive Elizabeth-Jane realizes while visiting her mother's grave, sifting the fragments of forgotten ages for a complete 'scene' or unimpeded access to native customs is fraught with a sense of ruptured roots and ruined hopes:

> She seized on these days for her periodical visits to the spot where her mother lay buried – the still-used burial-ground of the old Roman-British city, whose curious feature was this, its continuity as a place of sepulture. Mrs Henchard's dust mingled with the dust of women who lay ornamented with glass hair-pins and amber necklaces, and men who held in their mouths coins of Hadrian, Posthumus, and the Constantines. (*TMOC* p. 204)

Hardy's stress on 'the Empire' (*TMOC* p. 140) forcibly reminds us that the 'men who held in their mouths coins of Hadrian' were both tireless minions and unwitting victims of a centralized and imperial administration that maintained its sway through acts of supposedly condign punishment. The name 'Posthumus', like Weydon-*Priors*, reveals a grimly relished irony: Hardy signals his own addiction to myriad necromantic figurations and all things 'obsolete' (Tandon, 2003, pp. 472–89). However, in this episode Hardy's standpoint is more aggressively sardonic, as the palpable toughness of 'remnants' (*TMOC* p. 67) that have weathered time's unflinching rigour ('glass hair-pins') are measured against the abject and debased condition of their once illustrious possessors ('dust'). The luxurious props and adornments of public, dynamic life in the distant past, implying femininity as lavishly decorated spectacle ('amber necklaces') contrast with the dreary stillness of residual remains. For Dud No-Man in *Maiden Castle* this continuity of 'sepulture' supplies an unexpected fund of solace, sensory stimulation and even sublime reassurance:

> Dorchester seemed [. . .to be] one deep vase of thick-pressed *pot-pourri* – a subtle perfume that was like the sweet dust of long-buried generations, a consecrated secular dust from which all that was foul in mortality had long since evaporated, leaving only a thrice-purged residue, a holy deposit, the dust of what was inviolable in ashes, indestructible in embers, destined to perish only with our human senses. (*MC* p. 390)

For Powys, human decay is winnowed of its desolating associations and reveals instead a fragrant and enabling 'holy deposit'. Hardy, by contrast, cannot conceive of this continuity without being alerted to a heritage of blight and pollution whose harrowing bleakness is unleavened by the mischievous brio which mobilizes the Egdon seniors in their 'dance of death' on Rainbarrow's summit.

Susan Henchard's 'dust' in the Casterbridge graveyard is by no means as perilously corrupting and infectious as the numberless layers of toxic ash under which the once mighty metropolis is buried in Richard Jefferies's *After London*. However, her vitiated remains highlight the unwholesome residues to which the dispossessed members of a rustic underclass are repeatedly exposed: the mortmain of the past is a 'thick hoar' which cloaks the land of the evicted and the exploited, 'deadening footfalls' (*TMOC* p. 7). In the third chapter, the 'highroad into the village of Weydon-Priors was again carpeted with dust. The trees had put on as of yore their aspect of dingy green' (*TMOC* p. 8). The 'dingy green', as Bharat Tandon avers, ominously echoes Susan's sullen first impression of 'the blackened-green stage of colour that the doomed leaves pass through dingy, and yellow, and red' (*TMOC* p. 7). '[W]ell-nigh ruined' by 'drink' as a young man, the middle-aged Henchard hopes to bring to 'fruition' a 'scheme' for rebuilding his fortunes, yet the bold pursuit of filthy lucre results in so much 'dust and ash' (*TMOC* p. 129); the bankrupt former mayor's countenance is marked by 'a film of ash' (*TMOC* p. 219); 'a cloud of dust' (*TMOC* p. 265) heralds the Royal visit to Casterbridge. Farfrae notices at one point that Elizabeth-Jane's 'dress' is 'still sown' with wheat husks and 'dust' (*TMOC* p. 95); and her perceived want of social finesse 'disgrace[s]' her step-father Henchard 'to the dust' (*TMOC* p. 132), presaging his grim proximity to the debased detritus of Casterbridge society – Mixen Lane.

That Hardy so diligently exploits the multifarious associations of 'dust' and 'ash' in a novel obsessed with ruinous acts of fury and fraudulence as well as the relics of remnant primitives is unsurprising; what is more striking is how his roving archaeological sensibility permits ostensibly trite local occurrences to evince 'certain peculiarities of reverberation' (*TMOC* p. 275), until they adumbrate precipitous and revolutionary change. 'Time' is indeed a 'magician' (*TMOC* p. 35), bringing together the polluted and the pristine; and the narrator spans countless generations to disinter affiliations and uncanny correspondences that would otherwise remain cloaked. So the dour and unadorned steadiness of Hardy's opening gambit, with its drab topographical data – 'a road neither straight nor crooked, neither level nor hilly, bordered by hedges, trees, and other vegetation' (*TMOC* p. 70) – augurs a more wide-ranging, and portentous vista: 'the voice of a weak bird' sings an 'old evening song that might doubtless have been heard on the hill at the same hour, and with the self-same trills, quavers [. . .] at any sunset of that season for centuries untold' (*TMOC* p. 7).

When Susan Henchard espies at the King's Arms banquet the scornfully sober spouse who once abandoned her, she is flabbergasted at the extent of his transmutation from fractious wage-labourer and shoddy opportunist to the paragon of bourgeois probity: 'When last she had seen him he was sitting in a corduroy jacket, fustian waistcoat and breeches, and tanned leather leggings, with a basin of hot furmity before him' (*TMOC* p. 35). Hardy compresses the time-span between the sumptuous mayoral meal and the earlier tableau of a tattered furmity tent, whose chthonic 'law' suspends chivalric etiquette and overturns the sacramental union of Christian matrimony. And 'dishing the dirt' on Henchard's ignominious 'secret' takes a mere 'four-and-twenty hours' as snide innuendo races through the leafy avenues of the sedate county town: 'there was not a person in Casterbridge who remained unacquainted with the story of Henchard's mad freak at Weydon-Priors fair, long years before [. . .] the act having lain as dead and buried ever since, the interspace of years was unperceived' (*TMOC* p. 291).

So Hardy's imaginative excavation delights in 'contrarious inconsistencies' (*TMOC* p. 319) and affords the sharpest contrast to the sober dictates of archaeological reconstruction which J. Romilly Allen expounded in 1884: to comprehend the layers of a 'parish' past one must subdivide 'Time' into 'periods, either consisting of so many actual years, beginning and terminating at a known date, or into eras' (Allen, 1885, p. 240). Yet in Casterbridge there is radical 'unrestraint as to [temporal] boundaries' (*TMOC* p. 61), thwarting the imperial instinct to rationalize time as the monitoring and mapping of a succession of simultaneously apprehended clock or calendar events. This may explain Hardy's blithe indifference to any structuring principle of historical chronology when moving his 'Man of Character' between a dizzying array of metaphorical positions. Henchard is measured against Achilles, Oedipus and other classical Greek figures; Roman historical luminaries like Caesar and Brutus; Biblical personages such as Cain, Samson and Saul; even Shakespearean tragic protagonists such as Macbeth and King Lear are brought into the equation (Moses, 1995, p. 32). This manoeuvre intimates a temporal sensation that is highly subjective, discontinuous, indeterminate and vertiginous; productively disturbing a conventional narrative's artificial attempts at crisp, coherent linearity:

> Other clocks struck eight from time to time – one gloomily from the gaol, another from the gable of an alms-house [. . .] so that chronologists of the advanced school were appreciably on their way to the next hour before the whole business of the old one was satisfactorily wound up. (*TMOC* p. 31)

'Wound up' wittily puns on the concept of an imminent commercial collapse. 'Time' proves that Henchard lacks the keen assurance to keep his own enterprise afloat when threatened by Farfrae's mystery cult of money which augurs a modish concept of agriculture as a highly cutthroat industry subject to the fluctuations of international trade. As with the discordant striking of the town 'clocks', Hardy draws rich possibilities from the general dealer Buzzford's eccentrically skewed perception of a tumultuous Wessex heritage which conflates the recent and the 'hoary', the endemic and the exotic:

> 'Casterbridge is a old, hoary place o' wickedness, by all account. 'Tis recorded in history that we rebelled against the King one or two hundred years ago, in the time of the Romans, and that lots of us was hanged on Gallows Hill, and quartered, and our different jints sent about the country like butcher's meat; and for my part I can well believe it.' (*TMOC* p. 121)

Hardy contrives a sarcastic sounding of contested chronicles through this amusingly wayward local pundit whose historical pastiche – full of blunders, foibles and frailties – scrambles 'fact' to suit his own rhetorical tics. For Buzzford it is storytelling flair, not dispassionate precision which matters. That he confuses the Duke of Monmouth's ill-fated 'Pitchfork Rebellion' against James II in 1685, and the retribution which awaited the insurgents at the hands of Judge Jeffreys, with the age of Hadrian and the Roman occupation indicates that there is, ultimately, a common thread binding these seismic events across the centuries – the unwritten 'law' that makes 'mortal [. . .] combat' (*TMOC* p. 116) its gloomy centrepiece. It is this facet which is missing from Daniel Defoe's *Tour through England and Wales*: 'Dorchester is indeed a pleasant agreeable town to live in [. . .] a man who coveted a retreat in this world might as agreeably spend his time and as well in Dorchester, as in any town I know in England' (Defoe, 1927, I, pp. 210–11). 'If you seek continuous history' according to F. J. Harvey Darton, 'here' in Dorchester 'is richness' (Darton, 1922, p. 41).

Yet as Buzzford's muddled 'lecture' reveals, it is economic, social and religious 'history' inextricably tied to images of 'butcher's meat', whether it be Sweyn's sacking of the district in Saxon times after the Romans departed; the 'drums and tramplings' (Darton, 1922, p. 41) as rival armies passed through its streets during the English Civil War; the gross indignities suffered by the local populace under the Bloody Assize and during the Napoleonic Wars; the torture and public execution of Mary Channing; or the town's association with the unfortunate Tolpuddle 'conspirators'. The competing voices of the Casterbridge 'clocks' discloses one of the novel's most memorable satires of circumstance: no matter how much Henchard strives to bury his own shameful past and 'autochthonous' ancestral 'roots' (Musselwhite, 2003, p. 53), these 'traces' take on a 'ghastly' existence of their own (it is no accident that some of the local scamps call a pinched and pallid Susan 'The Ghost'). One of Henchard's key traits is the nagging fear that his own instinctual longings will erode the rigid boundaries he has drawn to define, and defend, the existential vacuum he labels 'character'. Henchard hopes that the spasm of inebriated frustration which ended 'his early married life at Weydon Fair was unrecorded in the family history' (*TMOC* p. 67). Yet after his first meeting with the adult Elizabeth-Jane, Henchard gazed 'at the opposite wall as if he read his history' of incontinent excess and 'subterfuge' there (*TMOC* pp. 62, 69). Such 'survivals' conspire to strip Henchard of what he seems to cherish most as churchwarden and chief magistrate of Casterbridge – the opulent props of selfhood which the skimmity-ride lampoons by parading the former mayor as a 'stuffed figure' with a 'false face' (Franklin, 2008, p. 426).

As David Musselwhite convincingly contends, for all his assumption of autocratic status Henchard never expunges the native within, personified by the dishevelled and raucously defiant furmity-hag who seeks refuge in the 'nether parts of Casterbridge' (*TMOC* p. 334). Henchard is himself an unsightly ethnographic specimen, bearing the 'marks of the beast' (*TMOC* p. 200) regarding

his own obscure provenance. Henchard projects himself as a proudly unvarnished, plain-speaking 'Wessex man' (Franklin, 2008, pp. 426–48); but Hardy's
laconic opening gambit implies that the future mayor, like the ambitious young
Scot, is in flight from a vague and unspecified locality ('an obviously long
journey' [*TMOC* p. 69]). Moreover, 'something fetichistic' (*TMOC* p. 19) resides
in Henchard's beliefs. In *Primitive Manners and Customs* (1879), James A. Farrer
defined the 'the fetichistic mode of thought' as 'undoubtedly a low, and to us
an absurd one. Burnings in effigy may probably be traced to it, and the stories
so common in the annals of witchcraft of waxen images stuck with pins or
burned, in order to injure a person they represented, undoubtedly belong to it'
(Farrer, 1879, p. 281). For A. C. Lyall,

> In the rudest stage of religion, the line between the most abject Fetichism –
> perhaps only the worship of certain queer objects – and witchcraft is very
> difficult to be traced by us to whom from our great intervening intellectual
> distance both kinds of superstition seems indistinguishable in type and
> character. (Lyall, 1873, p. 430)

For Henchard the rhythms of diurnal existence and the customary commercial
codes are tinged by 'abject' and unaccountable impulses. Towards the end of
the novel, he worries whether 'somebody has been roasting a waxen effigy of
me, or stirring an unholy brew to confound me! I don't believe in such power;
and yet – what if they should ha' been doing it!' (*TMOC* p. 190). Are we to align
Henchard as 'Man of Character' with the narrator's notion that 'Character is
Fate' (*TMOC* p. 185)? On occasions, the text demonstrates clearly that
Henchard's misfortunes are triggered by his own intemperate folly and aimless
petulance (he 'knew no moderation in his requests and impulses' [*TMOC* p. 76]).
Yet there are other instances where the antiquarian narrator underwrites
and bolsters the 'fetichism' of this hubristic and 'reckless misadventurer'
(*TMOC* p. 295) who mutters darkly about 'the scheme of some sinister intelligence' or tribal demon 'bent on punishing him' (*TMOC* p. 127). Does 'this man
of moods, glooms, and superstitions' (*TMOC* p. 250) seem justified in construing
this locale as a physical register of rapine, a site of baleful 'exhalations'?
    Bronislaw Malinowski codified the 'goal' of interwar ethnography as the
resolve 'to grasp the native's point of view, his relation to life, to realize *his* vision
of *his* world' (Malinowski, 1922, p. 25). But we never 'grasp' the full significance
of Henchard's 'native' condition. He is an anthropological conundrum, unable
to process metaphysical 'abstraction[s]' (*TMOC* p. 41) and blasé about the
basic lesson expressed by the eminent interwar archaeologist O. G. S. Crawford:
'the rise of civilization was dependent upon *bread*' (Crawford, 1955, p. 174).
Henchard is positioned as the last living legacy of extrovert 'virility' inherited
from the earliest British tribes (*TMOC* p. 274). The 'State of Hostility' formulated by John McLennan in the 1860s to explicate base or depraved customs
among 'primitive' peoples, evokes the increasingly paranoid milieu in which
Henchard finds himself; and partly explains the vehemence with which the

former mayor assails and repudiates those whom he believes are conspiring against him:

> Whoever is not with you is against you. All who are not of your immediate group are your enemies. It is not so much that there are frequent and sanguinary encounters as that at any moment there may be an encounter. There is a total absence of security [. . .] actual combats are just frequent enough to sustain perpetual distrust and fear. (McLennan, 1896, pp. 78–79)

But Henchard's gladiatorial prowess is ineffective in the modern economic 'arena' of enlightened industry that Farfrae swiftly dominates. Henchard finds 'penmanship' a 'tantalizing art': he is 'mentally and physically unfit for grubbing subtleties from soiled paper' (*TMOC* p. 76). Henchard is ill-equipped from an evolutionary standpoint: he bears out James Frazer's thesis that the members of a rural underclass, no matter how well 'they are drilled by their betters into an appearance of civilization, remain barbarians and savages at heart' (Frazer, 1908, p. 3). Henchard feels there is something inherently mean and unnatural, even tainted ('soiled paper') in the observances of accurate book-keeping and the calm scrutiny of risk. Meanwhile, Farfrae shows admirable 'dexterity' in 'clearing up the numerical fogs which had been allowed to grow so thick in Henchard's books' (*TMOC* p. 76).

Whereas Henchard is consumed by insular atavisms, obsessed by vendettas and 'revivals of dead days' (*TMOC* p. 244), Farfrae behaves like a participant-observer of an unfamiliar 'low' culture; treating Casterbridge as an exercise in 'fieldwork', given its remoteness from the metropolitan centre: to the 'liege subjects of Labour, the England of those days was a continent, and a mile a geographical degree' (*TMOC* p. 27). The Scot appears more sophisticated than the desultory, unschooled amateur antiquarian; nor does he typify Frazer's 'armchair anthropologist'. This oddly anonymous figure immerses himself in the municipal life of the district, calibrating its indigenous customs, and eventually clinches the partial trust of the 'tribe' (*TMOC* p. 61) – but without blunting his canny sense of cultural apartness. Farfrae embodies perhaps the condition of ethnographic modernity which James Clifford defines as 'rootless, mobile [. . .] a state of being in culture, while looking at culture'. This is not a 'predicament' for the Scot; rather he turns it to material advantage, and as a sturdy means of self-protection (Clifford, 1997, pp. 3, 9). The Scot is 'one of those men upon whom an incident is never absolutely lost. He revised impressions from a subsequent point of view, and the impulsive judgement of the moment was not always his permanent one' (*TMOC* p. 240). He balances vicarious participation in an alien culture with critical scrutiny of it from a more measured perspective. That Elizabeth-Jane finds Farfrae to be 'impassioned' as he regales a rapt crowd with his 'fascinating melodies' (*TMOC* p. 56) pays ironic tribute to the Scot's ability to 'impersonate' an affable, glib and winning warmth – camouflaging a watchful distance and a 'comfortably indifferent tone' (*TMOC* p. 246). Even when he exposes the grievous limitations of his

former employer's commercial tactics, Farfrae seems immune to gloating
triumphalism. This is 'the art that conceals art' (*TMOC* p. 96), allowing a
Scottish 'stranger' (*TMOC* p. 39) to make himself at home in a bustling market
town that 'looked Roman' and 'announced' Rome 'in every street, alley, and
precinct' (*TMOC* p. 71). Farfrae discovers in the topography not so much
a locus of irreclaimable savagery and wild disorder but instead a reassuring
residue of imperial bureaucracy – the perfect ethnographic 'laboratory' for his
experiments in impersonal business methods. Farfrae identifies with this
ancient bequest because, as Mary Butts claims in her preface to *The Macedonian*
(1933), the Romans' 'deepest instincts were for administration' (1994, p. 3).

Farfrae's imperial scrutiny of this 'old-fashioned' enclave (*TMOC* p. 45)
affords a sharp contrast to Henchard's need to obliterate the distance between
himself and the objects he surveys: he must touch and taste the fresh produce
of this 'fertile country' (*TMOC* p. 64) before estimating its cash-value; he
literally embraces the young Scot as a long-lost brother; he threatens to destroy
Farfrae and Lucetta 'in the heat of action' yet finds that to 'accomplish the
deed by oral poison' was beyond 'the nerve of his enmity' (*TMOC* p. 246). Infu-
riated by Abel Whittle's abject failure to 'clock in' of a morning, Henchard
personally drags this unfortunate from bed and marches him 'half-naked'
through 'Back Street' (*TMOC* p. 99). Farfrae, who cultivates a qualified rapport
with the 'native' workforce, is dismayed by this unlovely spectacle of rough justice.
However, his employer ripostes, 'Tis not tyrannical! [. . .] It is to make him
remember' (*TMOC* p. 170). For Henchard, the most crucial life-lessons must be
learnt though cleansing discomfort and Spartan physical discipline: one cannot
create a 'memory' without some form of 'sacrifice', as the public slaying of Mary
Channing provides only too lurid a testimony.

Farfrae's cautiously weighed engagements with the Casterbridge 'tribe' throws
into bold relief Henchard's destructive volatility (Jackson-Houlston, 1999, p. 154).
And it is typical of this 'paranoiac parvenu' (Musselwhite, 2003, p. 61) that he
cannot countenance the supposedly 'low' or 'primitive' provenance of those
he deems as 'family'. Although Elizabeth-Jane is initially discomposed by the
Casterbridge folk and their 'grim broad way of talking about themselves' (*TMOC*
p. 57), her own 'grievous failing' was 'her occasional pretty and picturesque
use of dialect words – those terrible marks of the beast to the truly genteel'
(*TMOC* p. 200). These verbal tics and homely cadences are for Henchard exas-
perating reminders of an atavistic past whose voice from 'centuries untold'
(*TMOC* p. 7) must be silenced; just as Mary Channing's mouth is stuffed with a
'swab' to 'stop her cries':

> The sharp reprimand was not lost upon [Elizabeth-Jane], and in time it came
> to pass that for 'fay' she said 'succeed'; and that she no longer spoke of
> 'dumbledores' [. . .]; no longer said of young men and women that they
> 'walked together' but that they were 'engaged'; that she grew to talk of
> 'greggles' as 'wild-hyacinths'. (*TMOC* p. 200)

These supposedly unladylike 'dialect words' (*TMOC* p. 138) are philological survivals which violate the rules of standard 'dictionaries' and classroom 'grammar-books' (*TMOC* p. 97). Like unruly 'spirits from the grave' (*TMOC* p. 247) these terms disturb the sober modulations of a principally Latinate register anchored in 'the Roman characteristics of the town she lived in' (*TMOC* p. 63). Hardy's friend William Barnes demonstrated that sociolects are themselves 'past-marked' (*TMOC* p. 82) records: vernacular locutions eroded by an incredibly 'long procession of years' (*TMOC* p. 21). For Charles Newton, in his essay 'On the Study of Archaeology', valuable evidence of bygone times is found in

> those archaic words, inflections, and idioms, which literature has either rejected or forgotten, which, once general, have become provincial, and are retained only in the mother-tongue of the peasantry. [. . .] These obsolete and rare forms of speech are to the philologist what the extinct Faunas and Floras of the primeval world are to the comparative anatomist and the botanist. (Newton, 1850, pp. 3–4)

Henchard's social and economic eclipse by Farfrae renders the 'Man of Character' an 'obsolete' relic. Though in striving to extinguish himself from the face of Wessex, Henchard simultaneously contributes to his own myth as a 'rare' form of life: he adds his name to a 'crumpled scrap of paper' that instructs those left behind not to 'remember' him (*TMOC* p. 333). And the name does survive amid the 'rubble' and 'scraps' of the 'hay-barn' which was once the busy headquarters of his trade: 'A smear of decisive lead-coloured paint had been laid on to obliterate Henchard's name, though its letters dimly loomed through, like ships in a fog' (*TMOC* p. 221). The 'smear' carries a faint echo of the 'soiled paper' and 'numerical fog' of Henchard's lamentable account books (*TMOC* p. 76). Like the Romano-British dust of bygone ages, his 'name' indicates a 'substratum' (*TMOC* p. 82), a culture of the harassed, the overborne and the evicted; just beneath the crust of new and improved roads, footpaths and waterways that will soon engulf this bucolic milieu.

In the next chapter, I address Richard Jefferies's imaginative enterprise to grapple with the complex problems of layered organic continuity. His abiding preoccupation with the ruins of time is evidenced by his need to uncover a framework of inclusive relatedness that could function as a rite of reconciliation with his Wiltshire homeland. Both Hardy and Jefferies offer a type of 'psychotopographic' literary experience in which inner processes are projected onto an exterior bucolic terrain (Ebbatson, 2006, p. 63). Indeed, Jefferies's highly charged account of his mystical immersion in the primeval contours of the Wiltshire downs in *The Story of My Heart* powerfully echoes the experiences of the furze-cutting Clym. However, as is clear from Jefferies's later fable *After London*, this archaeological and ecological saga can only end by raising more vexed questions about how 'survivals' inform the present and future condition of England.

Chapter 3

Archaeophobia: A Fear of Old Things

Pilgrimage into Wild Places

Wiltshire looks large on the map of England, a great green county, yet it never appears to be a favourite one to those who go on rambles in the land. At all events I am unable to bring to mind an instance of a lover of Wiltshire who was not a native or a resident [. . .] Listen to any half-dozen of your friends discussing the places they have visited, or intend visiting, comparing notes about the counties, towns, churches, castles, scenery – all that draws them and satisfies their nature, and the chances are that they will not even mention Wiltshire [. . .] for there is nothing striking in Wiltshire, at all events to those that love nature first.

(Hudson, 1910, pp. 1–2)

'Wiltshire' represents a complex topographical code that casual day-trippers, seeking brief respite from 'the prison of the pavement' (Massingham, 1942, p. 14), cannot unravel, according to W. H. Hudson's 1910 survey of southern England, *A Shepherd's Life*. That this locale fails to satisfy the suburban nature-lover is an essential part of its appeal to Hudson, and to E. M. Forster in *The Longest Journey* (1907): 'Here is the heart of our island: the Chilterns, the North Downs, the South Downs radiate hence. The fibres of England unite in Wiltshire, and did we condescend to worship her, here we should erect our national shrine' (Forster, p. 132). Forster's rapt conception of the 'Wiltshire' downs as mnemonic topography posits a prized heritage of agricultural 'Englishness' (Cucullu, 1998, pp. 237–59). Here are tangible traces of a 'nationalist archaeology', marked, as Bruce Trigger contends, by a tendency 'to glorify the "primitive vigour" and creativeness of people assumed to be national ancestors' (Trigger, 1984, pp. 355–70).

Forster's sense of the south Wiltshire downs as 'the heart of our island', carrying pronounced sacral overtones, is crucial to understanding *The Story of My Heart* by Richard Jefferies. In this spiritual autobiography Jefferies re-imagines his birthplace and its numerous prehistoric 'shrines' as a 'key to unlock the magic door into the past' (Massingham, 1988, p. 29). The natal home becomes the locus of a 'marvellous' and 'supernatural' bond, 'just outside the pale of common thought' (*SH* p. 44), that may yet reconfigure England's threadbare mythic and national narratives:

> Dreamy in appearance, I was breathing full of existence; I was aware of the grass blades, the flowers, the leaves on hawthorn and tree. I seemed to live more largely through them, as if each were a pore through which I drank. The grasshoppers called and leaped, the greenfinches sang, the blackbirds happily fluted, all the air hummed with life. I was plunged deep in existence, and with all that existence I prayed.
>
> Through every grass blade in the thousand, thousand grasses; through the million leaves, veined and edge-cut, on bush and tree; through the song-notes and the marked feathers of the birds; through the insects' hum and the colour of the butterflies; through the soft warm air, the flecks of clouds dissolving – I used them all for prayer. (*SH* p. 24)

Critics have frequently noted that Richard Jefferies and Thomas Hardy led 'parallel lives': both men were born in the 1840s and their myriad fictional and journalistic projects 'excavated' in sedulous detail West-Country folklore, village myths, botany and ornithology (Clarke, 2002, pp. 17–20). Jefferies uncovers a recuperative sense of the numinous in the spatial patterns of diurnal life, an 'ecstasy of exquisite enjoyment' (*SH* p. 122), which dissolves the markers of possessive individualism and echoes Clym's insight into the antique communion between furze-cutters and the Egdon wilderness. Through its symbolic use of season and setting, as well as in the broad pattern of figurative tropes, *The Story* decries too rigorously analytical 'modes of thought' (*SH* p. 45) that frame universal laws totally divorced from natural phenomena. Jefferies, in a memorably bizarre conceit, likens himself to the 'Caveman primordial' for whom 'twelve thousand years' of 'written tradition' (*SH* p. 45) are as nothing when compared to the fund of cathartic grace epitomized by the sweep, curve and exuberant diversity of the Wiltshire downs. Like in his earlier *Wild Life in a Southern County* (1879), the opening gambit revels in the exultant peace of 'the grassy mound and trenches of an ancient earthwork': 'drowsy warmth' infused by 'the happy hum of bees' (1879, p. 17). Here Jefferies expresses animistic affinity with an expanse that Oswald Crawfurd evoked in the 1898 *Idler* as a measureless primeval cemetery, saturated in the archaic past and studded with myriad stone circles: 'changeless since the Saxons and Danes fought for mastery in England' (Crawfurd, 1898, p. 292).

The Story renders a milieu of unkempt, thronging profusion as the palpable forms of 'greenfinches', 'blackbirds', 'butterflies' and 'grasshoppers' compete for space in a patch of 'grass'. The familiar figures and forms of a natural cosmos seem 'like exterior nerves and veins for the conveyance of feeling' (*SH* p. 122) to Jefferies. As the 1884 *Pall Mall Gazette* noted, this was his 'innate talent' for putting himself 'instinctively *en rapport* with the dim intelligence of birds and beasts and insects and fishes' ([Anon.], '*Life of the Fields*', 1884).

Jefferies brings the human eye preternaturally close to flora (leaves 'veined and edge-cut') and deploys the transfiguring effects of sunlight to delineate this busy menagerie. Just as the sensuous ambience of the sandy Egdon slopes has a largely purgative effect on the neurasthenic Clym, who rediscovers a partially submerged mental state, making 'the incipient marks of time and thought' less 'perceptible' on his face (*RN* p. 207), so Jefferies secures a 'dreamy' liberation from 'the petty circumstances' and 'annoyances of existence' (*SH* p. 18). He becomes a transparent vehicle for the shy, fugitive and evanescent sensations that entrance him. The bucolic minutiae in Jefferies's account function as psychological counters and outline his emerging consciousness concretely instead of through woolly abstraction. This pagan 'prayer', with its intricate deployment and interplay of primal and elemental motifs, maps those 'spots of time' conceptualized by Saree Makdisi as 'self-enclosed and self-referential enclaves of the anti-modern' (Makdisi, 1998, p. 12). Jefferies projects himself as 'earthborn – autochthon' (Jefferies, *Red Deer*, 1884, p. 161), by enumerating specific sensory effects. He juxtaposes the numinous – the rapt reaction to sunlight, 'hawthorn', 'tree' – and the seemingly drab quotidian details of 'dry chalky earth' falling through his fingers: this combination leads to multiplied perception, as he hides his face in the 'grass' (*SH* pp. 18–20).

Both Hardy and Jefferies are preoccupied by notions of self-emancipation from the legion pressures of a fevered but facile modernity. However, salient and substantial differences are manifest between the two writers. A key representational and historical imperative energizes the narrative trajectory of both *The Return of the Native* and *The Mayor of Casterbridge*: we are never permitted to forget Hardy's obsession with the nascent sciences of humankind and how they bring to nineteenth-century fiction myriad formal and expressive possibilities. Through Tylor's anthropology Hardy conceived of Dorset culture both as a shared, coherent mode of daily life to be chronicled as well as a network of meanings to be deciphered. Moreover, Hardy records in his notebooks that history 'depends upon the relation between the organism & the environment' (Björk, 1985, I, p. 132). Yet Clym's dilemma enacts, in its unresolved tensions, the 'difficulty' of securing any ecstatic renewal through the brusque disavowal of controlled intellection (Ebbatson, 2006, pp. 63–70). For Jefferies by contrast, spiritual trance, suspension of diurnal actuality and spontaneous articulations of the unconscious are vital; affording highly individualized points of view that undermine the generic and sentimental constraints of mimetic realism, with its dependence on genealogical stability. George E. Dartnell, in his 1893 overview of Jefferies's life for the *Wiltshire Archaeological and Natural History Society* ponders this habit, which aggressively 'breaks the continuity of the narrative':

> [Jefferies] never really attained the gift of selecting and proportioning his materials, and so working them up into one harmonious whole. Hardy can do better in this line – if he chooses. Take *The Woodlanders*, for example. The plot (as also with Jefferies) is not the pleasantest part of the book, but

when we escape from it to the hayfield or the winter woodlands what wonderful pictures he gives us! He can subordinate the lesser to the greater – as that tree-planting episode proves. (Dartnell, 1893, p. 77)

Here Jefferies is construed as a figure largely disdainful of, even bored by, standard novelistic practice which decrees the fastidious tailoring and presentation of narrative. As a result, *The Story*, with its impish delight in reverie rather than sober record, inspiration rather than cognition, is for Dartnell 'too morbid and mystical to arrest our sympathy, or to secure our convictions' (Dartnell, 1893, p. 79). Edward Thomas reads *The Story's* marked preference for divination over diagnosis, trance over concrete particularities of present time, as a defiantly poetic flourish whose musical motifs attain an 'absolute, more than logical, unity' (Thomas, 1909, p. 186).

By prioritizing the tentatively provisional, fluid and polysemic potencies of language in his imaginative excavations, Jefferies has, according to M. R. Hoste, 'something which Hardy surely lacks, a noble and lofty ideal, an innate belief in and admiration of moral as well as physical beauty and purity' (Hoste, 1900, p. 229). It is more accurate to say that *The Story of My Heart* promotes 'an innate belief' in temporal rupture as well as the interpenetration of landscape and human consciousness to de-familiarize the customary (Ebbatson, 2006, pp. 63–80), and evade the trammels of deterministic causality in a search for 'intense soul-emotion'. Committed to an arcane revelation of being which smudges lyrical description and meditation, Jefferies chronicles a feeling for the Wessex soil not so much as a plentiful resource (as it is for Clym the furze-cutter or Henchard the corn-factor) but as a sanctuary and metaphysical solace – 'visible, tangible wealth [. . .] a possession, not a profit' (Jefferies, *The Hills and the Vale*, 1980b, p. 101). Unlike the primarily verbal Clym, whose self-righteous oratory goads the apathetic heath-men towards the path of purposeful and progressive advance, Jefferies espouses an eloquent silence in which the voluntary promptings of the ego are stifled, and the mind separated 'from external present influences'; compelling it, 'in falling back upon itself, to recognize its own depth and powers' (*The Hills and the Vale*, p. 36). This is what commentators soon after Jefferies's death called his 'intense spiritual sensibility' ([Anon.], 'Richard Jefferies', 1909b, p. 223): the magus whose primal creativity was reflected in his bid to release the imprisoned spirit of his homeland. Such subliminal communion Jefferies implies, with its affirmation of elemental links and elaborate patterns of archetypal imagery, cannot be translated completely by the emergent discourses of archaeology, geology and sociology.

What is most striking about Jefferies's depiction of rural Wiltshire in *The Story* is its radical ambivalence towards the scientific theories which frame and enrich Hardy's imaginative archaeology. The critical construction of Jefferies as an 'ethnographer of gamekeeping' and 'amateur anthropologist' (Morris, 2006, p. 7), who is attentive to the 'origin of superstition' (*SH* p. 95) and the semiotic status of recovered relics, does not tally with the profound change of 'heart' imbuing this spiritual autobiography (Grimble, 2004, pp. 96–110). In the opening extract, a fleeting modern moment conveyed by the lulling warmth of the air, the clear shapes, the living insects' 'hum' is anchored in the sediment of aeons of geological and historical movement. The second chapter shows Jefferies attuned to the impossibly remote dimensions of time implicit in the scene, as he modulates from the cosmic to the microscopic:

> through space to the old time of tree-ferns, of the lizard flying through the air, the lizard-dragon wallowing in sea-foam, the mountainous creatures, twice-elephantine, feeding on land; all the crooked sequence of life. The dragon-fly which passed me traced a continuous descent from the fly marked on stone in those days. (*SH* p. 26)

This account is strongly reminiscent of Clym Yeobright ensconced in 'a nest of vivid green', where 'lizards' and 'grass-hoppers' bespeak the 'ancient world of the carboniferous period, when the forms of plants were few, and of the fern kind' (*RN* pp. 205–206). Jefferies's visualization of vegetative and organic data which connotes 'old time' also enacts what T. H. Huxley termed 'retrospective prophecy': 'the reconstruction in human imagination of events which have vanished and ceased to be' (Huxley, 1901, p. 6). In 1869, J. R. Green remarked that 'History [. . .] we are told by publishers, is the most unpopular of all branches of literature at the present day, but it is only unpopular because it seems more and more to sever itself from all that can touch the heart of a people' (Green, 1869, p. xi). But Jefferies, through a canny compression of discrete time-periods, makes what might have seemed an irrevocably absent past a piercingly vivid and immediate 'presence', indeed an intransigent actuality. The specific images – 'the lizard-dragon' and 'mountainous creatures' – invoke Gideon Algernon Mantell's immensely popular two-volume work *The Wonders of Geology* (1838)[1] whose 'Retrospect' at the close of the first volume depicts 'innumerable dragon-forms' and 'monsters of the reptile tribe, so huge that nothing among the existing races can compare with them, basking on the banks of its rivers, and roaming through its forests'. Jefferies's thought-adventure through 'periods of unfathomable antiquity' (Mantell, 1838, I, p. 447) promises a sustained exhumation of the 'buried life' of his home district of north-east Wiltshire, whose 'great swelling downs' bear 'on their broad shoulders traces of ancient hill forts'. However, he confesses that his once zealous 'interest in archaeological matters' is 'long since extinct' like the fossilized creatures found in rocks and riverbeds (*SH* p. 103).

As a bracing cultural phenomenon that truly came of age during his lifetime, Jefferies apprehended better than most how excavation as a research tool had 'considerably cleared away' the 'mist of antiquity' (Jefferies, 1896, p. 1); altering his chiefly metropolitan readership's perception and reception of the ancient world, as well as amplifying the results of surface observation and record. In an 1875 piece for *The Graphic* he proclaimed the untouched splendour of 'Marlborough Forest' as a region of immanent depths; he appealed to the educated wayfarer's 'taste for archaeological studies, especially the prehistoric': the 'edge of the forest melts away upon downs that bear grander specimens than can be seen elsewhere. Stonehenge and Avebury are near' (*The Hills and the Vale*, p. 34). The village of Avebury is situated in Wiltshire's Kennet valley almost 11 kilometres west of Marlborough, and 30 kilometres north of Stonehenge. As Jefferies would have known, the chalk downlands of this area boast 'the largest concentration of prehistoric monuments' in Western Europe (Edwards, 2000, p. 65). Following his death, myriad critics portrayed Jefferies as the very epitome of an acute archaeological consciousness. A contributor to the 1889 *Quarterly Review* fashioned Jefferies as the 'curious inquiring youth' sitting by 'deserted fosse and nameless barrow' drawing in 'the spirit of the past', and who 'learned how it lives in the present' ([Anon.], 'Richard Jefferies', 1889a, p. 228). His birthplace Coate Farm and the grassy, largely treeless terrain to the south of Swindon – especially Liddington Hill and Ashbourne Chase – were replete with tumuli, hill-forts and stone circles. In his early journalism these landmarks carry a talismanic potency; and G. Goldney, writing for the 1874 *British Architect*, paid tribute to these imperilled prehistoric residues:

> Wiltshire is rich in objects of antiquity, and possesses a mass of illustrations from which institutions emanate. We have castles and towns of different periods, ages and races; tombs, barrows, and Druidical temples, tessellated pavements, Roman villas, great Roman roads [. . .] With such materials before us we have all the temptations requisite to induce us to become archaeologists. (Goldney, 1874, p. 179)

The 'explorations' of the mostly Bronze Age prehistoric burial mounds of Wiltshire by Sir Richard Colt Hoare were, in J. Romilly Allen's words, 'the first systematic attempt to explore British sepulchral remains, and the collection he formed' epitomized 'one of the finest ever made in this country' (Allen, 1885, p. 234). Other 'eminent archaeologists' were intimately associated with the Wiltshire 'parish': John Aubrey 'by residence', and John Britton 'by birth' ([Anon.], 'Proposed Monuments', 1857, p. 203). The *Wiltshire Archaeological and Natural History Society* was formed in 1853 partly to purchase Britton's 'extensive library' of topographical and antiquarian manuscripts and to extend his researches into the county's ample residual remains (Rogers and Crowley, 1994, pp. 410–11; Chandler, 1996). Jefferies read a paper entitled 'Swindon: Its History and Antiquities' to the *Society* in September 1873, and he wrote to his aunt Ellen that his neighbourhood was a veritable 'mine for an antiquary' (qtd. in Morris, 2006, p. 37). A contributor to the 1869 *Quarterly Review* amplified this notion:

> What may be our relationship to the builders of the temples and barrows of Wiltshire we are unaware; but, ancestors of our own or not, they were

a powerful and an enlightened people. No work within the four seas, in modern times, has equalled the grandeur of their masonry. The only parallel is to be sought in the ruins, attributed to giant-builders, of the megalithic walls of Tiryns and contemporary cities, or in the structure of the Pyramids themselves. ([Anon.], 'Pre-Historic England', 1869b, p. 396–97)

According to the critic John Chandler, Jefferies claimed as early as 1861 to have begun gathering and classifying local lore for an antiquarian survey of Swindon and its environs, which was eventually published as a series of articles in the *North Wilts Herald* and *Swindon Advertiser* between 1867 and 1872 (Chandler, 1996, pp. 14–24). In his *History of Swindon* Jefferies demonstrates a detailed knowledge of the area between his natal home, Avebury and White Horse Hill, evoking a place

> alive with the dead. Not a step can be taken which does not lead to some token of antiquity. Turn up the turf and you shall find coins, arrow-heads, and bones [. . .] Ascend the downs and pause in astonishment before the vast fortifications of a former era. (Jefferies, 1896, pp. 144)

And in 1875, for *Frasers Magazine*, Jefferies contributed 'The Story of Swindon', gauging how the 'potent magician' of 'Steam' had affected the lives of those 'who dwell farther back out of the track of modern life' (*The Hills and the Vale*, 1980, pp. 114, 133).

Jefferies's passionate interest in field archaeology and natural history was underpinned by a journalistic career which gave short shrift to the hackneyed techniques of historical and genealogical enquiry – poring over pedigrees, musty manuscripts and copying inscriptions from 'weird cavernous crypts' (*The Hills and the Vale*, 1980, p. 36). Rather than replicating the tone of conventional county histories (mimicked in Jefferies's own 1873 *Memoir of the Goddards of North Wiltshire*), which affirmed the local landowner's smug pride in property, ties to the past and responsibilities for the future, Jefferies prioritized exhaustive fieldwork as a salutary physical and mental exercise for all: his modest 1873 handbook *Reporting; Editing and Authorship* avows that 'the reporter, while going about the country studying as he goes its topography, antiquities, traditions and general characteristics', will have plentiful 'opportunities of amassing materials for original sketches in the paper' (Jefferies, 1896, p. 3). His 1877 article 'Unequal Agriculture' for *Fraser's Magazine* 'ponders' deeply out in the field so as to refine a distinctive archaeological perspective:

> The plough is at work here also, such a plough as was used when the Corn Laws were in existence, [. . .] principally made from the tree – the tree which furnishes the African savage at this day with the crooked branch with which to scratch the earth, which furnished the ancient agriculturists of the Nile Valley with their primitive implements. It is drawn by dull, patient oxen,

plodding onwards now just as they were depicted upon the tombs and temples, the graves and worshipping places, of races who had their being three thousand years ago. Think of the suns that have shone since then [. . .] of the human teeth that have ground that grain, and are now hidden in the abyss of earth; yet still the oxen plod on, like slow Time itself, here this day in our land of steam and telegraph. (Jefferies, *The Hills and the Vale*, 1980b, pp. 136–37)

In this essay, the aggressively modern steam-ploughing engine in one field suggests to Jefferies 'the crude force' which 'may have existed in the mastodon or other unwieldy monster of the prehistoric ages'. However, in the next field he uncovers images of sedate, unchanging rhythms over the centuries, implying bucolic lethargy ('dull, patient oxen'). The primitive plough is ranged against a febrile present whose principal innovations play bewildering games with traditional conceptions of slow, plodding 'Time' framed by hoary agricultural and ecclesiastical calendars. From the humble agrarian prop of the 'plough' Jefferies fashions an elaborate and plangent vision of unbroken continuities, which oversteps ethnic, regional and national boundaries. Like a comparative anthropologist in the mould of E. B. Tylor, Jefferies seizes upon those esoteric rituals which unite the Wiltshire land-labourer with the 'African savage at this day' as well as 'ancient' farmers. This passage also reminds us that it is the perception of 'remarkable contrasts' and odd incongruities – the sight of the primitive 'crooked branch' scratching away in a 'land of steam and telegraph' – which represents, according to his 'Story of Swindon', a 'perfect epitome of the spirit of the nineteenth century' (*The Hills and the Vale*, 1980, p. 112). Wiltshire was, according to the 1880 *Examiner*, 'one of the most rural, not to say, primitive, of our forty English counties' ([Anon.], 'A hedgerow philosopher', 1880a, p. 1023); yet even here, Jefferies implies, are intimations of 'go-ahead ways' (Grimble, 2004, pp. 129–30).

Jefferies's energetic forays into local historiography during the 1870s, comparing 'modern associations' with what lies 'hidden in the abyss of earth', are all the more arresting when measured against his bullish repudiation of such intellectual pursuits in *The Story of My Heart*. The fierce intensity of his narrative cannot be assigned merely to an exasperated impatience with the petty snobberies which marred the study of parochial lore and legend at mid-century – a stifling social 'scene' dominated by the complacent cant of vicarage and manor-house (Chandler, 1996, pp. 14–18). By unearthing the preserved relics of human antiquity, such as 'bits of shaped glass' and 'rude flint' (*SH* p. 117), late-Victorian archaeology sought to pique the modern audience's appetite for an emotional 'encounter' across centuries that purged the distant past of the coarse, the untidy and the chaotic. However, Jefferies's *Story* queries the capacity of excavated artefacts to transmit the ambience of a lost locality; or to grant access to historical annals irradiated by the analytical disciplines of sober scrutiny, taxonomy and imaginative reconstruction. For Jefferies, archaeologists who sought a conceptual, cultural and historical classification which would lend coherence to the fragments of flawed records arrogate a certain kind of 'knowledge' which masquerades as spurious 'authority'. How can a science of systematic excavation help us grasp better the ineffably ancient thought-processes of 'priests who worshipped' the 'beetle' (*SH* p. 117) for instance?

> [T]o go back as far as possible, the study and labour expended on Egyptian inscriptions and papyri, which contain nothing but doubtful, because laudatory history, invocations to idols, and similar matters: all these labours are in vain. Take a broom and sweep the papyri away into the dust. The Assyrian terra-cotta tablets, some recording fables, and some even sadder – contracts between men whose bodies were dust twenty centuries since – take a hammer and demolish them. Set a battery to beat down the pyramids, and a mind battery to destroy the deadening influence of tradition. The Greek statue lives to this day, and has the highest use of all, the use of true beauty. [. . .] Egyptian and Assyrian, medieval and eighteenth-century culture, miscalled, are all alike mere dust. (*SH* p. 87)

Jefferies calibrates the Greek statue's 'true beauty' against the choking residues which had become 'strangely eloquent' to prehistoric archaeologists, who 'lent a voice to the dumb past' by sifting barrows, peat-bogs, shell-mounds, and lake-habitations ([Anon.], 'Pre-Historic Records', 1879a, p. 805). Jefferies reacts to these deposits with the unfeigned disgust of a sanitary reformer exhausted by the onerous challenges of waste management. In this extract 'history', like the blighted metropolis itself in *After London*, is a vast agglomeration of pestiferous matter, and a continual memorial of decay, stripped of any quaintly 'picturesque' connotations ([Anon.], 'Dust', 1868a, p. 630). Far from inspiring a neo-Romantic paean to sublime dereliction, Jefferies construes the refuse of 'history' as a rank affront to the civilized senses. Mere 'dust' increases, deepens and befouls the modern moment and, like other acute social embarrassments, has to be speedily disposed of – in this case swept away with a 'broom' (*SH* p. 87). Jefferies implies that the strivings of remote and even proximate precursors should be eclipsed rather than emulated: he exalts 'soul-life' as a condition of *becoming* instead of *having been*. As a contributor to the 1866 *Good Words* remarked: 'what to an ordinary observer can have descended lower in the material scale than the dust-heap? There mundane things seem to have reached the last stage' of 'repulsiveness, and deformity' ([Anon.], 'Dust Ho!' 1866b, p. 645). P. B. Shelley's thrilling secrets of the birth of time become in Jefferies's evocation an archaeological 'dust-heap' which acts as a depressing brake on creative zest. This standpoint sharply contrasts with how Hardy reacted to the demand from an informed, ebullient reading public that the dust of 'geological time' (*SH* p. 104) be transfigured by the aesthetic motifs of narrative prose fiction. It is Hardy's opening gambit to *The Return of the Native*, rather than the abstract stringency of mathematical formulae, which helps 'to realize our conceptions of the enormous lapse of past time', drawing attention to other conditions of existence ([Anon.], 'Lyell', 1851, p. 412).

Jefferies impugns the fruitless, retrograde and enfeebling 'labours' of reconstructing the meaning of discredited pagan relics such as Egyptian 'inscriptions and papyri'. The most one can hope for is an occasional fleeting perception through his own numinous and visionary flights. As H. S. Salt remarked on Jefferies's memoir soon after its publication, it is curious that the author 'discards the most cherished axioms of modern scientific enquiry', given that his 'own powers of observation were extraordinarily keen' (Salt, 1888, p. 164). *The Pall Mall Gazette* censured Jefferies's 'depreciatory' comments on 'human efforts in the past, of which he seems to forget that his own ideals must be a product' ([Anon.], 'Richard Jefferies' late essays', 1889b, p. 125).

The chief problem with Jefferies's mystical geography of Wiltshire is that its rejection of historical hindsight and orthodox chronological markers – mechanical 'time has never existed and never will, it is a purely artificial arrangement' (*SH* p. 30) – supplies scant insight into his own artistic excavations as an ever-evolving process. So he aligns 'Egyptian', 'Assyrian', 'medieval' and 'eighteenth century' artefacts with a 'deadening' influence that immures felt experience in outworn 'tradition'. That Jefferies singles out the 'Assyrian terra-cotta tablets' and later in *The Story* 'winged men on the Assyrian bas-reliefs' (*SH* p. 115) is suggestive. Such references conjure the excavations of Sir Austen Henry Layard, who established the vanished city of Nineveh as 'an archaeological fact' during his two expeditions of 1845–1847 and 1849–1851 (Pearson, 2006b, pp. 42–45; Malley, 1996, pp. 152–70). To 'remember Nineveh' and 'the bearded bulls of stone' (*SH* p. 70) according to Shawn Malley, 'was nothing short of a national pastime, such that this hitherto obscure and distant world quickly became absorbed into Britain's own historical consciousness' (Malley, 1996, p. 153). As Schliemann's discovery of Homer's Troy would do in the 1870s, Layard's discoveries 'left a permanent mark on the public's consciousness of antiquity and archaeological heritage' (Pearson, 2006b, p. 42). Layard's hugely successful two-volume account of his wanderings and the excavations, *Nineveh and Its Remains* (1848) depicts the 'ruins in Assyria and Babylonia' as 'formed of mere earth and rubbish [. . .] A great vitrified mass of brick-work near the Euphrates, surrounded by the accumulated rubbish of ages' (Layard, 1848, I, pp. xx–xxi). Yet Layard's text avows that this 'rubbish', which had for 'twenty-five centuries' hidden 'from the eye of man' winged human-headed lions (Layard, 1853, p. 71), inspires commentators to sift the jumbled, malleable amalgam of a lost civilization for a public eager to know more about the sites of the Tigris-Euphrates valley.

Jefferies belittles the spectacular 'Assyrian' finds, such as 'the painted chambers', and the Egyptian pharaonic bequest 'held on the mummy's withered breast' (*SH* p. 70) as a pale surrogate of the past. That he interprets this hoard hidden 'in the laborious sarcophagus' (*SH* p. 70) as 'mere dust' rather than living memories may of course reflect his own dismay at the self-serving Wiltshire squirarchy and clerisy who corraled archaeology, geography and sociology as exclusively genteel, rarefied pursuits. However, Jefferies makes a more incisive point: he targets the delusive dreams of archaeologists who aimed to flatter their compatriots by trumpeting ancestral virtues and contriving a glorious national narrative from the 'sand and failing rivers' of 'Assyria' (*SH* p. 70); a predestined sequence of canonical 'facts' quite literally of depth and commanding substance (Malley, 1996; Zimmerman, 2008). What *The Story* clearly documents is that for Jefferies, disinterred cultural forms such as 'Aztec coloured-string writings and rayed stones', or the 'uncertain marks left of the sunken Polynesian continent' (*SH* p. 71) are not emblematic icons or cherished instruments from 'deep' archaeological time, returning to regale late-Victorian audiences. The very dishevelment and fragmentation of recovered remnants from the 'aged caves of India' (*SH* p. 115), manifest the unfeasibility of ontological empathy and connection; we are left with 'hieroglyphs as useless as those of Memphis' (*SH* p. 71). For the 1909 *Edinburgh Review* the stark force of this repudiation typifies 'the morbid, furious self-analysis' which mars so much of *The Story*, with its 'wild surmising' and 'extraordinary farrago and jumble of incongruous ideas'; showing 'a Jefferies exiled from his own native resources, struck down with mortal sickness [. . .] overstrained and hysterical' ([Anon.], 'Richard Jefferies', 1909b, p. 226). The bitterness imbuing Jefferies's attitude towards 'commonplace papyri' (*SH* p. 70) is even more striking when compared to the numerous 'laudatory' assessments of classical archaeology in middlebrow journals such as the *Quarterly Review*.

> The present century is remarkable for the great extension of the dominion of Science [. . .] Ancient, long-lost, utterly forgotten history, has left traces that were long unintelligible, but that have of late found a voice. The cuneiform characters, which were used both by Persian and Assyrian scribes, are no lon-ger entirely unintelligible; the hieroglyphics of Egypt are, to a great extent, unlocked; and philology has found a clue that enables us to trace certain descents, and even certain geographical movements, of branches of the great human family, to a period long antecedent to our earliest quasi-historic memories [. . .] Even the grandest engineering feats of the age of iron and of steam fall short, in some respects, of the efforts of our pre-historic ancestors. ([Anon.], 'Pre-Historic England', 1869b, p. 396)

This reviewer promotes the exhumation and resurrection fantasy in the rising profession of archaeology, evoking antiquity as a beguiling spectral presence ('traces', 'found a voice'), whose purpose is to remind Victorians that the conservation and display of excavated remains should not be one of orchestrat-ing static, heavily policed sites. Rather than fostering the impression of an unbridgeable gulf between past and present, we should value a 'great human family' in which awe for the 'efforts' of 'our pre-historic' ancestry is key. Wordless wonder for 'the grandest engineering feats of the age of iron' both justifies the assiduous recovery, taxonomy and safeguarding of material vestiges and gives them durable worth as well as poignant human associations. Recovered curios, such as the scrolls of ancient archives or the stone monuments of long-vanished empires, become mystical fragments that, even when wrested from their original cultural context, possess the potency to broadcast whispers of the oldest ways.

For Jefferies, this mawkish regard for the 'Persian and Assyrian scribes' is little more than a fatuous poetic indulgence. In response to surfacing archaeological trinkets, he argues that we should 'take a hammer' and 'demolish' the 'Assyrian terra-cotta tablets' because excavators are unable to garner credible diagnostic data about their spatial provenance, chronological assignment or resonant links with other exotic trophies. Moreover, he views in these 'ages past' (*SH* p. 101) the transmission of a curse rather than a benediction:

> The truth is we die through our ancestors; we are murdered by our ancestors. Their dead hands stretch forth from the tomb and drag us down to their mouldering bones. We in our turn are now at this moment preparing death for our unborn posterity. [. . .] All the labour and the toil of so many millions continued through such vistas of time, down to those millions who at this hour are rushing to and fro in London, have accumulated nothing for us. (*SH* p. 101)

While Jefferies derides the aesthetic figurations of necromancy that archaeologists employed to trace the lineaments of prehistoric belief systems, his *Story* mobilizes Gothic motifs, such as the dead hand of the ancestral past laying a poisonous weight on productive change and 'preparing death for our unborn posterity'. In Jefferies's account, those who dare to trace 'vistas of time' are lost in the sepulchral gloom of a brutish past, amid 'mouldering bones'.

Jefferies construes disinterred relics not as glamorous medals but as base and unintelligible slivers; the remote past is 'indistinguishable noise not to be resolved' (*SH* p. 70). In 1880, when archaeologists discovered the royal tombs of Tutankhamun's predecessor Khuenaten, the so-called heretic king, they interpreted and structured their findings to demonstrate that the Egyptians had foresworn a sordid plurality of savage deities and embraced monotheism as well as sober civic virtues that prioritized sage self-restraint, rational clarity and mutual respect. Nineteenth-century excavators, according to Jefferies, sought to confirm, substantiate as well as memorialize the beginnings of prestigious modern institutions. In this process, 'possession was tantamount to appropriation of ancient Assyrian culture' (Malley, 1996, p. 160). By recovering the metropolis of the great Assyrian Empire from the 'barren shores of the Tigris', excavators offered a fresh perspective on providential patterning, in addition to reminding British readers of their innate ties to 'the great human family' in the curios Layard had unearthed ([Anon.], 'Layard's Nineveh', 1849a, p. 446). For the *Westminster and Foreign Quarterly Review,*

> Assyria [. . .] may be regarded as the nation which, with Egypt, laid the foundation of that stupendous fabric of the earth's civilisation, which, progressively rising and accumulating under the intellect of ages, received, as it were, its next story in the medieval era of Greece and Italy, and is now raising its superstructure in the tardy enlightenment of Western Europe. ([Anon.], 'Review of *Nineveh*', 1849c, pp. 332–33)

For Jefferies, this crusade to situate Assyria and 'the lore of the arrow-headed writing' (*SH* p. 70) in a cultural continuum crowned by a Britain nation which was, according to Alfred Lord Tennyson, in the foremost files of time was a blatant fabrication of 'laudatory history' from very 'doubtful', incomplete evidence (*SH* p. 87). Because they can no longer be part of the same object, these shards and splinters seem, in the words of one sceptical reviewer, merely 'fossil remains' from 'the rubbish of Assyria' (Crolley, 1850, p. 367). As Layard himself remarked, if commentators persisted in abstracting the Assyrian finds from pressing social and cultural concerns, the vestiges would be no better than 'scattered wrecks on the solitary shore' (Layard, 1853, p. 91).

Jefferies's debunking stance towards the 'glamour of modern sciences and discoveries' reveals deep unease about core issues of difference, cultural memory, 'erasure' (*SH* p. 74) and oblivion. Against his haughty dismissal of Egyptian and Assyrian lore as 'past accumulations of casuistry' (*SH* p. 74), *The Story of My Heart* cherishes 'the Greek statue' as an artefact that 'lives to this day': the power of 'old association', to employ Hardy's terminology, is crucial – a touchstone of towering and 'true beauty'. Jefferies's 'Greek statue', like his conception of the Wiltshire turf, is a welcome exit point from the dispiritingly bleak features of a historical framework that has divulged irrefutable proofs of disjunction, belatedness, and deletion ('the fierce heat of the human furnace' [*SH* p. 70]), rather than a copious reserve to be tapped and venerated. His 'Greek statue' interrupts the temporal process and engenders heightened consciousness: 'Now is eternity; now is the immortal life' (*SH* p. 39).

The Story, given its eloquent insistence on the fructifying potencies of 'the earth', paradoxically resists any desire scientifically to excavate it. Plumbing the 'depths' of the archaeological and evolutionary record discloses raw data from which Jefferies recoils, especially when 'geological time' (*SH* p. 102) yields such stark 'traces' of the 'monstrous' and 'anti-human'. These survivals reveal 'the crooked sequence of life' (*SH* p. 26) which threatens to overturn his static and perennial standard of 'true beauty':

> How extraordinary, strange, and incomprehensible are the creatures out of the depths of the sea! The distorted fishes; the ghastly cuttles; the hideous

eel-like shapes; the crawling shell-encrusted things; the centipede-like
beings; monstrous forms, to see which gives a shock to the brain. They shock
the mind because they exhibit an absence of design. There is no idea in
them. (*SH* p. 50)

William Wordsworth anticipated the day when the 'remotest discoveries of the
chemist, the botanist, or mineralogist will be as proper objects of the poet's art
as any upon which it can be employed' (qtd. in Knoepflmacher and Tennyson,
1977, p. xviii). But Jefferies makes the bottom dropping out of history seem like
an existential 'shock', revealing 'an absence' of balanced design or directing
intelligence to which the human 'mind' can barely adjust. 'Shell-encrusted
things' and 'hideous eel-like shapes' adumbrate all that is abject in the shadowy
primordial past; a reading of the cosmos as prone to lawless caprice. That there
may be a shared genetic legacy between Jefferies and these 'distorted' and
'strange' creatures engenders a tone of disgusted disbelief.

Unlike the 'ghastly' beings from the 'depths of the sea', there is an empower-
ing 'design' in his familiar Wiltshire surroundings; but this is not simply an
'idea' of unruffled and unproblematic bucolic splendour.

There was an entrenchment on the summit, and going down into the fosse
I walked round it slowly to recover breath. On the south-western side there
was a spot where the outer bank had partially slipped, leaving a gap. There
the view was over a broad plain, beautiful with wheat, and enclosed by a
perfect amphitheatre of green hills. [. . .]

I was utterly alone with the sun and the earth. Lying down on the grass,
I spoke in my soul to the earth [. . .] I thought of the earth's firmness – I felt
it bear me up; through the grassy couch there came an influence as if I could
hear the great earth speaking to me. (*SH* pp. 18–19)

In the forbidding solitude of this site, Jefferies is acutely conscious of the
tension between the 'transport' he receives from a lived-in, time-crusted terrain
that bears him 'up', and the fraught feeling for human tribes who have been
dragged down and defeated by bitter struggles to survive over 'immense time'
(*SH* p. 26). Simon Grimble discerns the 'rhetoric of violence and a post-
apocalyptic landscape' in key phases of *The Story*, and argues that the source of
this is Jefferies's lack of a 'strong and conscious sense of cultural life as battle-
ground' (Grimble, 2004, pp. 97–99). But the historical rootedness of this 'grassy
couch' in Wiltshire, its apparently stable and soothing rhythms, do not elide
what Barbara Bender terms 'a proprietorial palimpsest': the 'flanks of the hills'
(*SH* p. 26) proclaim a doggedly contested chronicle of class ferment as well as
fierce unrest (Bender, 1993, p. 245). However much *The Story of My Heart* seeks
to deny the excavating consciousness that imbues Hardy's Wessex Novels, the
primeval past returns through repeated reminders of the deserted earthworks
and tumuli that dot the distant uplands around Jefferies's home.

Whatever restful aura the 'grassy couch' implies only serves to highlight the repressive rubble of bygone battles: the 'amphitheatre' and the 'entrenchment' on the summit (*SH* pp. 18–19). Although Jefferies strives to render the Wiltshire downs as a neutral space, *The Story of My Heart* cannot ignore that this terrain, like Egdon Heath and the 'ancient borough' of Casterbridge, bears multifarious physical scars of former strife, and the proximity of death is especially pronounced. Yet he reflects that natural phenomena have an existence independent of human agency, 'an incomprehensible religion in itself rather than the medium for revealing the doctrines of any particular religious system' (Lymington, 1887, p. 249).

> For themselves they are, and not for us. Their glory fills the mind with rapture but for a while, and it learns that they are, like carven idols, wholly careless and indifferent to our fate [. . .] Its hills speak of death as well as of life, and we know that for man there is nothing on earth really but man. (Jefferies, *Field and Hedgerow*, 1889, p. 264)

Jefferies remarks the camps, with their mound and fosse, and the prehistoric tracks – suggesting that they invoke the ancient Britons, or perhaps, in an echo of Hardy, the 'eagles of old Rome' (Jefferies, *Wild Life*, 1879, p. 69). As Eric Jones argues, far from being 'a place of tranquillity' (*AR* p. 50), Jefferies Land 'was and is the unintended product of actual violence, inefficient economic processes and what in any other English-speaking country would be recognised as grotesque social inequities' (Jones, 2005, pp. 83–93).

Salvaging the Hunter

The Wiltshire downs appear 'haunted by history' (Raine, 1994, p. 169), whose latest enactment is between Jefferies the custodian of a securely bounded terrain, rich in local connections and inflections, and those who convert nature into a sterile object for scientific or practical control. The 'amphitheatre of green hills' and the 'fosse' (*SH* pp. 18–19) are unnerving memorials of vicious 'blood sports': a harsh competitive fight for supremacy at multifarious moments in time:

> It is strange to think of, yet it is true enough, that beautiful as the country is, with its green meadows and graceful trees, its streams and forests and peaceful homesteads, it would be difficult to find an acre of ground that has not been stained with blood. A melancholy reflection this, that carries the mind backwards, while the thrush sings on the bough, through the nameless skirmishes of the Civil War, the cruel assassinations of the rival Roses, down to the axes of the Saxons and the ghastly wounds they made. Everywhere under the flowers are the dead. (Jefferies, 1978, pp. 52–53)

Dissension is an inextricable part of this vista, however much a sense of harmonious beauty may seem to dilute, or even occlude it, and this tension defines Jefferies's testimony from the outset (Grimble, 2004). The earth-fort in *The Story of My Heart* also evokes the primitive past of brute strength still operant in Jefferies's own instinctual impulses. He projects himself not as 'high-priest of Pan and Pomona' ([Anon.], 'A hedgerow philosopher', 1880a, p. 1022) but as an anthropological entity who comprehends his milieu only when he has tangible contact with it. This partially explains his highly charged references to 'Julius Caesar', and the celebration of the bust of this figure in the British Museum:

> I always stepped aside, too, to look awhile at the head of Julius Caesar. The domes of the swelling temples of his broad head are full of mind, evident to the eye as a globe is full of substance to the sense of feeling in the hands that hold it. [. . .]
>
> The one man filled with mind; the one man without avarice, anger, pettiness, littleness; the one man generous and truly great of all history. It is enough to make one despair to think of the mere brutes butting to death the great-minded Caesar. He comes nearest to the ideal of a design-power arranging the affairs of the world for good in practical things. (*SH* pp. 64–66)

Against the frightening absence of 'directing intelligence' (*SH* p. 94) in the hideous 'sea-creatures' (*SH* p. 50), Jefferies excavates a heroic version of Caesar elevated above 'the mere brutes' of the petty present; whose example comforts those individuals depressed by the 'ceaseless hum' of crowded London thoroughfares (*SH* p. 64). This is a more complex response than M. R. Hoste's judgement that Jefferies 'surely had some secret sympathy with all wild creatures that quickened his marvellous powers of observation' (Hoste, 1900, p. 227). Jefferies – through his cult of 'the great-minded Caesar' – also seeks to subjugate and suppress that which threatens or offends him. Here are intimations of that 'close observer of nature' who was 'too introspective to be an altogether healthy judge of men' ([Anon.], '*The Story*', 1902, p. 554), according to 1902 *Academy and Literature*.

In *The Amateur Poacher*, Jefferies invites the reader to remove himself from history through roving thought-adventure: 'Let us get out of these indoor narrow modern days, whose twelve hours have become somehow shortened, into the sunlight and the pure wind. A something that the ancients called divine can be found and felt there still' (Jefferies, 1978, p. 352). Obeying the call of what the 'ancients' termed 'divine' in the Wiltshire soil also entails the need to obey a politically charismatic and imperious chieftain who can restructure 'the affairs of the world'. Jefferies longs to wield 'an iron mace' with which to 'crush the savage beast and hammer him down' (*SH* p. 80) – an ominous echo of taking a 'hammer' to 'demolish' the venerable Assyrian relics (*SH* p. 87) in the eighth chapter. In such instances the quest for a 'fullness' of physical vigour,

leading to 'a deeper desire of soul-life' (*SH* p. 81) acquires an alarming resonance, melding mawkish sentimentality with barely concealed ferocity. '[W]hat
Jefferies himself most needs deliverance from', according to the 1909 *Edinburgh
Review*, 'is his own fevered and hysterical emotionalism' ([Anon.], 'Richard
Jefferies', 1909b, p. 229). At these moments, his imaginative landscape is
charged with a furious rejection of his own bodily frailties, rather than 'generous' metaphysical and visionary possibilities. *The Story of My Heart* is littered with
instances in which the becalmed rustic hinterland refurbishes a damaged or
etiolated masculinity. But in craving 'the physical perfection which was never
his' ([Anon.], '*The Story of My Heart*', 1902, p. 554), Jefferies seems to endorse
the terms of proto-fascist pastoral:

> My heart looks back and sympathises with all the joy and life of ancient time.
> With the circling dance burned in still attitude on the vase; with the chase
> and the hunter eagerly pursuing, whose javelin trembles to be thrown; with
> the extreme fury of feeling, the whirl of joy in the warriors from Marathon to
> the last battle of Rome, not with the slaughter but with the passion – the life
> in the passion. (*SH* p. 84)

Though Jefferies warns of the perils of winsome nostalgia, remarking 'that time
cannot be put back on the dial' (*SH* p. 33), he indulges an imaginative reconstruction of 'the dimmest past' (*SH* p. 23) that insistently lauds the 'severe
discipline' of a 'Spartan' regime (*SH* p. 85). He qualifies his rapt reverence for
these 'warriors' by arguing it is the rowdy exuberance of 'passion', not battle-
field bravado ('the flush of strength to face sharp pain joyfully' [*SH* p. 84]) or
wholesale 'slaughter' which inspires him. This fantasy, in which Jefferies envies
'Nero' and 'the unwearied strength of Ninus' the eponymous founder of
Nineveh (*SH* p. 80), is anchored in 'extreme fury of feeling' as a channel of
recuperative grace. Indeed, the power of sunlight links Jefferies 'through the
ages to that past consciousness' epitomized by 'Sesostris' (*SH* p. 23), the legendary king of ancient Egypt who led a military expedition into parts of Europe, as
related by Herodotus.

Contemporary commentators scorned this affection for Caesar and Sesostris
as a distracting strain of 'morbid, furious self-analysis' ([Anon.], 'Richard
Jefferies', 1909b, p. 226). Jefferies summons these figures as part of his
earnest, though peculiarly problematic search for a standard of extrovert
virility – 'the vehemence of the spear' (*SH* p. 81) – against which 'the philo-
sophies of old time past' and the 'discoveries of modern research' seem as
'nothing to it' (*SH* p. 121):

> For the flesh, this arm of mine, the limbs of others gracefully moving, let me
> find something that will give them greater perfection [. . .] something after
> the manner of those ideal limbs and muscles sculpted of old, these in the
> flesh and real. [. . .] I believe in the human form; let me find something,

some method, by which that form may achieve the utmost beauty. Its beauty is like an arrow, which may be shot at distance according to the strength of the bow. (*SH* p. 33)

The issue of correct or balanced perspective is central to Jefferies as he ascends the Wiltshire downs (Grimble, 2004, pp. 72–75). But his viewpoint here is couched in the crudest terms of sabre-rattling martial rhetoric – 'watching troops marching in rhythmic order' (*SH* p. 84) – which ill accords with Edward Thomas's thesis of a serene and 'unflinchingly true revelation of a human spirit' (Thomas, 1909, p. 173). Jefferies recalls lying on a prehistoric tumulus, and dwells on his feelings of coexistence with a primitive warrior of ancient England:

There were grass-grown tumuli on the hills to which of old I used to walk, sit down at the foot of one of them, and think. Some warrior had been interred there in the ante-historic times. [. . .] I felt at that moment that I was like the spirit of the man whose body was interred in the tumulus: I could understand and feel his existence the same as my own. He was as real to me two thousand years after interment as those I had seen in the body. The abstract personality of the dead seemed as existent as thought. As my thought could slip back the twenty centuries in a moment to the forest-days when he hurled the spear, or shot with the bow, hunting the deer, and could return again as swiftly to this moment, so his spirit could endure from then till now, and the time was nothing. (*SH* p. 36)

The 'grass-grown tumuli' adumbrates a mental disposition radically different from that which he argues is synonymous with the emasculating repression of suburban mores. Yet by the Edwardian period, as Ronald Pearsall comments: 'the countryside was treated as a phenomenon especially laid on by the Almighty for the edification of town-dwellers' (Pearsall, 1973, p. 119). Does Jefferies actively collude with this fantasy, exploiting the brittle pastoralism of an Arnoldian scholar-gypsy? His impassioned endeavour to disclose a paradigm of inclusive relatedness or a rite of reconciliation with elemental nature ends in failure and dissatisfaction. Furthermore, as he demonstrates in *After London*, the provenance of this gaunt but majestically sombre terrain and the experiences of the tribes who once subsisted on it cannot be convincingly recaptured, only invoked through the mannered artifice of lyrical rhetoric.

That Jefferies feels a formidable connection with 'the spirit of the man whose body was interred in the tumulus' indicates how the *Story*, while resistant to archaeological methodology, is nevertheless concerned with rescuing a fructifying force; asking how the ostensibly 'abstract personality of the dead' conditions the modern moment. That the 'thought' of Jefferies can 'slip back [. . .] twenty centuries in a moment' reflects a fascination not only with the cultural fossils of earlier epochs that are a salient part of the present-day environment, but also with psychological 'survivals'. Sir John Lubbock's *The Origin of Civilisation* (1870) posited that 'some ideas' are 'rooted in our minds, as fossils are imbedded in the soil' (Lubbock, 1870, p. 1). This implies, however, that ancient beliefs, although lodged in the human mind, cannot actively shape current behaviour. Jefferies conceives of himself in a way which bears out R. R. Marett's 1917 observation that imperceptible though resistless energies can overtake conscious promptings: 'savage impulses' always remain 'dormant in the heart of civilised man', ready to 'spring to life again' (Marett, 1917, p. 14).

It is the 'savage' spirit of the 'ante-historic' warrior 'hunting the deer' with whom Jefferies identifies, which is revealing about his own exact self-construction. Within the space of a few decades the predominant view of geological time had shifted from that which could be comprehended imaginatively, to that which could only be grasped mathematically. This represented, according to the 1869 *North British Review*, 'one of the most important [. . .] scientific discussions of the present century' ([Anon.], 1869a, p. 406). But geological science could only express the earth's true age by exploiting increasingly limited and recondite methods of presenting results. A *Quarterly Review* correspondent averred

> Geology, although it carries us back to the remotest periods of time, is itself almost a science of yesterday. Not on the wings of an airy imagination, but on the most solid foundation beneath our feet, it bears us back through uncounted ages; and yet it is eminently a science of the present century; a science, the very skirts of whose glory could only be dimly descried by the most far-seeing master-minds of earlier times. ([Anon.], 'The Geological Observer', 1856, p. 71)

Yet the 'far-seeing' Jefferies evokes the *idea* of 'the remotest periods of time' by conjuring up the revenant of a long-dead hunter from the 'forest-days': an imaginative distillation of a wide sweep of time within which human habits and codes arrogate a special resonance. The warrior's world is not a twilight terrain of undifferentiated dread, but a possibility for physical and spiritual refreshment. Jefferies's ardent faith in 'the wings of an airy imagination' is transmuted into a compelling inner myth that obviates misgivings about the deadening domesticity of suburban life.

The core problem with Jefferies's 'airy imagination' is that it adumbrates a sensibility which too quickly settles for panicked retreat into socially regressive nostalgia. As Edward Thomas notes, 'the revelation' of which Jefferies 'was in search' (Thomas, 1909, p. 162) could only be affirmed through blunt negation. The 'solitude' Jefferies cherishes for its power to induce 'irresistible idleness', a 'Nirvana of indifference' (Jefferies, *The Hills and the Vale*, 1980b, p. 32), has to be paid for by the lowly land-labourers largely absent from the 'Nature' he processes for a chiefly suburban audience. This fraught, self-lacerating awareness leads to rhetoric of seismic upheaval and intimations of a post-apocalyptic vista:

> The world would be the gainer if a Nile flood of new thought arose and swept away the past, concentrating the effort of all the races of the earth upon man's body, that it might reach an ideal of shape, and health, and happiness. (*SH* p. 94)

However, the dystopian fable *After London* ruthlessly debunks this naïve yearning for a 'Nile flood' to wash away the pernicious residues of 'earlier times'. If, as David Lowenthal asserts, English landscapes imply 'datable acts ascribed to ancestral precursors' (Lowenthal, 1994, p. 23), then what would happen if the environment had been purged of the monuments which speak of memorable human processes, predilections, interactions? *After London* envisages an England in which the intermediate steps between remote antiquity and the modern moment cannot be traced with limpid clarity or conviction. This 'island' has developed some time after an unspecified but devastating cataclysm; geological changes to England's terrain include the silting and flooding of rivers, the collapse of dams, the burying of towns, all of which creates a vast lake which stretches from the former mouth of the Severn to the rotten core of a ravaged London: 'from an elevation, therefore, there was nothing visible but endless forest and marsh' (*AL* p. 6).

The notion of 'barbarism once more flooding the world' (qtd. in Fowles, 1980, p. viii), as William Morris phrased it, is fully realized in the first section of *After London*. Jefferies shows that there can be no fulfilment of 'health' and 'happiness' in a terrain whose tangible connection with those valleys 'grooved in prehistoric times' (*SH* p. 125) has been obliterated. In his 1929 essay 'England Laid Waste' H. J. Massingham invites his audience to imagine a west country which for 'aeons after the last retreat of the glaciers [. . .] remained in her wild babyhood – forest, desert and the bare summit of the higher hills' (Massingham, 1988, p. 35). A conception similar to this 'wild babyhood' motivates Jefferies in *After London*, whose gloomy vistas paralyse the effort to transmute 'a temporal sequence into a spatial grid' (Bender, 1993, p. 2).

The Story seeks a condition of 'wildness' that permits the solitary wayfarer to commune with, and linger over, the fossil-rich palimpsest of Wiltshire; a narrative of escapist solace that retools the sublime for a predominantly suburban clientele (Grimble, 2004, pp. 24–31). *After London*, eschewing the often strident and hectoring style of the memoir, ranges that fey, aestheticized construct against a more visceral and disturbing panorama of 'degraded' and bestial tribes such as the 'Bushmen', whose 'savage frenzy' (*AL* p. 20) connotes a 'wildness' that cannot be domesticated or diluted by the literary quirks of a wistful scholar-gypsy. In 1905, A. Clutton-Brock figured Jefferies as 'a sad romancer, without spirit or hope enough for [William] Morris's vision of an England that has recovered all the beauty of the Middle Ages together with a new order of freedom' (Clutton-Brock, 1905, p. 108). If Jefferies's *Story* represents on one level a canny targeting of metropolitan readers disaffected with drab urban routines, *After London* shows the author slyly subverting his own status as 'that most potent magician of field and forest and hillside' ([Anon.], 'Review of *The Eulogy*', 1888). While *The Story* deplores 'false' evolutionary theory, the first part of *After London* embraces it, illustrating 'Darwinian concepts such as hybridity and extinction by describing the extinction of unfit domestic pets [. . .] and the interbreeding of the remaining dogs, leading to the survival of only three varieties' (Pamboukian, 2008, p. 12).

The opening gambit of *After London* erodes fairy tale convention by showing how the 'cunning artificers of the cities' are 'all departed' (*AL* p. 18); and the tangible triumphs of metropolitan modernity, such as the 'iron chariot' of the train and the 'magic wires of intelligence' (*AL* pp. 18–19) have been submerged by marshlands. What a late-Victorian readership would have taken for granted as technological innovations – formidable reminders of imperial sway – are construed by the amateur antiquarian narrator as fantastical or legendary lore; mere poetic tropes for ambitious balladeers in the future. As this narrator concedes: 'we have fuller knowledge of [. . .] extremely ancient times than of the people who immediately preceded us, and the Romans and the Greeks are more familiar to us than the men who [. . .] mounted to the skies' (*AL* p. 18). Jefferies evokes the 'site of the mightiest city of former days' (*AL* p. 206), now buried under the weight of its own accumulated debris: 'composed of the mouldered bodies of millions of men who had passed away' (*AL* p. 206). As Natalka Freeland indicates, the 'residents of Jefferies's imaginary future do not need to condemn the past by using its monuments to store their refuse: nature does it for them' (Freeland, 2005, p. 229).

In the 1880s, Jefferies would have been far from isolated in voicing a suspicion that the once robust body politic was sickening fast; newspaper and middlebrow magazine editors muttered darkly of bitter class strife, the ominous threat of German militarism, natural catastrophe and ravaging epidemics. However, Jefferies goes well beyond conventional auguries of apocalyptic destruction. His narrator's excavations reveal 'an unsuspected strength of remorseless logic' (Thomas, 1909, p. 256). A. Clutton-Brock, writing for the 1905 *Speaker* commended 'the eager and circumstantial manner in which Jefferies imagines his transformed England [. . .] It is a country quite familiar to us and yet of a country that has never been' (Clutton-Brock, 1905, p. 108). The *Athenaeum* elaborated this judgement: 'never' has Jefferies 'displayed a richer or more plausible imagination than in dealing with the geodetic and constructive aspects of his novel England, with its peculiar fauna and flora' ([Anon.], '*After London*', 1885d, p. 463).

Roaming a Savage Wessex

[T]he strange story is put into the mouth of a native chronicler [. . .] The mingled shrewdness and naivete of this imaginary chronicler's cursory remarks, the mixture of pert self-confidence and abject reverence for the superiority of 'the ancients' [in this] new, strange, and reverted England. There are elements in it that remind one of early Greece; others that remind one of medieval Italy, yet others that savour of Canada or Australia, of feudal Germany and feudal Japan, of barbaric Asia and barbaric Africa [. . .] All seems tentative, vague, shadowy. So individual a mind falls but ill into our conventional classifications; when it tries romances they are half science.

(Allen, 1885, p. 271)

According to Grant Allen's 1885 review, *After London* is a bravura and eclectic time-voyage whose archaeological sensibility demonstrates the 'scientific use of the imagination'. Given his own ambition to perfect the genre of time-travel romance rooted in evolutionary hypotheses – as attested by 'Pallinghurst Barrow' (1892) and *The British Barbarians: A Hill-Top Novel* (1892) – Allen was well placed to gauge Jefferies's literary fascination with moving through various cross-sections of the nation's history, or 'Looking Backward' to employ the title of Edward Bellamy's 1888 narrative. Allen's accolade is all the more striking given the fierce gusto with which *The Story* denigrates the epistemological power and kudos presumed by excavators who sought to determine history via the distribution of regional antiquities or as a series of settlement patterns (Daniels, 1998, p. 129). In *After London* Jefferies depicts Wessex as a 'loose group' of petty misgoverned states – a vision at once 'new', 'strange', and yet 'reverted'; his romance of the remote future is strewn with the lamentable 'remnant[s]' (*AL* p. 25) of forgotten tribes, recalling variously 'early Greece', 'feudal Japan' and 'barbaric Africa'. Whereas *Bevis* vividly delineates a parochial expanse merging colonial and feudal conceits, *After London* affords, according to the *Pall Mall Gazette* 'a distinct tinge of something more savage and more primitive' ([Anon.], '*After London*', 1885c, p. 165). Indeed, for Grant Allen, *After London*'s startling uniqueness resides in its erosion of existing sentimental and generic markers. Many contemporary critics conceded that the novel was 'so utterly unclassifiable a work' that 'we do not know how to review it without broaching half its story' ([Anon.], '*After London*', 1885c, p. 165).

As Clutton-Brock observed in 1905, *After London* reads like 'a real history and seems to be written by a historian with a living sense of his country's sorrows and fallen state' ('A Neglected Romance', 1905, p. 109). The unnamed chronicler combines the pithy 'objective' wisdom of an amateur antiquarian with the alertness to legend redolent of monkish medieval scribes such as Bede and Asser. The young protagonist of *After London*, Felix Aquila, shares the native chronicler's 'mingled shrewdness and naivete'. Felix's susceptibility to daydream, which smudges the boundaries between external verifiable fact and vivid fantasy, the

'abstract theories' (*AL* p. 172) of inductive science and the irrational promptings of superstitious dread, enhances rather than impedes his sweeping vision
of this 'novel England':

> [T]he whole map, as it were, of the known countries seemed to pass without
> volition before his mind. He saw the cities along the shores of the great Lake;
> he saw their internal condition, the weakness of the social fabric, the misery
> of the bondsmen. The uncertain action of the League, the only thread which
> bound the world together; the threatening aspect of the Cymry and the
> Irish; the dread north, the vast northern forests, from which at any time
> invading hosts might descend on the fertile south – it all went before his eyes.
> (*AL* p. 91)

Felix's perception of the 'whole map' affords on one level a visual plotting
of the shapes and outlines of a ravaged terrain that was once a coherent, self-
contained spatial entity. Yet he is more than 'a fully grown Bevis' here ([Anon.],
'Book Review', 1905, p. 1237); indeed he effortlessly assumes the panoptic
prestige of an aerial archaeologist, surveying the 'characteristic physiognomy'
of the 'body politic' in tough-minded, tangible terms as a field of exhaustive
information about 'geology, soils and natural vegetation' (Daniels, 1998, p. 113).
Felix appears to access the changing scales at which the excavator measures the
lineaments of the prehistoric past: at one moment offering a magisterial and
panoramic overview, taking in the configuration of coasts and the position of
major settlements; then illustrating the tiniest sliver of that once proud national
territory in 'breathtaking detail' (Darvill, 1996, p. 2). Jefferies in *The Story of My
Heart* portrays a Wiltshire homeland whose geography of material remains and
sites of commemorative ritual teeters on the brink of nebulous abstraction.
Felix by contrast envisages 'the known countries' with diagrammatic acuity: as
highly complex and volatile socio-political entities, moulded by the unrelenting
interchange of natural habitat and warlike human actions. His map – layered
with geological, demographic and administrative information – frames competing accounts of national belonging and even acerbically critiques the very
concept of the nation as a social and cultural formation (Daniels, 1998, p. 118).
Felix also manifests a keen responsiveness to what swarms beneath the civic
'surface' (*AL* p. 20), probing the grave 'internal condition' of a beleaguered
expanse whose 'fabric' – already weakened by the disappearance of bourgeois
capital and landed, county-based patrician clans – will soon unravel altogether
as the shadow of factional infighting menaces gallant efforts to uphold the
meagre 'benefits of civilization' (*AL* p. 19).

   This ability to ascertain political problems within 'the known countries' by
alluding to the frequently violent processes by which regional boundaries are
formulated and fixed, signals Jefferies's commitment radically to refashion and
retool the pastoral romance in *After London*, making it speak urgently to, and
about, sites of ethical as well as civic fragility: 'how' the body politic 'was held

together by brute force' (*AL* p. 71). Because of his lofty perception of the 'map', Felix moves beyond the stymied and ineffectual cadences of Jefferies's *Story*; rather he is positioned at the centre of a multifaceted national and mythic narrative (Grimble, 2004, pp. 99–105). That the feudal, military despotism in *After London* routinely ignores such signs of social ferment throws into sharp relief, according to Simon Grimble, a similar ignorance on the part of Jefferies's principally metropolitan readership; a group that still clung to the hope of a serene rustic hinterland and its beckoning spaciousness (Grimble, 2004, pp. 99–110). Jefferies sardonically overturns this fantasy by reinventing the 'south-western forests' (*AL* p. 11) as the locus of a resurgent Celtic race, of which the Welsh are now a superior 'tribe' proclaiming venerable credentials, in addition to sturdy links with a sacred terrain. Jefferies's 'interest' in 'archae-ological matters', haughtily foresworn as 'long since extinct' (*SH* p. 103) in *The Story*, nevertheless lends pressing intensity to his futuristic parable. The narrator of *After London* cultivates the tone of ethnographic solemnity when documenting the stark differences between our own era and his:

> [T]he Welsh, or, as they call themselves, the Cymry, say that the whole island was once theirs, and is theirs still by right of inheritance. They were the original people who possessed it ages before the arrival of those whom we call the ancients. Though they were driven into the mountains of the far distant west, they never forgot their language, ceased their customs, or gave up their aspirations to recover their own. This is now their aim, and until recently it seemed as if they were about to accomplish it. For they held all that country anciently called Cornwall, having crossed over the Severn, and marched down the southern shore. The rich land of Devon, part of Dorset [. . .] and most part of Somerset, acknowledged their rule. (*AL* p. 27)

The 'Cymry' are portrayed not as a cowed ethnic group bereft of stalwart leader-ship and with only residual autonomy at best, but as a tenacious and belligerent 'tribe', in which the supposedly outlying province of Wessex assumes a key strategic and archaeological importance. Jefferies may have read Thomas Nicholas's ethnological survey *The Pedigree of the English Race* (1868) which posits 'that all the people found by the Romans in possession of the British Isles belonged to the Celtic race [. . .]. Of these, the Cymry seem to have been pre-eminent. They occupied that part of the island which we now call England' ([Anon.], 'The Pedigree of the English', 1868b, p. 518). Indeed, an ostensibly inessential minority, lacking credible legal and cultural institutions – 'the lowest elements of the population', in the words of *The Pall Mall Gazette* – now practises highly effective guerrilla warfare ([Anon.], 'After London', 1885d, p. 146). Although Prime Minister Rosebery averred in 1882 that the Celtic domains were to the English but 'lesser gems' in the British crown (Lord Rosebery, 1921, II, pp. 111–12), Jefferies turns this around by declaring the 'centrality' of an ancillary district – a mischievous jibe perhaps at Edward Bulwer-Lytton's 1871 novel *The Coming Race* whose account of a subterranean master race 'looked forward to a triumph of intellect over matter' ([Anon.], 'The reader', 1885b, p. 499). Jefferies's conception of the 'Mystical West' contributes to and elaborates cultural and historical formations of the numinous; associating these 'far distant' counties with a different, Celtic kind of regional attachment that shuns the abject and craven associations of the 'Ancient Briton' (Stout, 2008, p. 59), enshrined in notable examples of mid-Victorian historical painting such as William Bell Scott's *Building a Roman Wall* (1855–1856).

Whereas the acolytes of E. B. Tylor conceived of the modern Celt as a 'prehistoric survival, with attributes that attested to a lowly place in the hierarchy of progress' (Stout, 2008, p. 57), the folklorist Alfred Nutt, a key figure in the romantic rehabilitation of this social category, argued that however much 'it may be regretted in certain quarters, the Celt is an abiding element in the imperial life of the British race' (qtd. in Stout, 2008, p. 121). This designation of the Celtic temperament, in which a once stigmatized and subjugated race – belittled as slovenly and treacherous in ethnic historiographies such as Robert Knox's *The Races of Men* (1862) – has reclaimed 'the whole island' as its rightful 'inheritance', does not necessarily bespeak a definable identity or a single myth of origin. However, Jefferies does imply that the Celt is inextricably linked with notions of arcane lore and multiplied perception. For Jefferies Wessex becomes a settlement, sanctuary and site of ritual enactment for another persecuted 'underclass' who were routinely pathologized in nineteenth-century nationalist narratives – the 'gipsies'. The 'movements of these people', according to Jefferies in *The Gamekeeper at Home* 'are so irregular that it is impossible to be always ready for them' (1978, p. 135).

> The gipsies are everywhere, but their stockades are most numerous in the south, along the sides of the green hills and plains, and especially round Stonehenge, where, on the great open plains, among the huge boulders, placed ages since in circles, they perform strange ceremonies and incantations. (*AL* p. 23)

What is notable about this formulation of the 'Romany' or 'Zingari' population (*AL* p. 21) is its validation of matrilineal groupings, in which women figure as 'progenitors and legators' (Lowenthal, 1997, p. 49). This concept challenges paternal rule and descent as the ostensibly 'natural', fixed and immutable form of social organization: 'among the gipsies a woman, and even a young girl often exercises supreme authority, but must be of sacred blood' (*AL* p. 23). The relapse into barbarism provides Jefferies with a rich opportunity to reflect urgent anthropological debates concerning the patriarchal theory of civil origins and the history of the matrimonial contract. Jefferies presents a matriarchal culture in which 'agriculture is practised, and flocks and herds are kept, but the work is entirely done by the women' (*AL* p. 22). The characterization of these priestess-rulers, whose dwellings are 'full of mystery and magic' (*AL* p. 22) illuminates ethnographic writings of the 1870s devoted to recovering the provenance of the clan as a primary social unit, with its affiliated institutions. Lewis Henry Morgan's *Systems of Consanguinity in the Human Family* (1871) and *Ancient Society* (1877), plus John F. McLennan's *Primitive Marriage* (1865) and *Patriarchal Theory* (1885) located the rudiments of monogamy and patriarchal society in a prior matriarchal state. These controversial findings supplied a signal anticipation of the turn comparative anthropology would take in the next 15 years, as feminist classicists such as Jane Ellen Harrison refined the notion of a matriarchal culture that greatly predated Olympian rule (Prins, 1999, pp. 43–81). In her *Prolegomena to the Study of Greek Religion* (1903), Harrison lavishly details the crucial importance of fertility, both vegetative and human, in ancient ceremonial and the darkly oracular potency of the goddess – or what Jefferies calls 'sorceresses' (*AL* p. 21). Harrison posits that agricultural ritual is the core element in the evolution of religion, superior to myth and theology. In a chapter entitled 'The Making of a Goddess' she argues that in the iconography of extant artefacts we uncover traces of an ancient matriarchal cult which was stifled by Olympian orthodoxy.

Since *The Story of My Heart* prioritizes the surviving 'gipsy' population in Wiltshire, we expect *After London* to show this group in a position of redoubtable strength. However, ongoing conflict prevents not only their control of the land, but also inhibits any curiosity in horizons beyond a narrow parochialism, what Jefferies calls in *The Story* a misplaced faith in 'the extremely local horizon, the contracted mental view' (*SH* p. 140). For Jefferies in *After London*, as for Hardy in *Tess of the d'Urbervilles*, the Neolithic ruin of Stonehenge is not only a heavily symbolic corner of Wessex, but crucial in the context of an evolving regional, and then national, identity. If for the medieval peasant the stones in their liminal milieu were revered and believed to have curative and procreative properties, for Hardy the monument suggests quite the opposite: the dogged endurance of a punitive, paranoid regime whose appetite for wanton violence masquerades as the austere rule of rational order and justice. Jefferies tests instead the rediscovery and reinvention of much earlier 'occult designs' (*AL* p. 26). For him the medieval aura of the site is both esoteric, baffling and yet comfortingly familiar: something open for renegotiation, and imbued with a specific construction of prehistoric mysticism, implied by 'strange ceremonies and incantations'. 'Every age has the Stonehenge it deserves – or desires' according to Jaquetta Hawkes (1967, p. 174); and Jefferies revisits John Aubrey's proposition that Stonehenge was not Roman or Danish but a Celtic site associated with Druidism.

Here Jefferies seems to conceive of Stonehenge in a manner reminiscent of how archaeologists currently construe the site's function during the medieval era, in which the Stonehenge downland was a common grazing expanse. In this instance, 'the material world was scarcely more than a sort of mask, behind which took place all the really important things'. Nature 'in the infinite details of its illusory manifestations [. . .] was conceived above all as the work of hidden

wills' (Bloch, 1962, I, p. 63). That the 'gipsies' enact 'strange ceremonies' connotes an arena in which mystical perception is legitimated by its connection to
ancestral divinities, while the stones evince a component of an enduring, if
syncretic folk culture that *After London* cherishes as one of the few remaining
echoes of a more vital past. As Deborah Epstein Nord explains, if 'Gypsies' are
depicted in literature as 'primitive, it is not only to underscore the ostensibly
under-evolved nature of their customs and traditions in relation to advanced
British culture, but also to suggest that they occupy a primal spot in the history
of civilisations and contain in their culture clues to essential humanity that
might otherwise be lost' (Nord, 2006, p. 9).

However, Jefferies does not so much articulate the 'essential humanity' of
this itinerant population as their unbridled capability for bellicose resistance:
vengeance becomes their fundamental 'religion and their social law' (*AL*
p. 23). The gipsies 'boast that their ancestry goes back so much farther than
the oldest we can claim'; in racial and ethnic terms they preserve 'the blood
of their race pure' because 'they never dwelt under permanent roofs, nor
bowed their knee to the prevalent religion. They remained apart, and still
continue after civilisation has disappeared, exactly the same as they were
before it commenced' (*AL* p. 22). This articulation of the primitive could be
misinterpreted as a trite neo-Romantic impulse which craves an *unmediated*
relationship to the unkempt hinterland. Jefferies sidesteps this tendency by
showing a less glibly sentimentalized version of otherness through the squalid
tribes of 'Bushmen', former beggars whose 'thirst for blood' (*AL* p. 20) is far
removed from the quaint illegalities and twilight 'mischief' canvassed in *The
Amateur Poacher.*

After London shows that there is no apex of sophisticated rational 'civilization'
(*AL* p. 22) against which to calibrate the deviant, the atavistic or the 'backward'
given that the future is construed not as 'evolution' (*AL* p. 173) but rather
as a profoundly unsettling retrogression, a dispersion and 'falling into decay'
(*AL* p. 73). As B. G. Johns warned in an 1887 article on 'The Literature of the
Streets', 'infinite peril lies in forgetting that [evolutionary] development may
be for evil as naturally, as inevitably for good: upwards to the stars or downward
to decay and death' (Johns, 1887, pp. 40–65). Significantly, when Felix moves
away from his birthplace and towards the site where the grand edifices of
London once stood, his body becomes 'marked' by a return to the benighted
native, insofar as he is affected by 'discoloration': 'As he leaned over the side to
dip water, [he] saw his reflection [. . .] his face was black, his clothes were black,
his hair black' (*AL* p. 211). Though Ruskin and many other mid-Victorian
cultural commentators conceived of a time when the metropolitan hub would
devour the outlying rural provinces, Jefferies shows instead unhusbanded
nature engulfing the 'cities' (*AL* p. 18). So a constellation of scattered and
acutely vulnerable outposts dot the shores of the inland lake. These barely
civilized zones are redolent, as W. J. Keith rightly notes, of a pre-Conquest
England: '[e]ach community was well acquainted with the bay before its

own city, and with the route to the next, but beyond that they were ignorant, and had no desire to learn' (*AL* p. 45).

In *After London*, there is no glorious return to the feudal framework as an antidote to a perceived 'effeminacy' in late-nineteenth-century metropolitan culture. Jefferies's parable is forthright in its recognition of a hidebound milieu 'rotten and corrupted, coarse to the last degree, and animated only by the lowest motives' (*AL* p. 171). For the seventeenth-century chronicler Edward Chamberlayne, the invading Romans and Saxons discerned England as 'such a precious spot of ground' that 'they *fenced* it in like a *Garden-Plot* with a mighty *Wall* and a monsterous *Dyke*' (Chamberlayne, 1671, I, p. 5) to repel the Scots and the Welsh. However, with an acerbic flourish, Jefferies mocks the ideology of imperialist Englishness by depicting how once opulent 'cities' are now 'kept in awe by troops of Welshmen, Irish, and even the western Scots' (*AL* p. 26). *After London* impugns the habit of many mid-Victorian archaeologists and ethnologists to gauge history as a vertical continuum in which non-Western natives and their 'primitive' cultures were rendered childlike, helpless and rooted to the very bottom of the social evolutionary scale (Morgan, 1877, p. 9).

By detailing England's exposure to the depredations of terrorizing Scots, Welsh, and Irish, Jefferies satirizes the ethnographic mode elaborated by E. B. Tylor's *Primitive Culture*. Where there was once a single people there are now only residual remnants; the 'State' becomes a hollow concept (*AL* p. 25), split between myriad feudal overlords: all 'hostile hordes' (*AL* p. 140) locked into an endless spiral of internecine rivalry. Jefferies, by fashioning this once 'untainted' nation (*AL* p. 22) as a locus of chaotic heterogeneity and profound otherness, complicates the inflexible and totalizing perspective of one's culture promulgated by Tylor, Frazer and their evolutionary disciples. Whereas Sir Charles Newton glibly predicted an ennobling future of never-ending advancement based on appreciation for archaeological treasures from an exotic past, Jefferies realizes to some extent Hardy's concept of historical narrative in *The Mayor of Casterbridge*: a grave undercurrent of deranged excess breaks through the brittle membrane of civilized intercourse.

The concept of excavating the 'feudal' as a site of atavistic 'depredation' (*AL* p. 21), 'vile motives' (*AL* p. 26) and 'endless war' (*AL* p. 21) is all the more unsettling since Jefferies, in earlier rural journalism, glamorizes the 'old feudal days' and its robust modern embodiment in the 'experienced hunter' (*AL* p. 21). In *The Gamekeeper at Home* (1878), for instance, Jefferies maps the parochial culture in which this type operates, revealing an intermediate caste between the affluent local landowners and agricultural labourers (Grimble, 2004). The gamekeeper's sturdy, taciturn assurance and adventurous independence of mind is tied to his status as a watchful and wise outsider with *inside* knowledge. That he is not necessarily a native to the region over which he presides evinces a sovereign singularity rather than slavish acquiescence in the obtuse directives of his social 'betters'. Consequently, he is not worried by the trifling and muddled strictures of the parish hierarchy:

> There is a solidity in his very footstep, and he stands like an oak. He meets
> your eye full and unshirkingly, yet without insolence; not as the labourers do
> who either stare with sullen ill-will or look on the earth. In brief, freedom and
> constant contact with nature have made him every inch a man; and here in
> this nineteenth century of civilised effeminacy may be seen some relic of what
> men were in the old feudal days when they dwelt practically in the woods.
> (Jefferies, *The Gamekeeper*, 1978, pp. 11–12)

With malevolent glee, *After London* punctures this hackneyed 'feudal' ideal
of dwelling 'practically in the woods'. Such a winsomely nostalgic model of
terse virility cannot survive in a perilous milieu which conceals roaming
'banditti' (*AL* p. 25) and parasitic 'Bushmen' who exploit 'the darkness of the
night' (*AL* p. 23).

The Poisonous Past

The antiquarian narrator's stoical disabused wisdom in this version of 'wild
Wessex', coupled with his reluctance to indulge in pietistic moralizing, suggests
that the relapse into barbarism does not adumbrate divine 'interposition'
(*AL* p. 217) or savage judgement. *After London*, as Simon Grimble notes, is more
menacing in its theological resonances: far from being the harbinger of providential patterning, Jefferies codes the cataclysm as an event which may have
sprung from any number of possible causes: sobering evidence not of a
fresh moral order but rather a desolating randomness, or monstrous caprice
(Grimble, 2004, pp. 99–110). Felix's 'voyage of discovery' (*AL* p. 200) may lead
him to a hitherto uncharted 'Paradise' (*AL* p. 211) of 'extraordinary fertility'
(*AL* p. 74). He does after all, survive the sulphurous wastes of London, and he
is appointed chieftain of a new tribe. Could Englishness, as a sustainable set of
beliefs, be reinvigorated by Felix's technological savvy? The conclusion implies
not emphatic assurance but rather a deliberate and unsettling vagueness: it is
likely that Felix may never even reach 'home'.

Many of the 1885 reviews sidelined or overlooked the grave anthropological
and evolutionary implications of Jefferies's text. The 'deserted and utterly
extinct city of London' emblematizes a shattered nation, in whose 'stratified
[. . .] rocks' (*AL* p. 206) we read a record of irreversible declension. Even the
tempting prospect of disinterring treasure from the once thriving capital is
treated in nightmarish terms:

> [Felix] stumbled over a heap of something which he did not observe, as it was
> black like the level ground. It emitted a metallic sound, and looking he saw
> that he had kicked his foot against a great heap of money. The coins were

black as ink; he picked up a handful and went on. [. . .] the finding of the
heap of blackened money touched a chord of memory. These skeletons were
the miserable relics of men who had ventured, in search of ancient treasures,
into the deadly marshes over the site of the mightiest city of former days.
(*AL* pp. 205–206)

Here London is both archaeological dig and imperial scene of crime: 'Ghastly
beings haunted this *site* of so many' transgressions (*AL* p. 206; my italics).
'Our painters', according to the 1866 *Good Words*, 'fond as they are of giving us
pictures of still life, have never attempted a dust-heap, and yet nothing is so still
as the dust. If a man might be allowed to moralize over such an unsavoury
object, the first thing that would strike him would be the painful sense of
desolation it exhibits' ([Anon.], 'Dust Ho!', 1866b, p. 645). Jefferies offers a
desolating vision of London as a 'still life': the vast poisonous husk functions as
a ghastly 'exhibit' that nobody, except the most foolhardy, would dare survey.

The Mayor of Casterbridge illustrates the palpable toughness of 'coins of
Hadrian, Posthumus, and the Constantines', tokens which have resisted, unlike
their owners, 'Time's effacing fingers', in the form of social, dynastic and
religious revolutions ([Anon.], 'Races of the old world', 1864a, p. 455). The
coins in *After London* are irredeemably 'blackened' vestiges of a dirty and
discredited heritage which prompted and rewarded squalid self-interest. This
bitterly sardonic perception of wealth as Ruskin's 'illth' (qtd. in Freeland, 2005,
p. 230) is perhaps unsurprising in a novel which depicts nomadic communities
fleeing in terror from anything that resembles the physical ruins of 'former
days', an epoch that quickly fades into a dim twilight of doubt and bewildered
conjecture. Indeed, the 'reign' of terror expressed in this novel is not one in
which, according to Francis Galton in 1869, 'the race is perhaps able to recover
its tone' (qtd. in Pick, 1989, p. 38). Yet some of the early reviews posited that
this material conjures up a post-apocalyptic idyll in which man has reached a
civilized maturity by progressing backwards; any intimations of reversion are
cancelled out by the expected return to a simpler, more integrated regime in
which 'humans and nature peacefully coexist in a sort of eternal present'
(Hauser, 2007, p. 203). But Jefferies is explicit in showing that the 'geography'
of this Wessex (*AL* p. 34), far from being warm, wooded and harmonious, is
actually relict and balkanized – a battered platform upon which atavistic fealty
is gauged through unruly confrontation between tribal indigenes.

In its 1885 assessment of *After London* the *Quarterly Review* seized upon
the eerie resonance of 'the great metropolis having sunk into a horrible
mephitic swamp':

the conception, though merely that of the romancer, does not deal with the
absolutely impossible: witness the present condition of Nineveh, of Babylon,
of Egypt, and of other centres of ancient civilization. It may be humiliating to
contemplate such a catastrophe, but we dare not say that it shall not occur;

and Mr. Jefferies brings it before us in a strikingly realistic way. ([Anon.], '*After London, or Wild England*, 1885e, pp. 197–98)

The ancient centres of Nineveh, Babylon and Egypt, which Jefferies abjured as 'mere dust' in *The Story of My Heart*, convey a grim message to this contributor, whose patronizing regard for the 'romance' genre as a whole does not diminish his appreciation of *After London*'s 'realistic' prediction of turbulent upheaval. The *Quarterly* reviewer is also alert to how the entangled bank has become a monstrous entity in Jefferies's novel: 'the brambles and briars had choked up and blocked the former roads, which were as impassable as the fields' (*AL* p. 3). There was not 'a single open place [. . .] where a man could walk' (*AL* p. 3). Insular isolation leads not to settled continuities or rooted verities but rather to a biting sense of radical estrangement. The opening gambit toys with the suggestion of a pastoral reversion to the soothing intimacies of an oral tradition: 'The old men say that their fathers told them' (*AL* p. 1). However, narrative as well as topographical 'tracks' are difficult to discern: the roads and paths are overrun and concealed by grasses and 'heaps of refuse' (*AL* p. 9). These crucial lines of communication – which not only permitted the passage of goods and trade in the past but also adumbrated a progressive teleology – are now effaced, 'full of leaves and dead branches' (*AL* p. 3). *After London* shows undergrowth gaining a foothold in the new 'topsoil' (*AL* pp. 4–5), with venerable landmarks slowly disappearing beneath the surface. Visible boundary markers, which afford a definite shape and image to the region, have been forgotten; everywhere 'the lower lands adjacent to the streams had become marshes' (*AL* p. 3).

In 1926, the nature writer Anthony Collet contended that the rustic lane was a core structuring principle of English terrain, 'form[ing] boundaries so old as to show plainly that they are not the footpaths of yesterday'. He goes on, '[w]herever in our walks between village and village we find a track utterly overgrown and deserted, a sanctuary of butterflies and adders, we may be fairly sure that it was of importance when most modern highways were quagmires' (Collett, 1926, pp. 182–84). But for Jefferies, the tangible, historically rooted England that was formerly found down such lanes is no longer apparent, let alone accessible (Harrington, 2002). This loss of local pathways and 'roads' upon which to 'walk' implies a deeper anxiety, when compared to Hardy's piercing stress on the geographical and historic significance of 'tracks' and 'traces' as clarifying principles of 'place'. Recent scholars such as Allison Adler Kroll and Scott Rode have variously shown that local landmarks, rather than the jamborees enacted upon them, help us envision and re-vision Wessex history in Hardy's fiction. The road encircling Casterbridge, the verdant path through the secluded nook of Little Hintock in *The Woodlanders*, the trail into the lush Blackmore Vale in *Tess*, and the trek into Marygreen in *Jude the Obscure* – all of these paths throw into sharp focus competing concepts of citizenship; as well as how human settlements are coordinated both within the region and in relation to the world at large (Rode, 2006, pp. 20–25; Kroll, 2009, pp. 335–52). In *The Face of England* (1932) Edmund Blunden expresses elegiac longing through images of overgrown tracks and forlorn walkways: '[p]aths that were as good as roads are overwhelmed with nettles and briars; or the stiles that admitted to them are uprooted, and wire fences run in their stead' (p. 108). Blunden, like his admired predecessor Hardy, indicates that keen cultural self-understanding is chiefly dependent upon the visible presence of avenues which facilitate trade and migration – the disappearance of which leads in *After London* to existential emptiness.

Given the novel's persistent focus on the conversion of the 'country' and its route-ways into 'an immense forest' (*AL* p. 3), and how 'the duty of saving and protecting life' (*AL* p. 121) is usurped by the wayward promptings of personal gain, it is uncertain whether Felix Aquila can ever occupy a meaningful place in a Wessex where 'humanity' (*AL* p. 121) itself has gone to seed. As a modest but crucial counterbalance to this glum prognosis, Jefferies directs us to the closely bounded and intimate landscape of his childhood. Despite the remorseless erosion of the geographical 'palimpsest', and the loss of the value of ritual observance in cementing communal togetherness and cooperation, there lingers an arresting reminder of a vital Wessex 'tradition', as in the pointed references to 'White Horse' vale:

> As [Felix] drew near White Horse, five white terns, or sea-swallows flew over [. . .] The headland, wooded to its ridge, now rose high against the sky; ash and nut tree and hawthorn had concealed the ancient graven figure of the horse upon its side, but the tradition was not forgotten, and the site retained its name. (*AL* p. 135)

As Jefferies would have known from his own diligent antiquarian pursuits as a young journalist, the southwest seacoast was identified with an array of chalk figures, such as the Cerne Giant, which has subsequently become a cultural icon. Indeed, as H. G. Archer noted in his 1903 article for *Good Words*, 'this form of memorial or landmark is peculiar to this island, and that in no other part of the world has it ever been known to be perpetrated' (Archer, 1903, p. 187). Thomas Hughes's *The Scouring of the White Horse* eulogizes this 'colossal figure cut out in the turf, and giving the name to a whole district' (1857, pp. vii–viii). Jefferies's *History of Swindon and its Environs* contains a vivid account of the figure, the scouring of 1857 and Hughes's novel (1896, pp. 123–26). Hughes's exhortation to his fellow 'west-countrymen' in *The Scouring of the White Horse* to 'let no old custom, which has a meaning, however rude, die out, if it can be kept alive' (*TSWH* pp. xii) acquires bitterly sardonic force in *After London*. For Jefferies, the 'straits' of 'White Horse' convey a poignant resonance in a novel where ardent affiliation with 'some primordial natural fundament [. . .] made and remade by many centuries of native folk' (Lowenthal, 1994, p. 20) has frayed. Society is 'overgrown' and cut off from many of its historic and cultural roots, while the bulk of written 'records' are defaced or 'destroyed' (*AL* p. 15) altogether. Yet the 'ancient *graven* figure', whose outline has been obliterated due to the chalky indentations gradually filling with sediment and 'long grass' (*AL* p. 4), still vouchsafes a cluster of evocative legends that encrypt clues about the nation in its moment of origin.

Far from being, in the judgement of the 1905 *Saturday Review* 'a carefully elaborated bid for popularity' ([Anon.], 'Book Review', 1905, p. 1237), *After London* is a determinedly sombre opus whose attitude to Felix's future prospects is at best vexed, and which shows the English as having forfeited their cultural identity as benevolent 'stewards' of 'an enduring yet evolving' territorial bequest (Lowenthal, 1994, p. 22). However, the location of the White Horse on the edge of the Berkshire Downs still allows for imaginative engagement with this bedraggled nation's internal geography, its bitterly contested frontiers, numerous spheres of control and zones of political intrigue (Daniels, 1998, p. 112). According to Geoffrey Ashe, the 'presence of the White Horse can, with certainty, be documented as far back as Henry II and, based on its resemblance to the horse figures depicted on ancient Celtic coins from the last centuries B.C.' (Ashe, 1932, p. 57). So in a novel that foresees Celtic tribes reclaiming Wessex from their once redoubtable and ruthless overlords, the 'White Horse' vale is a muted 'protest against the lawlessness and brutality of the time' (*AL* p. 122). The Horse evokes a tribal emblem that adumbrates the 'archaeology of ethnicity' (Jones, 1997, p. 4); and provides a 'marvel' of a different order from that of Stonehenge, whose purpose in *After London* is firmly tied to the enactment of 'magical' ceremonies (Hawkins, 2000, p. 385).

Stonehenge supplies a striking site of 'magic' in John Cowper Powys's *A Glastonbury Romance*, which opens the next chapter. Like Jefferies, Powys is exceptionally attuned to the Wessex turf as a script whose richly multiplicitous meanings vouchsafe moments of animistic insight. Jefferies moves to a point in his literary career where biting disillusionment stifles the pursuit of 'wonder become a state, an impregnation of being' (*AWM* p. 140). Powys by contrast strives to override moribund metropolitan precepts by reinvigorating the west country as a hinterland alive with ancestral harmonies and hints of a metaphysical and sexual sublime.

Chapter 4

Mystical Secrets and Lies

Romancing the Stones

John Cowper is in many ways so English. One can search his novels in vain for
the slightest indication that he has ever set foot outside the counties of Dorset
and Somerset [. . .] *Ulysses* is seen to have recaptured the vast simultaneous
rhythm of a Dublin day, so Mr. Powys is able to communicate a constant sense
of the whole life of Glastonbury in progress, as distinct from an arbitrarily
imagined plot of which the scene happens to be Glastonbury. But in attaining
this end, he has made use of a more tremendous design than Joyce, given it
more organic unity [. . .] The detail, that is, has the cumulative effect of a
description of some locality, made on the spot by an old native.

(Theobald, 1932, p. 36)

Why is Powys's sensibility 'so English', according to J. R. Theobald's 1932 review
of *A Glastonbury Romance*? On one level Englishness is a national ideology, an
identifiable melange of principles and practices, tied to an assiduous mapping
of archaic, 'native' cultural forms in 'Dorset and Somerset'. Theobald contends
that Powys is preoccupied by conserving, and reconfiguring earlier romance
tropes; a distinctively 'English' mode whose narrative logic is grounded in the
'accumulated intenseness of the past as present' (Evans, 1937, p. 12), disclosing
piquant incongruities and unforeseen continuities, the fortuitous and the
grotesque. Theobald implies that Powys accords Glastonbury town the status
of chief protagonist and *genius loci*, transcending 'an arbitrarily imagined plot'.
This 'Land of Glamour and Illusion' (*GR* p. 755) is not a type of historical fossil
but a *site* of violent strangeness in which chronic victims of rapine have sought
to rebuild their lives; which bears the ragged residue of insurrectionary
tradition and boasts a bizarre dishevelled verve, even empathetic sentience:
'Glastonbury [. . .] in her sleep' seems 'an actual [. . .] Creature!' (*GR* p. 723)
To Owen Evans the town is 'magic-charged' (*GR* p. 927) and replete with
elemental, astral and phantasmal entities; 'the guide books make their great
mistake [. . .] in treating Glastonbury as a fragment of history, instead of

something that's *making* history' (*GR* p. 830). Whereas Joyce's *Ulysses* achieves a thorough architectonic and semiotic reordering of the nineteenth-century novel, Powys's 'tremendous design' keeps faith with, anthologizes, deepens and enlarges core novelistic tropes synonymous with esteemed Victorian precursors such as Hardy. Theobald also points out that *A Glastonbury Romance* operates as a sanctuary for the mock-epic transcendental apparatus which the regnant social realism of the interwar period could not adequately distil. This is apparent from 'the moment when John Crow drinks the water from the Slaughtering Stone at Stonehenge' to the baroque excess of the novel's peroration which depicts the 'towers of Cybele' (Theobald, 1932, p. 36).

> When they reached the thorn tree John [Crow] stopped and drew a deep breath. He [. . .] stared across the dark strip of downland turf before him, staggered and thunderstruck. Stonehenge! He had never expected anything like this. He had expected the imposing, but *this* was the overpowering. 'This is England', he thought in his heart. 'This is my England. This is still alive. This is no dead Ruin like Glastonbury. I am glad I've come to this before I died!' (*GR* p. 82)

For John Crow '[w]alking towards the West Country' alongside the 'long-winded antiquary' Owen Evans is like 'walking towards some mysterious celestial Fount wherein pain was transmuted into an unknown element' (*GR* p. 79). John's spellbound awe signals immersion in this 'unknown element', as he approaches the 'Great Stone Circle' (*GR* p. 83), 8 miles north of Salisbury. For him the 'identity of that great space of downland' (*GR* p. 81), does not signify a remote, arcane or unreachable past. On the contrary, he grasps a sense of 'England' as a refuge for the errant, the unmoored, the nomadic and the heterogeneous; undercutting any desperate appeal to ethnic provenance, or collective 'race memories' (*GR* p. 108). This episode self-consciously evokes another literary rendering of 'the towering monoliths and trilithons', though filtered through the camera 'eye' of 'Hardy' (*GR* p. 205) in a memorable moment of vision from *Tess of the d'Urbervilles*. John Crow avers that 'stone-worship is the oldest of all religions,' whose enduring majesty is 'easier to sympathise with than any other religion' (*GR* p. 84). For Thomas Kendrick, in his *The Druids: A Study in Keltic Prehistory* (1927), 'the Kelticized population of Wessex took advantage of the ancient *national* sanctity of the old circle-site on Salisbury Plain to construct thereupon a temple for their faith that should serve as a rallying-point [. . .] for Druidism' (Kendrick, 1927, p. 155–56). However, the 'message' apprehended by John Crow on the 'silent Plain' (*GR* p. 86) produces neither a 'savoured melancholy' nor a frayed 'nostalgia' (Corbett et al., 2002, p. xiii) for Druidism; rather he registers a 'heathen' liberty from all the hidebound and humourless dictates of civilized constraint (Duncan, 2003, p. 81). This freedom in shape-shifting he will later construe as the 'revelation as to the value of inconsistency' and stupefied bewilderment; resisting the interwar preservationist campaign to salvage a single or 'essential' national identity, as exemplified by Cyril Fox's seminal text *The Personality of Britain* (1932). Instead John Crow delights in mimicry, masquerade and the profligacy of social identities that affirm burlesque inflation, sophomore 'silliness' and 'conceit' (*GR* p. 508). Like his protagonist, Powys himself is 'liberated' not only from the crude distortions of national chauvinism but also from the tedious 'burden' of 'assuming any definite mask or any consistent role' (*GR* p. 87).

Whereas Tess Durbeyfield flings herself, in a last forlorn gesture of bitter futility, on the Stone of Sacrifice, John Crow 'seemed to have been given a sort of exultant protean fluidity. He felt an intense desire to make a fool of himself, to act like a clown, a zany, an imbecile [. . .] under these huge blocks of immemorial stone he felt a wild ecstatic happiness in being exactly as he was' (*GR* p. 87). It is this impish glee that enables John fully to indulge his wayward heretical imagination, moving beyond the terms of staid Christian culture or narrow nationalist archaeology to negotiate between varieties of mystical trance 'outside the sphere' (*GR* p. 909) of cool sceptical enquiry.

That John Crow's buoyant conception of 'England' amid the wild treeless isolation of Stonehenge is tied to notions of legerdemain and the ribald repertoire of a 'zany' makes Glen Cavaliero's judgement of *A Glastonbury Romance*'s 'great weakness', all the more curious:

> too often what are acceptable as superbly imaginative insights and intuitions of an infinitely suggestive nature are presented as dogmas uttered with a kind of pseudo-gnomic wisdom which lend themselves all too readily to the accusation that [. . .] Powys was a crank. (Cavaliero, 1973, p. 67)

But the opposite seems to be true, as Powys's literary excavations subvert the stylistic and formal boundaries of religious rhetoric, its strains of 'stony human fanaticism' (*GR* p. 227), and bombastic 'street-corner harangues' (*GR* p. 339). The narrator cultivates 'watchful detachment' (*GR* p. 440), even a quizzical scepticism, when tracking those who foster the fixed verities and glib certainties of 'the bookish doctrinaire' (*GR* p. 444), like the 'communistic' firebrand Dave Spear. Whether it is through the lens of Red Robinson's 'destructive Jacobinism' or Paul Trent's 'incorrigible anarchism' (*GR* p. 1061), Powys refuses to underwrite any single dogmatic definition of Glastonbury's 'immemorial Mystery' (*GR* p. 112). Powys depicts a dizzying array of standpoints towards the town's personality. He focuses especially on the characters' cartographic preoccupation with space and place, as well as the existential trials that result, such as Owen Evans's fraught pursuit of '[s]craps, and morsels and fragments, mythical, historical, natural, supernatural, as long as they had some bearing, however remote, upon the life of Merlin' (*GR* p. 169). Like Bert Cole, the narrator surveys this 'panorama of existence' with 'unpossessive relish' (*GR* p. 164), conveying a 'jumbled-up and squeezed-together epitome of life's various dimensions' (*GR* p. xiv).

John Crow's rapt reaction to Stonehenge becomes a yardstick by which to calibrate the nuances of mystical sensation emanating from the 'jumbled-up' and repressive rubble of Glastonbury:

> John began to say to himself that it was nothing else than this very low-lying character of the country that made it such a fatal receptacle for the superstitions of two thousand years! [. . .] Why, the land reeked with the honey lotus of all the superstitions of the world! Here they had come, here they had taken refuge, driven into flight by the great dragon-headed ships and the long bright spears of his own heathen ancestry! And here, caught by these fatal low-lying flats they had lingered; lingered and clung till they grew rotten and miasmic [. . .] God! This place must be charged [. . .] with all the sweet-sickly religious lies that had ever medicined the world! (*GR* p. 108)

That John compares the 'living' deities of Stonehenge (*GR* p. 381) to the moribund and ravaged 'Ruin' of Glastonbury is telling, given that the town has its own fluid 'residue of unused power' generated by immeasurable 'aeons of past races' (*GR* p. 291), sufficient to rival that imbuing the hushed sanctity of the standing stones (*GR* p. 367). Just as the 'landscape' seems to be 'a lie' to one of Graham Swift's disenchanted characters in the novel *Out of this World* (1988), so to John Crow's 'vagabond fancy' (*GR* p. 920), Glastonbury appears a seedbed for all the falsehoods and 'fake-miracles' (*GR* p. 350) that accrue to habitations of ostensible 'mystic influence' (*GR* p. 149) over the centuries (Maxwell, 1990, pp. 193–213).

Despite his dogged resistance to the 'heady, opiate fumes of the Glastonbury legends' (*GR* p. 373), John Crow becomes increasingly susceptible to the narcotic hex of 'this mystical spot' whose 'enchanted soil' was 'fed by the bones of untold centuries' (*GR* p. 165). That Glastonbury is 'the lowest pastoral country in the land of England' (*GR* p. 108), represents much more than a sober reference to altitude or topographical peculiarity (Maxwell, 1990, pp. 193–200). John suggests that Glastonbury is mired in 'sickly' superstition (*GR* p. 279); this 'bedlam of follies' (*GR* 941) is a hoard of 'low' and baleful untruths (*GR* p. 299) that stall the adjudications of 'fact' (*GR* p. 530). At the most trivial extreme is the pretty 'lie' that the budding lothario Tom Barter rehearses to flatter buxom 'provincial young ladies' (*GR* p. 516). Angela Beere mulls over how 'people have been driven on by the *Unreal* – by lies, and illusions, and fables [. . .] to the point of killing the only thing they've ever loved!' (*GR* p. 1101). For John, however, construing 'the general *lie* of the land' and its 'natural landmarks' (*GR* p. 225; my italics) is more about exposing and subverting 'poppycock about the Holy Grail' and the antiquarian 'gibberish' (*GR* p. 350) fostered by 'faddists' and 'soft heads' (*GR* p. 444). It is no accident that, as Richard Maxwell persuasively argues, John Crow perceives this 'rotten' and 'miasmic' locale in a chapter called 'Hic Jacet' ('here lies').

In a novel obsessed with the 'true secret of dealing with earth-life below the sun' (*GR* p. 28) the Latin phrase 'Hic Jacet' boasts an intricate and unexpected patterning. But Glastonbury is far from seeming a medley of 'dead husks' (*GR* p. 4), ossified relics and outworn customs; it adumbrates potencies that go 'further back than History' (*GR* p. 12) and cannot be disavowed as 'a mass of fantastic and gruesome fairy-tales' (*GR* p. 930). The narrator argues that we must 'allow that at certain epochs in the life of any history-charged spot there whirls up an abnormal stir and fume and frenzy among the invisible elements and forces that emanate from the soil' (*GR* p. 813). Owen Evans proclaims that in 'any given spot on the earth's surface [. . .] the consciousnesses of men are flowing and floating just below the blind material surface' (*GR* p. 847). No matter how 'materialistic' John Crow may claim to be, decrying 'the Grail story' as 'a learned lie' (*GR* p. 679), he is compelled to *learn* that what *lies* 'deep down below' the unwholesome surface of railways and roads, associated in legend with King Arthur, Morgan Le Fay and 'old Celtic magicians' (*GR* p. 1095), is crucial to his own intellectual growth.

Powys clearly delights in the punning possibilities which 'here lies' permits in a novel devoted to stirring up 'buried layers' (*GR* p. 1171), and piecing together the scattered fragments of forgotten faiths (Maxwell, 1990, pp. 194–200). Glastonbury is after all a 'wind-blown, gossamer-light vortex' from which multifarious sects and coteries have 'sucked their life-blood':

> Everyone who came to this spot seemed to draw something from it, attracted by a magnetism too powerful for anyone to resist, but as different people approached it they changed its chemistry, though not its identity, so that upon none of them it had the same psychic effect. [. . .] Older than Christianity, older than the Druids, older than the gods of Norsemen or Romans, older than the gods of Neolithic men, this many-named Mystery had been handed down to subsequent generations by three psychic channels; by the channel of popular renown, by the channel of inspired poetry, and by the channel of individual experience. (*GR* p. 112)

Just as John Crow is overcome by the 'magnetism' of Stonehenge, so too do various Glastonbury pilgrims divine a comparable 'Mystery' in the town, touching upon legacies that have little to do with broken statues and memorial inscriptions. The stress on 'psychic channels' adumbrates Powys's keen interest in a bequest that signals a memory of some occult ceremonial, rather than its physical persistence, which might spur new creations. What pilgrims 'draw' from this site is a notion that 'curiosity' itself boasts a numinous, transformative potency. 'Chemistry' is crucial here: the novel esteems an elliptical tradition that never becomes enshrined in 'categorical mandates' (*GR* p. 1005), ossified models or static trophies; this is why Powys sets such great store by John Crow's elated experience of Stonehenge, which lauds adaptability, audacious experiment, debunking wit and metamorphosis. Yet the 'appetite' for fresh sensation and for inventing new pasts that spurn bland historical facts, while it prompts the strong-minded towards the transcendent, can also push the susceptible and the feckless, like the tormented Owen Evans, into the lower levels of criminal intent, tapping 'a dark reservoir of our race's psychic garbage' (*GR* p. 833).

While this 'low-lying' expanse, embossed with long and round earthworks, bears discernible traces of all the 'hunted' and 'trapped victims [. . .] since the tribes of men had first come there', (*GR* p. 641), the town now offers refuge to the *lowly* and bellicose descendants of those very same tribal 'victims'. Predatory and parasitic behaviour is sedimented into the numberless strata of the Glastonbury tradition. This is implied by the description of Old Jones's curiosity shop, 'a hieroglyph of antiquarianism' (Bann, 1999, p. xvii), whose shabby and jumbled obscurity reveals the town 'layer by layer through the centuries', in 'certain significant petrifactions, certain frozen gestures of the flowing spirit of life' (*GR* pp. 354–55). The pageant that occurs at the book's (epi)centre strives to reanimate 'certain frozen gestures' through a wildly syncretic staging of the Arthurian, Judeo-Christian and 'heathen' chronicles of the Grail legend, a romance revival which Powys depicts 'as a thoroughly modernist piece of performance art' (Duncan, 2003, p. 91).

As the pageant demonstrates, Glastonbury has become a historic palimpsest, a topographical 'scroll of flickering enigmas' (*GR* p. 437). Among it 'lies' the Grail, which had 'attracted these various cults to itself with an indifference as to their divergency from one another that was almost cruel' (*GR* pp. 756–57). The foundation of Powys's work is, according to Jerome McGann, 'so accretive and (in pagan rather than Christian terms) salvific' (McGann, 2006, p. 176). But the Grail is not a stable or 'Absolute' standard of measurement in this novel; nor is it conceived straightforwardly as a bridge or transition between two more notable points of reference. On the contrary it is marked by a shifting and restive ambiguity. As John Crow avers, there are 'several ways of taking the Grail-cult' (*GR* p. 337) and no binding, redemptive or compensatory thread underpins the disparate fugitive impressions which cluster about this 'sacred' trophy. In the preface written 20 years after the novel first appeared for the 1955 edition, Powys reflected that 'Its heroine is the Grail. Its hero is the Life poured into the Grail. Its message is that no one Receptacle of Life and no one Fountain of Life poured into that Receptacle can contain or explain what the world offers us' (*GR* p. xiii). And so the maddening elusiveness of the Grail, 'that something' which 'has been dropped upon our planet, dropped within the earthly atmosphere that surrounds Glastonbury' (*GR* p. 471) according to Johnny Geard, permits the tireless narrator to inspect a 'thrilling mixture of contradictions' (*GR* p. 672). This memento seems to excite a lofty 'spiritual grandeur' on the one hand, while on the other the 'presence of the Grail in that spot' becomes a mellow charm, even an 'aphrodisiac', 'digging deep channels for the amorous life of those who touch' the Wessex 'soil' (*GR* p. 818).

Glastonbury's '*genius loci*' (*GR* p. 9), inextricably enmeshed with the occult 'Grail secret', implies another type of lying: sinking back to savour an 'oasis of sensuous, West-Country peace' (*GR* p. 332). The pregnant Nell Zoyland wishes to 'lie down' when overwhelmed by a 'wave of drowsy indifference' (*GR* p. 479); Johnny Geard heals Mrs Petherton by lying down beside her on a bed of 'blessed' repose (*GR* p. 297). Waves of 'delicious languor' emanate from this 'district' like a 'thin, penetrating anaesthetic', and posses a definite healing power (*GR* p. 684) for John Crow, who locates 'fathomless peace of mind, in idolising a girl's body' (*GR* p. 649). The 'ravishing and transporting satisfaction' (*GR* p. 864) fostered by this supernatural object functions as a spiritual nutriment, supplying a condition of ecstatic forgetfulness to 'neophytes', washing 'their *minds clean*' (*GR* p. 139). Several chapters after 'Hic Jacet', the bullish captain of industry Philip Crow, owner of Wookey Hole caves and implacably opposed to Johnny Geard's 'new religious cult' (*GR* p. 818), flies over the region in an airplane. This formidable, 'hawk-nosed' man (*GR* p. 30) exults in the Audenesque position of panoptic prestige, objectifying and abstracting the terrain as 'the hawk or the helmeted airman' sees it:

> Philip recognised the general lie of the land tonight and its natural landmarks more quickly than most passengers would have done in one of their first ascents. So might some hawk-eye among his Norman ancestors have surveyed the landscape from the high keep of some newly built castle [. . .] It was of the planetary earth, a sensitised round orb circling through space, not of any calm earth-mother, lying back upon her secret life, that his mind was full. (*GR* p. 231)

The 'life' of 'Glastonbury herself' murmurs 'softly in her long historic trance of the past' (*GR* p. 988). But to this ludicrously anti-romantic futurist, who combines the roles of 'pilot, harpooner' and macho 'big-game hunter' (*GR* p. 30), the earth mother and her 'primal sap of creation' (*GR* p. 545), symbolizing lavish liberality and soothing rhythms of cyclical recurrence, are unworthy of conservation. It is ironic that in an age of aerial archaeology, marked by pioneering publications such as *Wessex from the Air* by Alexander Keiller and O. G. S. Crawford in 1928, Philip has no sincere interest in surveying or photographing the lineaments of deserted Neolithic settlements, Roman roads, Iron Age hill-forts, chalk figures and round barrows from his elevated, glamorous and god-like perspective (Hauser, 2007). Philip avows, with acquisitive avarice, that the chalky soil of the Wessex downs, and its graven images of a resilient English past, will be 'dominated absolutely by Science' (*GR* p. 226), and subsequently turned to a swift, possibly illegal profit. It is a measure of Philip's obtuse narrowness, and his belief that the past of successive conquests and clearances can be cordoned off or sundered from the social and cultural formation of modernity, that this deforested region of southern England seems to him an unlovely, inert expanse. He is impervious to the 'most exquisite' reveries of 'absorption' that Sam Dekker enjoys when 'liberated from possessiveness, from ambition, from the exigencies of desire' (*GR* p. 969). Philip cannot apprehend the sacred solace or 'delicious drowsiness' that flows through other characters 'like a ripple of warm etherealised honey' (*GR* p. 719). Instead he positions himself as the 'man to blow' Arthur and the Holy Grail 'sky-high' (*GR* p. 228).

Owen Evans's 'private quest' (*GR* p. 138) for the Grail secret throws into bold relief the more unsettling connotations of 'Hic Jacet'. Evans, gripped and appalled by his own sadistic fantasy of delivering 'a killing blow' by 'an iron bar' (*GR* p. 139), tries to exorcise this mark of the beast through the Grail's purgative influence (*GR* p. 149), repeating to himself the mantra '*Hic . . . jacet . . . Arturus*' (*GR* p. 183). In the pageant at the novel's midpoint he plays the crucified Christ which affords him a grisly vision of all the distressing scenes that have been played out in the deprived nooks and crannies of Glastonbury: '"It is God and He is lying to me", thought Mr. Evans. "He is lying to me. People lie to the condemned for whom there is no hope"' (*GR* p. 618). That Powys links Evans's surreptitious sadism to his obsession with the rare, the recondite and the atavistic buttresses an orthodox literary perception of the antiquarian, promoted by Robert Burton's *The Anatomy of Melancholy* (1621) and Sir Walter Scott's Jonathan Oldbuck in *The Antiquary* (1816), as addicted to collecting tangible mementos and documentary traces that are – in every sense – much 'dirtier' than those permitted by socially certified nostalgia (Peltz and Myrone, 1999, p. 3). Such a dilettante dabbler, in Scott's novel, undertakes his search as a respite from, rather than as 'a bridge' to current socio-political concerns and priorities (Kidd, 2000, pp. 108). The secret 'cabinets' of Evans's mind are replete with 'rotten and stinking' vestiges, 'the better for being mouldy and worm-eaten': this pathetic and guilt-ridden figure has, Powys implies, become irrevocably tainted by the occult icons that he has consecrated his life to picking over, classifying and fetishizing (Earle, 1899, p. 14). That Evans turns against his own bodily and mental frailties in the pageant, divulges a more ominous facet of the *genius loci*, a potency which affirms not unblemished purity or delicate equipoise but rather 'exceptional stir[s] of heightened consciousness' (*GR* p. 1), even chaotic upheaval triggered by a 'heterogeneous mob of invaders' (*GR* p. 584).

Aboriginal Sins

Surveying the musty, seldom-visited library at Mark's Court, Johnny Geard

> became suddenly conscious, with a grim exultation, of the long history of the human race. And he felt as if every movement in that history had been a thing of books and would always be a thing of books! He thought of the great books that have moulded history – books like Plato, Rousseau, Marx – and there came over him an overpowering sense of the dramatic pliancy, suggestibility, malleability, of the masses of human beings. (*GR* p. 439)

However, what Geard learns is that the chthonic 'recklessness of the Glastonbury tradition' (*GR* p. 585) exposes a substratum of human want, misery and 'homicidal violence' (*GR* p. 139) that cannot be adequately encoded within yellowing tomes and 'folios' (*GR* p. 439). As vehicles for cutting-edge and insurgent ideas books do 'mould' and shape the course of history; yet Powys also captures the sense that printed matter is itself putrid, mouldy, compromised and obsolescent: the dead hand of the past stymies efforts to help those mole-catchers and stonemasons who were little more than a cursory footnote in antiquarian octavos and quartos; who enjoyed no access to libraries and other sites of civic prestige. The novel demonstrates that an imaginative excavation, 'layer by layer through the centuries' only becomes telling and trenchant when it acknowledges the natives from the 'back alleys' of Bove Town and the sardonically named 'Paradise' (*GR* p. 269): the 'autochthones' (*GR* p. 1044) – a seething 'mass' of 'human beings' who are not so pliant after all. These indigenes are, according to Richard Maxwell, grotesque 'creatures', 'sprung from the soil and thus can combat the *genius* on its own terms' (Maxwell, 1990, p. 194). Running through the novel is an urgent debate about whether it is 'hard common sense' that typifies the bedrock of 'old England' (*GR* p. 444) or rather 'outburst[s] of barbarity' (*GR* p. 327); the feral glee, 'older anyway than History' (*GR* p. 106), with which Glastonbury's 'heathen aboriginals' (*GR* p. 966) perceive a Grail 'secret' that shatters the ponderous and pedantic antiquarian leanings of their more well-heeled neighbours: 'Glastonbury a person? [. . .] These old, obstinate, irrational indigenes of the place understood this wayward and mysterious Personality better than any philosophical triumvirate could do' (*GR* p. 1045).

What the aboriginals understand is that material legacies, the remnants of saints and sovereigns, say nothing to or about the *indigent* populace. Powys illustrates the autochthones' corrosively cynical sense that Glastonbury's musty treasures – the churches, temples and tombs – are little better than props of clerical repression. Owen Evans's commitment to the Grail as an 'occult escape' from 'all the pain in the world' (*GR* p. 170), regresses into a nauseated fascination with those fiery 'nondescripts' whose insight into 'the terrible magic of this spot' (*GR* p. 1113) highlights their status as abject 'failures in the merciless struggle of existence' (*GR* p. 269); descendants 'by centuries of inbreeding' (*GR* p. 966) of those subjugated tribes, such as the 'Cymry' who regain a measure of self-esteem as part of Richard Jefferies's dystopian vision in *After London*. The majority of the autochthons, such as the 'semi-imbecile beggar' Jimmy Bagge (*GR* p. 967), derive from the dingiest Glastonbury tenements; another member of this riotous clan, Finn Toller, intuits immediately the wellspring of Owen Evans's 'erotic aberrations' (*GR* p. 94) and 'wickedest' thoughts (*GR* p. 1034), for which the Grail may be a panacea. Toller 'had detected with that extraordinary clairvoyance which imbeciles share with children, that Mr. Evans had a morbid interest in physical violence' (*GR* p. 1033). Does this fractious underclass, 'forever revolting against both church and state' and strongly reminiscent of the unruly topers at Peter's Finger in *The Mayor of*

Casterbridge, personify the most enduring link with the 'old chthonian divinities of Tor Hill' (*GR* p. 967)? Powys is deliberately cryptic on this issue, and the novel frequently shows that the connection between the autochthonous poor and the Grail story's 'runic clue' handed down 'from far-off centuries' (*GR* p. 170) can be fiercely antagonistic, expressing a grim 'litany of chaos' (*GR* p. 524):

> In all human communities – indeed in all human groups – there are strange atavistic forces that are held in chains deep down under the surface. Like the imprisoned Titans, these [forces] dwell in the nether depths of human nature ready to break forth in blind scoriac fury under a given touch. In these violent upheavals of class against class there is something deeper than principle or opinion at stake. Skin against skin [. . .] blood against blood [. . .] nerves against nerves [. . .] rise up from incalculable depths. (*GR* pp. 591–92)

Like the denizens of Mixen Lane in Hardy's *Mayor,* Powys's 'aboriginals' (*GR* p. 842) pride themselves on a spirit of robust resistance to civic governance and the august 'principles of municipal ownership' (*GR* p. 170): their precursors had waylaid 'the lovely queen of Rex Arturus himself' (*GR* p. 584); offered food and shelter to 'the crafty Welshman' Owen Glendower (*GR* p. 584); endorsed Jack Cade's popular protest against toothless leadership and unjust taxes; rioted in John Wycliffe's honour; and participated in that 'sweet, honeysuckle bastard' Monmouth's abortive attempt to depose James II (Maxwell, 1990, pp. 194–208). The extent to which this 'destitute, drunken and half-witted people' (*GR* p. 583) from the slums extracts its primal vim from a 'Presence that had defeated the Principalities and Powers of this proud planet centuries before the Norsemen came to Byzantium' (*GR* p. 451), emerges as the most inscrutable puzzle – and as a grave challenge to the efficacy of Geard's elaborate Midsummer pageant. The first part of the performance is nearly derailed when the 'roughest elements of the town' try to murder Lord P., an impulsive yet stern articulation of 'malignity' (*GR* p. 967) against 'everything in these people's lives that they had suffered from' (*GR* p. 569). It is only through Geard's foolhardy courage that a tragedy is averted.

A core facet of the pageant's fascination is how the spectacle goads the autochthons to a pitch of vicious 'revolt against all the gregarious traditions of the human crowd' (*GR* p. 383). The Arthurian tableau engenders in them not simply a spirit of 'released roguery' (*GR* p. 384), but rather a 'scoriac fury', because this version of the past is typically employed by a self-aggrandizing, rooted elite which magnifies its legendary forebears. Arthur does not *belong* to the urban poor; antiquarian 'chatter about the old gods' (*GR* p. 728) fails to allay their 'hideous miseries' (*GR* p. 649). Arthur betokens rather the inherited social constraints that should be sloughed off – an iniquitous burden best consigned to the dust-heap of history. The enraged natives construe Arthur as merely another one of those conquerors who told the luckless and the lowly that they had no right to forge, let alone glorify, their own emblems of tradition. *The Mayor of Casterbridge* situates the Mixen Lane autochthons within a boisterous, dissident and oppositional subculture of seasonal celebrations that include fairgrounds, feasting and illicit revelry. The survival of the 'skimmity ride' suggests a capacity to mobilize mass protest against the treacheries and oppressions condoned by corrupt local magistrates. However, Powys says little about the behavioural codes, verbal mannerisms, rituals or ancestral annals which may lengthen and strengthen the corporate identity of the Bove Town derelicts; this underclass is specified by and through 'an inherent barbarism and crudity of rank human nature' (*GR* p. 1122), which clamours for the immediate overthrow of the debased day-order. Their violent insurgency during the pageant reverberates through the novel, as the later chapter 'Nature Seems Dead' attests. On the night of 10th December in Glastonbury, 'what really came back [. . .] were the *dreams* of the conquered, those disordered, extravagant, law-breaking dreams, out of which the Shrines of Glastonbury had originally been built' (*GR* p. 756). These 'dreams' carry a monitory significance, 'outrageously startling' and 'upsetting to all proprieties' (*GR* p. 522). The benediction of the Grail is bequeathed to those, like the 'miracle-worker' Geard, who are largely unaffected by a sense of imprisoning conventionality; yet even he is discomposed by the terrible 'radiations' that this supernatural curio transmits (*GR* p. 471).

Powys also indicates that Grail images appear most frequently in the sinister form of dreams, revealing 'little' images that exacerbate 'the infirmities' of Owen Evans's 'flesh' (*GR* p. 1172) and making the pursuit of 'paradisiac peace' (*GR* p. 729) a process of endless deferral. For Powys, the indigenous 'murmurings of obscure invocations' seem 'to recede and vanish away even as they are named among us' (*GR* p. 1174). The secret of the Grail, imaged on occasions as a mode of combating alienated frustration, and upholding the cause of the 'weak against the strong' (*GR* p. 1174) actually unleashes a fiendishly disruptive and factional animus: it can neither be exorcised completely nor usefully channelled into existing political systems, economic institutions or cultural traditions.

The interminable struggle between hierophants of the Grail and those figures of 'atavistic retrogression' (*GR* p. 309) who contest it will only be resolved, Powys implies, by individuals who can neutralize the pernicious power of dreams and instinctual drives that subsist below the crust of waking consciousness. John Crow's dream of pissing into the Holy Grail; Persephone Spear's vision of cavorting around a tree that is also a cross; Philip Crow's fantasy of bloodthirsty swagger in which he quells an insubordinate workforce of 'hot-heads' and 'cranks' (*GR* p. 677) – *A Glastonbury Romance* is marked by increasingly outlandish and heterodox projections (Maxwell, 1990, pp. 200–13). Yet it is the sadistic fantasy of Owen Evans, whose plight in an 'empty no-man's land' (*GR* p. 1046) of 'sapless sterility' (*GR* p. 167) utterly deglamorizes the concept of 'the submerged Neolithic man' swimming up in one, 'like a rising diver from the bottom of the atavistic sea' (*GR* p. 523). Finn Toller, as both nonplussed gull and unpitying tormentor, exploits the situation to bring the hapless antiquarian to his crisis point. Evans's preoccupation with the esoteric lore of his antecedents provides little defence against the 'corrosive poison' (*GR* p. 167) of his grisly hypothetical reveries. The Grail, instead of supplying visions of delicious release, plagues Evans with weird foreboding, thus reawakening an appetite which marriage cannot altogether assuage:

> [The Grail] was too ticklish a thing not to divide human souls in a disturbing and disconcerting manner, setting brother against brother and friend against friend. All the way down the centuries it had done this, breaking up ordinary normal human relations and exerting whenever it appeared, a startling, shocking, troubling effect. (*GR* pp. 780–81)

Evans's plight illustrates with especial force how 'curiosity', conflated with objects of primarily antiquarian interest in the early chapters, now signals the compulsive and diseased promptings of a collector of delinquent 'sensations' – Evans as a doomed voyeur of his own 'cloddish, murderous, desolate thoughts' (*GR* p. 833). This is the 'troubling effect' of 'that particular kind of drowsiness that comes to human beings when the pitiableness of all human affairs presses wearily upon them' (*GR* p. 833). When Evans enters a tavern he notes how 'there was not a man [. . .] who had not come to forget his troubles' (*GR* p. 1006). That Evans resolves to purchase a 'tumbler of pallid gold', a potent local libation, only commits him further to Toller's macabre enterprise (*GR* p. 1009). At this juncture the mob violence which erupted at the pageant threatens to repeat in miniature form when Dave Spear, director of a new Glastonbury commune, is nearly attacked by the mutinous 'Glaston folk', enraged by his self-righteous political posturing. Spear advocates a glibly sentimentalized autochthony replete with pious platitudes: 'the human race, sprung from the earth, returning to the earth, loving the earth' in a future where there will be 'no more Glastonbury', no danger of ancestral echoes paralyzing present action; only 'a temperate and united human race' (*GR* p. 1017).

Dave Spear's utopian yearning, anchored in 'temperate' and measured human instincts, throws into sharper relief Evans's calamitous struggle with homicidal urges. His wife Cordelia remains affectionate towards him 'in the way mothers are endeared to a deformed or an idiot child' (*GR* p. 1055). Her 'savage maternal protectiveness' supports Evans's now futile search for 'the Great Good Place, Esplumeoir', to which Merlin disappeared. The Wessex through which Evans travels is no longer a place where brave modern knights savour uninterrupted slumber. Instead a seismic social convulsion awaits the unwary and the stalwart alike. What Chris Baldick calls Powys's 'relentless interpenetrations of the trivial and the cosmic, the everyday and the timeless, a method that gives rise more often to bathos and exhaustion than to the spiritual insight it gropes for' (Baldick, 2004, p. 232), misses the point of Evans's odyssey: bathetic excess and spiritual aridity are mixed into the witches' brew that the Grail object contains. For Evans 'exhaustion' is an inescapable fate; for Johnny Geard by contrast it is rapt reconnection with a pagan goddess whose presence is felt at the moment when he chooses death by drowning:

> For the great goddess Cybele, whose forehead is crowned with the Turrets of the Impossible, moves through the generations from one twilight to another; and of her long journeying from cult to cult, from shrine to shrine, from revelation to revelation, there is no end. [. . .]
> [. . .] Made of a stuff more lasting than granite, older than basalt, harder than marble, and yet as insubstantial as the airiest mystery of thought, these Towers of the journeying Mother still trouble the dreams of men with their tremulous up-rising. (*GR* pp. 1172–73)

This pointed reference to 'the great goddess Cybele' evokes Hardy's *Tess* and its figuring of the bleakly inhospitable terrain around Flintcomb-Ash as a massive recumbent female, 'bosomed with semi-globular tumuli – as if Cybele the Many-breasted were supinely extended there' (*Tess*, 1988, p. 273). Given the hardened and unwelcoming surface of Flintcomb-Ash, it is apt that Cybele was thought to personify 'the earth in its primitive and savage state' (Guirand, 1966, p. 173). The flints of the 'starve-acre place' (*Tess*, 1988, p. 277) have fertile 'phallic shapes' – perhaps a reminder that in what J. G. Frazer termed a 'ghastly rite', Cybele's priests castrated themselves in entering the service of the divinity. Powys seizes upon these ominous associations, in signalling a substance 'more lasting than granite' which continues to oppress 'the dreams of men'.

Powys's *Maiden Castle*, like *A Glastonbury Romance*, focuses on a West-Country town 'charged' with the rich residue of 'centuries of human life' (*MC* p. 113), in this case Dorchester, as a site in which 'mystical "recognitions" from Neolithic times' (*MC* p. 134) might be quarried. Powys's Dorchester is a locale where 'long atavistic history' and tokens of technological modernity collide: 'over the bare crest of the prehistoric, Romanized camp' of Poundbury is an 'unexpected marvel': the 'Wireless' stations in the far distance, pointing to the 'great Future' (*MC* p. 138). It is partly this abiding fascination with incongruous juxtaposition that explains his self-construction as 'incorrigible bookworm':

> Of all our Wessex writers I am the most hopelessly and incredulously bookish. Yes, I am an incorrigible bookworm with a desperate mania for trying to write the sort of long romances I have always loved so intensely to read. (*GR* pp. x–xv)

Dud No-man, the increasingly flummoxed anti-hero of *Maiden Castle*, the first of Powys's novels to feature a published author as central protagonist, could also make this admission. Dud is an 'unsuccessful historian' (*MC* p. 24) because his status as 'a sardonic realist' is complicated by a fondness for 'romantic sensationalism' (*MC* p. 94); he can experience 'ecstatic trance' (*MC* p. 93) yet is also 'morbidly sensitive to social embarrassment' (*MC* p. 90). Like Hardy, he cherishes the potency of old association, such as the 'homely sense of a recurrent satisfaction' of 'human necessities' (*MC* p. 15); or 'the fungus of time settling down on a fragment of ancient broadcloth' (*MC* p. 84) – 'a totally different layer of reality' (*MC* p. 84). Powys's fictional framework is anchored in an often ebullient sense that the three central characters champion discrete yet overlapping strata of time: Enoch 'Uryen' Quirm craves reconnection with a recondite, Celtic mythic heritage; his 'progeny' Dud, as a proponent of historical romance, is attuned to the 'indelible stamp' Roman invaders have left upon Dorchester (*MC* p. 215) and he focuses especially on an appalling injustice from the eighteenth century – the legalized murder of Mary Channing. Dud does not simply espouse William Morris's definition of 'romance' – the 'capacity for a true conception of history, a power of making the past part of the present' (qtd. in Stout, 2008, p. 64) – but wishes to make that past a stinging affront to the modern moment. Dud's headstrong young mistress Wizzie Ravelston baulks at both Uryen's quasi-religious cant and Dud's antiquarian curiosity by setting her sights on a future of reborn possibilities in the 'New World'.

Dud's arrival in Dorchester to research the life and violent death of Mary Channing reveals how the past residual histories of this county town overturn any sanitized idea of bucolic 'repose' (*MC* p. 113). The unquiet spirit of Mary Channing, expressing the 'very mystery of Time' and 'the tune of some secret knowledge' (*MC* p. 15), does not merely recall *The Mayor of Casterbridge*, but also forcibly reminds informed readers of the circumstances in which Hardy drafted this novel. As Michael Millgate and Peter Casagrande explain, Hardy had moved back permanently to the bustling county town in 1885, after more than two decades spent in other parts of England; Powys moved to Dorchester in January 1935, after many decades of living and lecturing in the United States, to compose *Maiden Castle*. Indeed, 'these striking resembles to Hardy are not the most profoundly Hardyan aspect of this book' (Casagrande, 1999, p. 95). Powys's final Wessex Novel illuminates the vivid contrast between Dud's admiration for his literary father, 'the great Wessex author' (*MC* p. 24), who seems to brush local landmarks with ghostly fingertips, and his chaotically dishevelled biological parent, Uryen Quirm. At one point, Dud wishes to re-enact with his father a version of the ritual of unceasing assassination at the sacred grove of Nemi which opens Frazer's multivolume *Golden Bough*:

> [He] felt as if he and his father, isolated from all other living things in the mystic circle of Mai-Dun, were two prehistoric entities linked together by the invisible semen of paternity, but *for that very reason* destined to a struggle of measureless malignity, a struggle that could end only in the death of the one or of the other. (*MC* p. 244)

Dud's fraught reaction to 'the mystic circle of Mai-Dun' reflects 'a region charged with so many layers of suggestive antiquity' (*MC* p. 19) reaching back to 'the most primitive times' (*MC* p. 18). Dud is extraordinarily attuned to the layering of place, the numerous modes of pre-modern existence superimposed one on top of another:

> How massive and compact all the houses were in this old town! How they seemed to settle their patient stones into the solid earth just as if they were searching for the foundations of older buildings, which in their turn were reaching down to yet older ones. (*MC* p. 343)

Like these magically sentient buildings, many of the key characters in *Maiden Castle* search for the 'foundations' of more archaic and dignified structures. Even Dud's room in High East Street is decorated with 'palimpsest' wallpaper: the 'most agreeable aspect of it was the wall-paper, which was covered with little pink roses, though there was one small spot, where [. . .] a fragment of a much older paper hung disconsolately' in 'shreds' (*MC* p. 17).

The opening gambit to Powys's 'meticulous chronicle' (*MC* p. 53) pays tribute to a haunting Hardy: Dud, returning to Dorchester in November 1935, visits the cemetery on the Weymouth Road where the graves of his parents and his spouse Mona are located, all of whom had died in an 'epidemic' almost a decade earlier (*MC* p. 25). Thereafter, he finds himself purchasing, for 18 pounds, a much younger replacement for Mona, the wilful equestrienne Wizzie Ravelston, which slyly invokes – yet also sharply contrasts with – the brutal ritual of repudiating a long-suffering wife in *The Mayor of Casterbridge*. Although Dud feels like 'a "haggard knight-at-arms"' on 'the verge' of a 'great adventure' (*MC* p. 68), he has no phallic potency and is 'the reverse of amorous' (*MC* p. 29). His strong inclination to 'cerebral lovemaking' suggests a correspondence with the aesthete Jocelyn Pierston in what is technically Hardy's final published novel, *The Well-Beloved* (1897).

The morbidly fastidious and quixotic Pierston is like Dud, devoted to women yet both are 'nervously incapable of consummating marriage'. This 'nameless bastard, whose [. . .] virility was so weak, that he could neither "love" as other men or feel angry as other men' (*MC* p. 121), reinvents himself using a cryptonym that evokes the absurdly comic folk figure of Renaissance culture – the 'No-body'.[1] Dud's bargain buy is made at a circus near Dorchester, within sight of 'the curved outline of the Amphitheatre' (*MC* p. 72), an 'extraordinary legacy of the classic Empire' (*MC* p. 28) where Michael Henchard arranges a furtive and fraught meeting with Susan, the wife he had sold for 5 guineas as a shop-soiled 'article'. Dud's perception of the gaudy circus caravans engenders in him a 'confused sense of the queer continuity of things':

> Here in front of him rose the grassy outlines – just as they had remained for nearly two thousand years – of the Roman Circus, where scattered legionaries from Gaul, from Spain, from Africa, from Asia, and a few perhaps from Italy itself, after due libations to Mithras, to Venus Anadyomene, to Diana, to the

great goddess Isis, gathered to watch the butchery they loved, whereas now
the most exotic excitement that these school-boys and school-girls hoped for,
before their morning repetition of a prayer to the new 'Saviour', was the sight
of a Fat Woman or a Legless Dwarf. (*MC* p. 29)

That Dud discerns 'continuity' here says more about his own 'subterranean
senses' (*MC* p. 46) and need to reinvent the past to suit his own perverse
preconceptions. From polytheism to the worship of a single 'Saviour'; from
the 'butchery' of gladiatorial skirmish to the garish parades of freak-show enter-
tainers: all remind Dud of the human body's unappeasable appetites, the
craving for sanctuary, solace, piquant diversion and interpersonal connection. His
drive to transcend cheerless routine is expressed through solemn ritual observance as well as spectacular public entertainment. Dorchester itself provides an
apposite platform on which such an extravagant drama may be enacted.

Mai-Dun and Mortimer Wheeler

It is no accident that Mr. Powys who, judging by his novels, has a mystical
tendency towards pantheism [. . .] should choose to write about Dorset. Both
the countryside and the natives have qualities which it is very easy to translate
into terms such as 'ancient' and 'pagan'. I had decided to abstain from the
silly and obvious sport of Powys mocking – let's leave all that kind of thing to
[. . .] Stella Gibbons – but on opening *Maiden Castle* I found that Mr. Powys
had led off with a parody of himself. [. . .] Almost all the characters suffer
from obsessional symptoms.

(Richardson, 1937, p. 631)

Maurice Richardson's 1937 assessment of *Maiden Castle* for the *English Review*
derides Powys even as it purports to avoid 'mocking' such an easy and asinine
target. Richardson construes Powys, and his creation Dud No-Man, as a
po-faced pursuer of dark gods, in a literary climate that has rendered such
'mystical' illustrations of the soil's animistic grandeur redundant, even ridicu-
lous. Powys's insistent mapping of the myriad paths to physical, aesthetic
and spiritual rehabilitation – theosophy, occultism, psychoanalysis, primitive
mystery religions, nature worship – smacks of self-parody. For Richardson Powys
is a writer desperately clinging to a sexual politics and vitalist credo already
lampooned by Stella Gibbons in *Cold Comfort Farm.* This withering judgement is
revealing about the initial perception and reception of *Maiden Castle,* and also
raises core questions about Powys's visual and descriptive vibrancy. Can the
'ancient' and the 'pagan' be refreshed in a version of pastoral romance keenly
alert to the cultural clichés such terms evoke?
    What Richardson's damning review overlooks is that Powys – the 'Druid of
Wessex' according to Angus Wilson (Wilson, 1973) – and his reclusive creation,

the 'history-obsessed' antiquarian Dud No-Man (*MC* p. 27), are only too aware of the puerile excesses to which the acolyte, seeking an ecstatic merger with the earth, is prone. *Maiden Castle* is a highly self-conscious, searching and often acerbic interrogation of the numinous and its long, intricate genealogy; the conventions that regulate 'a mystical tendency towards pantheism' and why it is rooted in a specific topographical frame. The key ambiguity of the novel is that Dud's biological father 'Uryen' Quirm, who, like Johnny Geard in *A Glastonbury Romance*, seeks initiation 'into some level of life, older, deeper, less transitory' than the 'surface-appearance' of things (*MC* p. 27), may be no more than a mountebank mumbling 'incoherent gibberish' (*MC* p. 448) or a 'half-crazed fanatic' (*MC* p. 446). Alternatively, Uryen has been interpreted as an unjustly misconstrued 'sage' (*MC* p. 446), a revolutionary revivalist or shaman gathering 'the centuries together with the familiar continuity of unbroken tradition' (*MC* p. 15). As Dud himself stumbles towards a modicum of self-awareness, Uryen does not remain monolithic, but regresses and disintegrates physically as he finds comfort in 'a Golden Age in the remote past that can only be postulated if you refuse all evidence from history that does not please you' (Young, 1986, p. 255).

The excavation of ancient artefacts and potencies in *Maiden Castle* is not the hackneyed aesthetic folly that Maurice Richardson's derogatory review claims. Indeed, Powys takes his inspiration, and manifold plot details, from the sizeable team of archaeologists who were quite literally 'tapping' into 'the thick-growing, honey-sweet turf' (*MC* p. 360) in and around the great Iron Age hill-fort which this novel commemorates. As W. J. Keith has demonstrated, *Maiden Castle* both shadows and foreshadows notable archaeological 'events' which exercised a profound hold over the public imagination in the 1930s.[2] The dust-jacket to the first American edition of *Maiden Castle*, published by Simon and Schuster in 1936, asserts that 'John Cowper Powys has put into MAIDEN CASTLE the results of extensive historical and archaeological study'. While it is tempting to dismiss this claim as a canny piece of promotional puff, it is worth recalling that Powys's drafting of his narrative 'proceeded concurrently', with 'the most systematic excavation ever undertaken of the earthwork that gives the book its title' (Keith, 1988, p. 14).

The digs at Maiden Castle, which Powys delineates in his central chapters, were prosecuted under the supervision of R. E. M. Wheeler (1890–1976), 'probably the best-known British archaeologist of the twentieth century' (Stout, 2008, p. 267) and later knighted as Sir Mortimer Wheeler. That Powys designates Wheeler as 'His Lordship' in the novel (*MC* p. 386) connotes the roguish and wittily debunking tone that *Maiden Castle* finesses towards the chief practitioners of scientific archaeology (Stout, 2008, p. 229). Powys returned to Dorset from the United States in June 1934, and he must have been forcibly struck by the intense media scrutiny surrounding Wheeler's audacious undertaking, which began that summer. Though Wheeler announced in an August 1936 interview for the *Observer* that his work would finish 'within the next few

weeks,' the excavations continued until 1938. Over a hundred trained assist-
ants, postgraduate and research students as well as local volunteers took part in
each of the four seasons and represented, according to Jacquetta Hawkes,
'probably the largest force of the kind ever to be employed on a British dig
before or since' (1982, p. 163). Regional journalists reported that in the first
two years of exploration many thousands of sightseers had inspected this area
2 miles south-west of Dorchester – 'a rush to the place from all parts of the
country' (*MC* p. 334) that impressed even Powys himself. Wheeler's complete
report on what he called a 'monstrous artefact' on the summit of a high open
chalk down, was published in 1943. He also issued, in association with the
Antiquaries Journal a succession of carefully pondered interim reports in the
mid-1930s, which assessed the structural development of the fortifications,
then related this to the complex cultural history of the myriad builders (Keith,
1988, pp. 14–17).

Although there is scant evidence in Powys's correspondence to suggest that
he scrutinized these erudite interim reports, he would have gleaned ample data
from national and local newspapers such as the *Evening Standard* and *Southern
Daily Echo,* as well as conversations with his brother Llewellyn (Krissdóttir and
Peers, 1998, p. 209). Wheeler staged regular and well-attended press days, and
in March 1935 Powys listened to Wheeler's lecture at the Dorchester Corn
Exchange (Stout, 2008, p. 229). 'Maiden Castle Capitulates' proclaimed the
Morning Post on 17 October 1934, 'Yielding Up Secrets to excavators' (qtd in
Stout, 2008, p. 228). Powys captures this excitement by referring at one point to
a 'momentous discovery' in the 'oldest portion of the earthworks' announced
by 'the local *Echo*' (*MC* p. 334). Moreover, Powys would have followed in
the footsteps of many other antiquarian pilgrims (such as T. E. Lawrence) by
visiting the site, which had become 'a highly successful public-relations exercise
for the new brand of archaeology' (Stout, 2008, p. 219).

Powys utilizes vivid details from Wheeler's archaeological account of the
site's abrupt configuration of bluffs and mounds to render a profoundly
sedimented history reaching beyond the Roman Empire to the ancient
Neolithic era. Powys's thought-adventure is sharpened and enriched by his
awareness of urgent contemporary debates regarding whether this branch of
science actually destroys, rather than 'revives' the primeval energies recovered
artefacts are supposed to contain. Uryen's antipathy towards the 'excavations'
(*MC* p. 360) – as well as the paradigms and promises of social evolutionary
thought imbuing them – throws into ironic relief the archaeological 'opera-
tions' for which Roger (Claudius) Cask ebulliently seeks subscriptions: 'It is
important that we should realize how scientific, in the best sense, modern
archaeology has become, getting rid of all the old romantic nonsense and studying the way our ancestors obtained their food-supply' (*MC* p. 164). Claudius's
desire to collect contributions, however nugatory, playfully evokes the words
of Wheeler's first interim report, in which he declared that excavations would
continue after 'an appeal for funds is issued by the Society of Antiquaries'

(Wheeler, 1935, p. 272). However, for Uryen, the 'Archaeological Society engaged in the Maiden Castle excavations' (*MC* p. 333), a formal institution with avowed public functions, is little better than a callous gang of vivisectionists, reducing 'the lavish and wasteful fertility of Nature' (*MC* p. 317) to a frozen, cheerless object of dispassionate survey; a process in which the amateur botanist Dunbar Wye is complicit by 'collecting, and drying, and keeping in portfolios, endless specimens' of the 'vegetation of the United Kingdom' (*MC* p. 335). Wizzie Ravelston's resistance to the uncovered relics mirrors Uryen's derisive scorn at the totalizing boasts of Wheeler's scientific archaeology. 'To *her* mind' the 'broken images from the dust-bins of antiquity meant nothing but desolate bits of pottery labelled with paper tags':

> Wizzie had been taken once by Sister Bridget to visit a provincial museum and she remembered how, as she followed the heavy black robes of the nun, the whole place had smelt of a sepulchre, and had suggested at the same time a conspiracy of one's godfathers and godmothers to take away even what excitement the bones of death possessed by putting them under glass cases. (*MC* p. 366)

Whatever 'excitement' and interest the 'bones of death' possess for Wizzie is only savoured through a tactile and resonantly innovative engagement. She embodies curiosity as a bold, seditious counter-discourse, which relishes the unsightly and discomfiting accretions of time. How can the 'provincial museum' distil the experiential essence of confronting remnants from an ancient ancestral past? The interwar archaeologist O. G. S. Crawford averred that the 'provincial museum' is 'a byword for dullness, dust and decrepitude. The very atmosphere reeks of decay, and the sight of a few skulls and stuffed birds completes the illusion of a charnel-house' (Crawford, 1921, p. 215). That Wizzie is an avid reader of romances demonstrates that the modes of a supposedly lowbrow narrative history trump the 'provincial museum' in the ability to pique and challenge the imagination to visualize what domestic life was like, especially for women, in the distant past. That the salvaged artefact is now left stranded in a 'glass case' reveals history as a sanitized and institutionalized discipline, not a continuous or nourishing tradition. The museum tries to abolish decay and thwarts sensual, energizing 'contact' or immersion in an alternative actuality. Such a mode of display renders the object quaint and atrophied; robbing it of its unique, intrinsic and irreducible character as the precious product of a specific era and locale. Wizzie seeks history as part of a living and vigorous present, richly layered in meanings that embrace the frailties, caprice and blemishes of fallible humanity. Her disaffection in this scene partly reflects how the husbanding, arrangement and transmission of an excavated national heritage has been snatched away from the public by the professional curator or 'expert', whose genial paternalism is subtly mocked. The curator's self-regarding stewardship rescues the artefact from dissolution,

Powys implies; but converting it from private property to national treasure also attenuates its status as a sumptuously storied curio and the personalized articulation of a historical outlook. Indeed, the 'heavy black robes of the nun' suggests the meek reliance on received authority which the museum epitomizes as a coercive, regulatory site 'where bodies, constantly under surveillance, were to be rendered docile' (Bennett, 1995, p. 89).

Wizzie's visceral indignation mirrors Powys's trenchant sense of the 'provincial museum' as one of the last bulwarks and bastions of historiographical ignorance about the intimacies of women's affective response: they are a passive minority largely irrelevant to, even disqualified from, participation in ancient British history. *Maiden Castle* also illustrates the key difference between unearthed 'arte-facts' and museum 'exhibits': the former store up, and promise to unleash the 'Beyond'; the unruly and heterodox promptings of felt sensation – 'all the wild prayers, all the desperate imprecations that had been addressed to them on the summit of Mai-Dun before the last stone had been added to Stonehenge' (*MC* p. 383). The exhibits, such as 'the enthroned Demeter' in the sculpture galleries of 'the British Museum' (*MC* p. 366), a secular cathedral to the exotic spoils of empire, present a misleadingly neutral image of the relic, unsullied by social and political ambitions. The Demeter is evacuated of oppositional resonance by those who cleanse and repackage it to fit an ostensibly progressive, 'improving' ethos. But for Wizzie, the assembled data is neither accurate nor pleasurable. While Uryen and Wizzie connect the evolving science of archaeology to specific constructions of power (murdering to dissect) and prestige (stale hegemonic maleness), Powys shows a rapt fascination with its procedures and practitioners in the mid-1930s.

By illustrating Uryen's aversion to the Mai-Dun digs Powys could dramatize and calibrate a long local tradition of suspicion towards the antiquarian collector, whose convictions, methods and activities divulge the subtly shifting and fiercely contested definitions of 'taste' during this era. After his initial forays around Dorchester, Dud expects to find a virulent 'prejudice against meddling with Maiden Castle' (*MC* p. 126). As Powys realized, few archaeologists could match John Milner's lofty ideal of 'the true antiquary':

> In searching [. . .] into these rude memorials of our forefathers, the true antiquary will ever respect their remains; and whilst he enters into their views by endeavouring to revive their memory, he will also as far as possible consult their wishes, in leaving to their bones their ancient place of sepulture. (Milner, 1886, p. 99)

Extending this critique, Charles Warne bemoaned the erosion of cherished ancestral legacies due to looting, and prefaced his *Celtic Tumuli of Dorset* (1866) with a stinging rebuke to the piratical amateur diggers of his home county who, instead of patiently studying the typology, distribution and relative chronology of various round barrows, rifled 'time-hallowed monuments for no better purpose than the indulgence of a craving acquisitiveness and the adornment of glass cases with ill-understood relics' (Warne, 1866, p. ii).

Given his lifelong interest in Hardy's oeuvre, Powys would have relished his predecessor's mordant story of Maiden Castle, 'A Tryst at an Ancient Earthwork', first published in *The Detroit Post* (15 March 1885) as 'Ancient Earthworks and What Two Enthusiastic Scientists Found Therein'. Hardy's scathing commentary on the artefacts wrested from the 'whole stupendous ruin' (*T* p. 171) by these archaeologists is suggestive: 'it is strange indeed that by merely peeling off a wrapper of modern accumulations we have lowered ourselves into an ancient world' (*T* p. 181). For Powys this evokes mechanized modernity itself, not as an irreducible force engulfing precious tracts of Wessex turf, but as a hastily manufactured, artificial and permeable film to be disposed of ('a wrapper'). Yet Hardy also prioritizes the chalk stratum of the hill out of which the earthwork is fashioned. For Gideon Mantell in the 1840s, devoted to popularizing natural history, the geological composition of this Dorset chalk, containing the fossilized fragments of ancient marine animal forms, afforded a perspective on a period in which momentous convulsions to the earth's surface had 'lifted the whole level of land in this region from the bottom of a shallow sea' (Pountney, 2001, p. 72).

Hardy could see this oval-shaped Iron Age fortress-town from his house, Max Gate, and he must have visited frequently a site whose 'associations' caused 'past and present' to become 'so confusedly mingled' (*T* p. 179). Mortimer Wheeler admiringly quotes Hardy's description of this extensive encampment, whose defences consist of three steep ramparts with deep fosses between, in his second interim report: '[Maiden Castle] is exceptional and, as to its great double entrances, unique in the scale and complexity of its defence-system; and in this respect may be regarded, not merely as the product of an era, but as the monument of some intensely individual and remarkable mind – in Thomas Hardy's words, "some remote mind capable of prospective reasoning to a far extent"' (Wheeler, 1935, p. 265). Hardy's acidic portrait of an elderly excavator engaged with the 'barbarous grandeurs of past time' (*T* p. 172) caricatures the activities of Edward Cunnington (1825–1916), the 'local Schliemann' of Dorchester, as Hardy sardonically dubbed him in a paper prepared for the *Dorset Natural History and Antiquarian Field Club* and read by Hardy himself on 13 May 1884.

Edward Cunnington made a name for himself in 1882 by opening the Clandon Barrow, 'on the north-western end of the chalk ridge crowned with the multi-period earthworks of Hod Hill and Maiden Castle' (Pearce and Bounia, 2000, pp. 3–4). Cunnington came from a well-known family of antiquarian collectors; his grandfather William (1754–1810) formed a key partnership with Sir Richard Colt Hoare in 1803 and they opened some 465 barrows together in Wiltshire (Pearce and Bounia, 2000, pp. 3–4). The 'professed and well-known antiquary', 'wrapt up in his own deep intentions' (*T* pp. 178–79) in Hardy's story unlawfully exhumes from Maiden Castle a complete mosaic proving Roman occupation, a 'fairly perfect' skeleton and a gilded statuette of Mercury (*T* p. 181). Hardy's antiquary embodies the point at which the excavator's petty vanities and self-serving exploitation of 'the mighty dead' (Pearce and Bounia, 2000, p. xiv) have overtaken any respectful sense of memorializing past achievements. Although he is prevailed upon to replace these finds, the beautiful statuette is located in the deceased excavator's possessions. His ardour 'for some special science' blunts 'the moral sense which would restrain' him 'from indulging it illegitimately' (*T* p. 180). How easily, Hardy hints, the ostensibly 'enlightened' pursuits of the scientific enquirer merge into the purblind greed and 'compulsive attachments' of the crooked 'collector' (Bann, 1999, p. xxi).

Hardy's sketch of a man lacking any strictness of integrity, Mortimer Wheeler regarded later as a 'burlesque account' of Cunnington's 'slight and ill-recorded excavations' (Wheeler, 1935, p. 265). Hardy's antiquary proclaims his belief that this capital of the British Iron Age tribe of the Durotriges, 'is not a Celtic stronghold exclusively, but also a Roman; the former people having probably contributed little more than the original framework which the latter took and adapted till it became the present imposing structure' (*T* p. 181). Wheeler's excavations greatly enriched and amplified knowledge of the earthwork's complex development through time (Keith, 1988, pp. 14–19). In the third chapter of *Maiden Castle* Powys makes his first allusions to Wheeler's undertaking, when Claudius summarizes the discoveries of the previous summer: 'A metal plate with a rough figure of Minerva upon it was dug up in the foundations of that Roman temple' (*MC* p. 164). Uryen, however, intervenes to speak of '*the other* votive image they dug up', which 'had nothing to do with Minerva or Rome either' (*MC* p. 166). It was 'a three-horned bull [. . .] with two human torsos impaled on its horns and another one transfixed on its up-curving tail' (*MC* p. 167). Powys cleverly fuses details of finds listed by Wheeler's report on the 1934 excavations in the 'area trenched by Cunnington in 1882' (Keith, 1988, pp. 14–19). In 1934 'a small votive bull of tinned bronze with the three horns familiar on votive bulls from eastern Gaul, and surmounted by three human busts, one with the head missing, came to light' (Wheeler, 1935, p. 272).

Powys describes a 'momentous discovery' in the novel's pivotal Midsummer Eve section:

> The unusually warm weather had stimulated the Archaeological Society engaged in the Maiden Castle excavations to begin their summer work earlier than was expected; and in the afternoon of Saturday the twenty-second the local *Echo* announced a momentous discovery.
>
> From the wording of this announcement it appeared that in the oldest portion of the earthworks, in a place where the digging had been undertaken for the first time, the remains of an extensive stone building had been discovered, of greater antiquity than the well-known Roman temple. (*MC* pp. 333–34)

Powys refers cryptically to 'the Great Discovery, as "It" – or "They" – rest[ing] there on that crude bench' (*MC* p. 369). These finds, which the main characters bicker about, comprise a 'woman's head', a 'headless torso', and an 'eyeless and earless beast-god' (*MC* p. 383). Mortimer Wheeler's actual excavations give no hint of such curios, though Powys's depiction of the 'woman's head' is strongly reminiscent of the 'Minerva' figurine unearthed by Edward Cunnington (Keith, 1988, pp. 14–18). Wheeler's 'votive bull' may also have shaped Powys's memorable illustration of the 'eyeless and earless beast-god'. While Cunnington and Wheeler provided Powys with a panoply of intriguing materials, it is also apparent, as W. J. Keith shows, that *Maiden Castle* refines ideas from the now widely discredited Diffusionist project, which set itself in opposition to the more orthodox scientific procedures of Tylorian anthropologists who posited 'the spontaneous birth of independent cultures with similar characteristics in various parts of the world' (Massingham, 1942, p. 54). O. G. S. Crawford disparaged the Diffusionists as 'a band of scientific adventurers' (Crawford, 1924, p. 101), who claimed that megalithic sites in Wessex were the work of 'flint-hunting mariners' who had journeyed from Ancient Egypt via Minoan Crete (Wright, 1996, p. 111). The chief advocate of this conjectural history was Grafton Elliot Smith (1871–1937). In the second edition of *Human History*, published 2 years before *Maiden Castle* in 1934, Smith proclaimed:

> The fundamental aim of this book is to throw light upon the truth concerning human nature and in particular to call attention to the fact that [. . .] man is by nature peaceful and truthful [. . .] the maintenance of peace is a matter of allowing man's innate qualities unimpeded expression. (Smith, 1934, p. 11)

Powys's novel interrogates not only primeval man's 'innate qualities', but also the social and political upshot of permitting such amorphous traits unfettered 'expression'. In *Maiden Castle*, Uryen seems to endorse Smith's highly inferential data when he laments the grievous 'limitations' of Wheeler's new-fangled archaeological 'methods' and the social philosophy of ethnographic evolution infusing them:

> Mai-Dun was a civilized *polis*, long before the Romans came [. . .] You must remember, lad [. . .] we're talking of the civilization that built Stonehenge and Avebury. Why should the dwellers in Mai-Dun be regarded as wretched earth-burrowers, when their contemporaries could build such monuments! (*MC* p. 239)

Uryen's speculations about Mai-Dun as a pre-modern community, 'a civilized *polis*' are crucial. He signals a belief not so much in a city-state, but rather a human collectivity whose proclamation of shared goals, aptitude for mutual recognition and compassionate alliance discards artificial distinctions between public and private, church and state, thought and feeling. Numinous intuitions were seamlessly woven into the fabric of quotidian life, and 'all citizens of the polis were thought to be part of a larger organic whole, and not autonomous agents who agreed to form some larger legal collective entity out of their individual wills' (Valdez Moses, 1995, p. 34). Mortimer Wheeler was also preoccupied by how the prehistoric peoples of Mai-Dun became civilized: 'it is perhaps as a citizen that man achieves the fullest scope for his various functions [. . .] Civilized man is a city-dweller' (qtd. in Stout, 2008, p. 222). Wheeler saw his own archaeological project as one of illustrating Maiden Castle not as some shadowy cluster of mean, ignoble dwellings or a workshop of wild nature, but as an ancient confederacy of steadfast, talented and autonomous producers, forged through shared personal experiences. This was Wheeler's blueprint for a very modern and resonant conception of urban existence in which communities saw themselves 'naturally embedded in time and space' (Cubitt, 1998, p. 5). In his interview with the *Observer* (30 August 1936) he opined that '[o]ur modern cities – London, Birmingham, Liverpool and the rest, are, in a real sense, the direct heirs of Maiden Castle and its followers' (qtd in Stout, 2008, p. 223). This claim, as Adam Stout explains, may have caught the eye of the prolific freelance journalist Harold John Massingham (1888–1952), a close 'friend' of Llewellyn Powys (Wright, 1996, p. 118), and an eloquent supporter of Diffusionist ideology. Massingham obviously relished the 'Battle of the Books raging' between Wheeler's neo-Darwinian disciples and the Diffusionists, and was 'enlisted as a light skirmisher' in support of his mentor Elliot Smith (Massingham, 1942, p. 54). In his 1942 memoir *Remembrance*, Massingham describes how he joined the anthropological staff at University College London, 'with a kind of roving commission to prospect the upland homes of prehistoric man in England' (1988, p. 30). Massingham's research into 'analogies between the hilltop settlements of our Celts and those of the pre-Hellenes about the Mediterranean' (1942, p. 54) was especially attuned to the tools, interests and beliefs of 'the men whose English capital was Avebury, and whose metropolitan area was the Wiltshire Downs' ([Anon.], 'Very Early Britons', 1926, p. 383).

The longest chapter in Massingham's miscellany of essays *In Praise of England* (1924) contains a signal account of 'Maiden Castle' in which the rural rambler's lyrical exuberance amid the enveloping quiet of the abandoned downs coalesces with the desire to play the triple role of agricultural historian, philosopher and amateur archaeologist. Massingham contends that the gigantic earthwork was probably conceived and constructed between the Avebury and Stonehenge periods (1924, p. 195). Wizzie grumbles to Jenny Dearth: 'Gracious! I've heard D. arguing with Mr. Quirm, till you'd have thought it was a matter of life and death, whether Maiden Castle was a town or a fort' (*MC* p. 307). Given Massingham's repeated ruses to unmask Wheeler's neo-Darwinian credo as 'the religion of the modern State' (Massingham, 1926, p. 16), it was a matter of paramount importance as to whether the prehistoric earthwork was a fortified camp, belonging to a riotous horde mired in brutish struggle, or the location of peace-loving, benign and self-sufficient communitarians. In *The Heritage of Man*'s section on 'The Origins of War' and *In Praise of England*'s essay on Maiden Castle, Massingham's theories are calculated to debunk the Tory Lord Birkenhead's then widely canvassed assertion that 'man from the very dawn of the world's history' has been a nomadic predator (qtd. in Thomas, 1924, p. 33) and his hilltop settlements the outcome of accident and unceasing strife. Massingham, having reclined on the ramparts of Maiden Castle, was unconvinced that this earthwork's tranquil immensities could be fashioned for purposes of fortification alone by marauding and 'wretched earth-burrowers'. Instead, he argues that this 'permanent capital settlement' was 'associated' with an immemorial tradition of 'religious ceremonial' (1924, p.195). Dud ponders Massingham's refined and sweetened notion of 'the natural peaceableness' of megalithic man, who 'slept without evil dreams' (Massingham, 1988, p. 67), rather than a pugnacious and acquisitive ancestry, living 'in miserable thatched holes, along with bones and cinders and potsherds' (*MC* p. 239):

> 'I wonder', [Dud] said to himself, 'whether it really *is* possible that if I'd come along this road ten thousand years ago I should now be gazing on the Cyclopean walls and towers and temples and parapets of a great, peaceful city of a far nobler civilization than ours, where war and torture and vivisection were unknown, where neither the pleasures of life were denied nor the paths to immortality discredited?' (*MC* pp. 230–31)

At the close of his first season of digs, Wheeler posited that the site may have once been 'a great, peaceful city'. However, by the time Wheeler embarked on his final season of digs, he had little confidence in the accuracy of his initial, rather sanguine speculations, which the *Dorset Daily Echo* (12 September 1934) chirpily summarized as 'Prehistoric Peace on Maiden Castle' (qtd in Stout, 2008, p. 220). Wheeler's 1934 excavations had already divulged many thousands of sling-stones and arrowheads, often in sizeable hoards, from pits. In 1936, traces of human ritual sacrifice were unearthed. Nearing the close of the enterprise, in August 1937, Wheeler and his team of diggers had 'hit upon the place where the British dead had been buried after their seemingly impregnable stronghold had fallen to a savage Roman attack' (Hawkes, 1982, p. 172) – in this case Vespasian's sacking of the fortress in about A.D. 43–44. Massingham's 'wilfully original' vision of Maiden Castle as a refuge for a dignified Neolithic community, in which organized hostilities were only prosecuted when a rapacious imperialism had infected a simple society of food-gatherers, now seemed preposterous to Wheeler and his team. Figuring this site as 'an escape from the mad misprision of values which we playfully call our civilisation', was well out of step with exhumed remains ([Anon], 'Nature and archaeology', 1924, p. 220). Instead of Massingham's conception of an august fellowship whose memorials 'were so perfectly blended with the natural scene' (Massingham, 1942, p. 55) – an obvious attempt to rescue the earliest English from charges of crass, bloodthirsty barbarism – Wheeler marshalled copious vestiges to support 'the Neo-Darwinian creed of endless trial by endless torment' ([Anon.], 'Very Early Britons', 1926, p. 384). Wheeler commented on the burials:

> The whole war cemetery as it lay exposed before us was eloquent of mingled piety and distraction; of weariness, of dread, of darkness, but yet now of complete forgetfulness. Surely no poor relic in the soil of Britain was ever more eloquent of high tragedy, more worthy of brooding comment from the presiding spirit of Hardy's own *Dynasts.* (Wheeler, 1935, p. 24)

Here, Wheeler depicts Maiden Castle as a primitive stage upon which spectacles of 'high tragedy' were played out to a grisly climax. His pointed reference to the author of *The Dynasts* is apt given that Hardy paid scrupulous attention to the pictorial composition of the photographic image ('The Castle of Mai-Dun') that was incorporated as an inserted frontispiece to the *Changed Man* short story collection in 1913. In his communications with the photographer Hermann Lea Hardy indicates that the earthwork's 'appallingly mournful' (*T* p. 173) and brooding intensity should be visually specified through 'Height and darkness' and by standing 'high up in the picture so that there may be not much sky' (Hardy, *Collected Letters*, 1988a, VII, p. 304). Hardy's preoccupation with conveying a sinister visual aura through the image harmonizes with his story's distinctive emphasis – as Wheeler remarked – on the earthwork's silhouetted shape and how the contours seem to absorb the midnight darkness. In his nocturnal rendering of the structure Hardy implements, according to Rob Pountney, 'melodramatic visual and acoustic devices to draw attention to this site's barbarous past' (2001, pp. 69–71). The 'hailstones' fly through 'the defile in battalions' (*T* p. 174) and the 'roar of the storm' is likened to a 'column of infantry', while 'lightning' bears 'a fanciful resemblance to swords moving in combat' (*T* p. 175). Through this careful delineation of an 'obtrusive personality that compels the senses to regard it' (*T* p. 171), Hardy implies the murderous and messy history promulgated by 'new students of the past' (*MC* p. 239). In opposition to these 'scholars' Uryen affirms nebulous experiences which never adhere easily to dominant ideology or to crude attempts at colonization. His increasingly frantic attempts to laud a highly personal and subjective response to prehistory, stressing 'the Power of the Underworld' that 'our race adored when they built Avebury and Maiden Castle and Stonehenge [. . .] when there were no wars' (*MC* p. 467) appear hectoring and naïve through the lens of Wheeler's extensive scrutiny of the site.

Debunking the Dark God of Dorchester?

It is when you set out for Maiden Castle, and begin to draw near to that immense stronghold, that the spirit of things very far off, very powerful, falls upon you. There is no time of year, no condition of light and shade, when the vast ramparts do not call up awe and wonder, and even pity: for the people who dug those trenches were a great race, and their power and their glory are utterly gone. But they live in soul. Maiden Castle, a thought made visible for ever, has still almost the strong power of a thought newly uttered into the world. To this day it dominates and hypnotizes.

(Darton, 1922, p. 41)

F. J. Harvey Darton's assessment of Maiden Castle implies that the energies of 'a great race' can still be tapped and utilized to irradiate urgent contemporary dilemmas. It is this aspiration which motivates Powys's 'Black Man of Glymes', Uryen Quirm. In a novel obsessed with excavating 'a region charged with' the accumulated layers of 'suggestive antiquity' (*MC* p. 19), it is fitting that Uryen himself is depicted as a besmirched archaeological 'find' – a dark grail or idol that poses philosophical conundrums and prompts manifold, even contradictory readings. In an 1871 article, Chris Benson remarked that within the 'mythical and traditional circle of which the Holy Grail is the centre exists a world of wonders; a world of strange and beautiful creations; a sphere abounding with fantastic pictures of the most glowing conceptions fraught with deep meaning' (Benson, 1871, p. 95). Even as Uryen's name sounds absurdly pretentious to Dud, 'like the name of a person in a book' (*MC* p. 231), so do the happenings of his life assume unearthly and strange configurations. Powys's depiction of Uryen is a 'fantastic' picture indeed, but one deliberately calculated to overhaul the glamorous and cathartic associations of 'deep meaning'; a picture which promises not the 'soul's serenity' as in Charles Williams's fictional reworking of the Grail legend *War in Heaven* (1930), but rather stunned surprise:

> Mr. Quirm's features were indeed nothing less than tremendous. Brow, nose, chin, all were modelled on a scale of abnormal massiveness that would have been awe-inspiring if the man's eyes had been different. But Mr. Quirm's eyes were dull, lifeless, colourless, opaque. They were empty of every gleam of human response. They neither softened nor warmed; they neither lightened nor darkened – they were simply *there*, as if someone had found a great antique mask with empty eye-sockets, and had inserted a couple of glass marbles into the holes. His head was covered with small, stiff, black curls, and so low did these curls grow on his brooding forehead that Dud was reminded of some gigantic bust he had seen once, but whether Greek or Roman he could not remember. His dominant impression of the man, as he recalled it afterwards, was of a half-vitalized corpse. (*MC* p. 55)

Dud's 'imagination' – which 'always seized upon the grotesque and even monstrous aspects of things' (*MC* p. 57) – finds in Uryen's striking lineaments ample material. For a writer given to musing over 'the various strata of social life that the place revealed, level upon level of quaint traditional differences between man and man' (*MC* p. 200), Uryen appears as a bizarre survival. Dud's initial impression registers both an eerie insubstantiality ('empty', 'lifeless') and a gross, even intimidating materiality. The archaic mask may be of primeval provenance, evoking an Easter Island statue (Wizzie remarks later that Uryen resembles 'a South Sea idol' [*MC* p. 371]). These images are complicated by the loftier Hellenic associations of a 'gigantic bust'; while the 'half-vitalized corpse' augurs the grisly future of corporeal and psychic disintegration that awaits this 'monstrous' figure: 'burying his intellect, his pride, his very soul at the bottom of an interior pit' (*MC* p. 371). Even as Uryen delivers a healing potion to his spouse Nancy, who suffers a heart attack in the vicinity of the town cenotaph, he smells like a corpse (*MC* p. 56) and 'the mortuary' scent of his breath seems 'an emanation from long-dead seaweed' (*MC* p. 461). His 'small, stiff, black curls' imply not actual human hair but a species of unsightly moss that grows on disease-ridden trees. Uryen's 'swarthy features' (*MC* p. 55) and 'dusky physiognomy' (*MC* p. 247) remind us of his affiliations with the original Uryen, a divinity who personifies the natural cycle of life and earth, who is coded as 'ardu, "black, dark, or dusky"' (Rhys, 1891, p. 256).

Dud's fraught reaction to the 'uncanny' figure (*MC* p. 57) who eventually announces himself as his 'begetter' (*MC* p. 254) indicates how Uryen's 'formidable magnetism' (*MC* p. 338) or 'stink' calls the parameters of social, ethnic and organic categories into question. Uryen's apparent eagerness to violate normative boundaries (of social decorum, of the body) underscores the very brittleness and artificiality of standard representational markers. He is 'a great sweltering toad' (*MC* p. 56) and his head resembles 'the woolly topknot of a mammoth ram' (*MC* p. 399); this 'strange beast' (*MC* p. 58) straddles both the human and paranormal domains. The most striking tangible evidence for Uryen's changeable and liminal status is vouchsafed by the mark of Bran, the Crow, 'scaly disfigurements' (*MC* p. 254) which he bears on his chest.

Dud's sharply observed account of Uryen is an attempt to fix a vague and fluid phenomenon that delights in affronting those who cling to glib taxonomic concepts, and who devise strategies for drawing narrow distinctions. Thuella thinks Uryen is 'more like a Chinaman than a Welshman' (*MC* p. 362); his hair has 'an African look' (*MC* p. 399), and Nancy, eager to puncture her spouse's pretensions to august and evasive inscrutability, says of him: 'He's not a simple man. He's *more* than a man' (*MC* p. 60). Uryen might be 'a miracle-worker' with his herbal concoctions (*MC* p. 61) who forswears 'old west-country names' (*MC* p. 60). Yet his mystical 'credentials' are a target for his long-suffering wife's 'furious sarcasm' about his being the 'greatest wonder after Maiden Castle and Poundbury and Maumbury Rings' (*MC* p. 59). Powys also discloses that Uryen is in part obscurely to blame for the death of Nancy's young son, Jimmy. Indeed, Uryen's bullying and intemperate muscularity is seen at its most disquieting when he attacks Old Funky. Uryen embodies and channels a heritage marked by

> Countless aeons of countless oppression, oppression of Neolithic men by metal-bearing men, of Durotriges by Romans, of Romanized Celts by Saxons, of Saxons by Normans, and, for centuries upon centuries, of all those who weren't 'gentry' by all those who were! (*MC* pp. 200–201)

Like his prototype, then, Uryen presides over a twilight domain of mortality and oracular perception. As Jennie Dearth claims, 'that Quirm man, over there, brings bad luck to everyone he comes near, by stirring up the old devils of this place' (*MC* p. 313).

Nancy Quirm's exasperated remarks show that Uryen, like Johnny Geard in *A Glastonbury Romance*, who claims to harness mediumistic or visionary gifts, combines the grandiose, the buffoonish and the bizarre. *Maiden Castle* insistently focuses on the grotesquely comic gulf between Uryen's lofty self-perception as the reincarnation of a Celtic mythological deity, and the tawdry, even squalid domestic and social dilemmas which assail him from every side. 'In him' according to Margaret Moran, 'the extraordinary has been domesticated, or the ordinary has so submerged itself within the mythical that the effect is the same' (Moran, 1990, p. 186). It is one of Powys's wittiest flourishes that while Uryen clings to the ceremonial observance of praying with his massive head immersed in water, this 'great hulking stinkard' (*MC* p. 59) seems oddly indifferent to the diurnal need for more modest ablutions:

> 'Just think of it, lad!' went on [Uryen], 'Mai-Dun, Poundbury, Maumbury Rings, all coming slowly back to life! I don't mean the dead in them', and the man, lowering his voice, drew nearer to our friend, drew so near, in fact, that the sour smell of his body under his seldom-changed clothes produced a physical revulsion that affected No-man like a wafture from decomposing mortality. (*MC* p. 174)

While Uryen's rapt rhetoric augurs a moment when the spirit of Dorchester's venerable landmarks come 'back to life', the unwashed robes of this self-baptized and erratic hierophant carry only the 'sour' whiff of a putrescent cadaver. The moribund stench functions as an ironic reminder of 'the old dark Homeric conception of death, with that terrifying multitude of the spirits of the dead surrounding us in their pitiful half-life' (*MC* p. 21). The riddling ambiguity with which Dud delineates Uryen reflects Powys's own sophisticated scepticism as to whether 'Scientific Excavation' accurately safeguards, or transmits, the 'great Power' (*MC* p. 447) of the 'sacred earthworks' (*MC* p. 359). Whereas *A Glastonbury Romance* vividly imagines an ancient Somerset town as the epicentre of chthonic verve, Uryen hopes the colossal ramparts of the forsaken citadel of Mai-Dun will become a shrine to those demoralized by a desiccated mainstream culture hurtling towards spiritual suicide. Explicating one of the finds from Mai-Dun, Uryen himself appears to undergo a transmutation:

> Uryen's massive features composed themselves like a dark stream on the surface of which an unknown animal has been swimming, leaving curious ripples. 'It's a three-horned bull', he said, 'with two human torsos impaled on its horns and another one transfixed on its up-curving tail. [. . .] It's not classical symbolism anyway, it goes back further; and when you talk of science you must remember that these things are like dark-finned fish embedded in ice. *They have life in them that can be revived.* [. . .] it is *not* science that can revive them. But go on with your excavations. [. . .] you must remember when you're dealing with *that* place you're vivisecting something different from a dog! But it doesn't matter. It's only a few hundred years against twenty thousand. [. . .] the secret escapes you! What you and your kind call Evolution I call Creation: and it would do no harm to just remind you that those who create can also destroy!' (*MC* p. 167)

Claudius prizes archaeological 'science' because the 'more you know about what *was*, the faster you can create what *will* be' (*MC* p. 126). O. G. S. Crawford, one of the most influential voices of British archaeology during the interwar period, disseminated this upbeat view of the indefatigable excavator labouring 'for the good of the race' in *Man and His Past* (1921):

> In our eyes a thousand years are but as yesterday. We deal wholesale in time; and having strengthened our vision by scanning the vistas of the past, we find that we can also view the future with less uncertainty. We may not be able yet, perhaps, to see far into it, we have acquired the time-habit of mind, and that is what matters. We no longer live from day to day; we take long views. (Crawford, 1921, p. 37)

For Claudius, as for Crawford's adherents, social 'evolution' imposes a crisp and enabling narrative upon 'great incalculable Nature' with its unnerving freaks of 'arbitrary waywardness' (*MC* p. 466). According to this reassuring credo, the bestialities of the past operate as a cautionary lesson to those social engineers who crave a more secure future that avoids the cataclysmic blunders which brought myriad ancient – and more recent – tribes to such an abrupt and ghastly end. Uryen rudely rebuffs these 'scientists' and mocks their misguided faith in evolutionary advance as historical sophistry at best, blatant idolatry at worst. Indeed, he aligns Claudius with an ancient Roman hegemony that, like Wheeler's materialist methodology, quashes an older, non-predacious reaction to the turf solitudes, in which the upholding of ecological equipoise – ensuring the steady supply of raw materials – was paramount. H. J. Massingham's 'wanderings through Wessex' (Massingham, 1988, p. 28) in the 1920s to inspect the historically integrated landscape around Maiden Castle – 'a wonder of the world' at 'his English door' (1924, p. 148) – marked a turning point in his personal and professional lives. He admired Wessex as a 'haunted land, magical, mysterious,

indefinable,' and construed Dorset as the 'peremptory shire' within that kingdom (Massingham, 1937, p. 15). To him, the 'Romans' – like Wheeler's team –
were 'brilliant but pedantic engineers' who thought in terms of technical
contrivance and abstract design (Massingham, 1988, p. 55); these figures of aloof,
sceptical detachment epitomized a 'Latin, geometrical cast of mind' and were
unwilling, or unable to embrace the more profound animistic perceptions of
the ancient British tribes they subjugated (Massingham, 1942, pp. 32, 93). Uryen
follows Massingham in expounding a different way of *knowing*, an acute sensitivity
to 'the peculiar effluence of places dyed in human associations' (Massingham,
1924b, p. 148) which trumps Wheeler's patiently planned, scientifically super-
vised and meticulously recorded digs. For Uryen there is no disharmony between
the fantastic, the forensic and the tall tale. This cheerfully mongrel mode fosters
alertness to 'those silent, ancient places where a dead people [. . .] to whom the
Greeks and Romans of one's schooldays are as children on the knee of time,
have left large signatures' (Massingham, 1924b, p. 148).

Uryen posits an imaginative blessing which scans O. G. S. Crawford's 'vistas of
the past', transforming the 'thick, crushing, heavy burdens of cruel antiquity'
(*MC* p. 368) into an inexhaustibly fecund and teeming 'Creation'. Dud's
personal quest is a coming to terms with the deceased and the 'moribund' (*MC*
p. 406), and in this narrative trajectory Uryen is the symbol of generative
sexuality (as Dud's father) as well as desuetude, despair and attenuation (the
dishevelled and repulsive 'corpse-god'). The arcane Celtic potencies that Uryen
believes are sedimented into the soil of the huge earthwork – such 'things
had been under the chalk when Caesar landed, under the chalk when the
Conqueror landed, under the chalk when Victoria was crowned!' (*MC* p. 383) –
are not tied to any credible reformist agenda. The novel canvasses a whole
gamut of social panaceas and topical, even prophetic theories which outline
the hazards of exalting laissez-faire liberalism and the venal institutions of the
centralized bureaucratic state at the expense of local autonomy (Goodway,
1984/1985, pp. 42–53). Teucer Wye evinces unalloyed enthusiasm for the
resiliently gentle benefits of a humanist ethos; by contrast his son Dunbar, a
buffoonish version of the Fascist stooge, dispenses Blackshirt tracts that 'nobody,
not even his wife, takes seriously' (*MC* p. 307); Jenny Dearth's partner Claudius
explains to anyone patient enough to listen that 'the only cure for everything is
to become a Communist' (*MC* p. 307). Uryen's disdain for censorious moralists
implies that these ideologically motivated figures should abjure 'the life of the
Masses' (*MC* p. 407) and the humiliating shifts and compromises synonymous
with the urban, state-centred disposition of interwar British socialism. Treating
his own stance as inflexibly disinterested and withdrawn from the shabby
arena of political partisanship, Uryen pleads for a spiritual virtue called '*Hiraeth*'
(*MC* p. 467) which shows how easily the intense privacy of lyrical inspiration
smudges into narcissistic morbidity (Goodway, pp. 45–50).

It is striking that the Celtic Uryen's chthonic perceptions, and his noncon-
formist programme for wise and gracious living, are never employed to buttress
a renascent Welsh nationalism, anchored in a Cymric impetus that 'between

1894 and 1922 had resulted in the creation of a host of national cultural institutions' (Stout, 2008, p. 169). Sir John Rhys, the first incumbent of the Chair of Celtic Studies established at Oxford in 1877, was instrumental in steering Welsh archaeology towards the revaluation of a more densely textured Celtic presence. However, Uryen reveals a pronounced aversion to the capitalist '*nation*' (*MC* p. 468) as a 'natural' and indispensable focus for political inspection and cultural comparison; he construes secular and bureaucratic state structures as ancillary to the more magisterial sweep and urgency of the mythical past (Cubitt, 1998, p. 15). His rhetoric shares little affinity with Theodore Watts-Dunton's 1906 introduction to George Borrow's *Wild Wales* which yearns for a free 'land of the Druids' (Watts-Dunton, pp. xi–xiv). Uryen's thinking is more in line with Rolf Gardiner's preservationist projects 'for the Wessex weal' in the 1930s: 'the unfolding of a new order of human society might depend on the contribution of small exemplary bodies rather than on mass-movements' (Gardiner, 1940–1941, p. 169). Indeed, Uryen comprehends his own ethnic heritage as a bridge to multiplied consciousness which spurns the findings of forensic science; it is resolutely 'detached from all movements of matter' and not 'transcribable in definite words' (*MC* p. 122): this is a generous bequest to all tribes, ethnicities and creeds. While Dud's initial reaction to the 'Black Man of Glymes', implies a redoubtable presence, Uryen is not a mere mouthpiece for a repressive patriarchal regime. Rather he unmasks 'the catastrophic menace' of mass movements such as Fascism and its unbridled aversion 'to feminism' (*MC* p. 336):

> 'What I would like to ask Mr. Wye', said Uryen suddenly, and something in his tone – perhaps the intonation of a man about to speak to men on the subject of politics – caused Mr. Cumber to assume his most alert office expression and grow serious, 'is whether you mightn't maintain that the Fascist movement in the world to-day is a reaction from Matriarchy?' (*MC* p. 226)

Do the excavated finds then – especially the 'woman's head' (*MC* p. 383) – indicate traces of a matriarchal cult; as signalled by Uryen's rapt reverence for 'the earth-goddess Caridwen' (*MC* p. 364), 'the great Phrygian mother' (*MC* p. 97) or Thuella's artistic rendering of 'the breasts of the earth' (*MC* p. 329), which recalls 'Diana Multimammia' in *The Mayor of Casterbridge*? It is true that Dud's 'baffled search for poise' (Burdett, 1935, p. 237) involves, like Wolf Solent's imaginative excavations, a partial disavowal of fatherly intonations and interference, whether it be the shrill, unavailing Platonism of Teucer Wye; Uryen's autochthony; and the haunting echoes of Hardy's fiction. However, Uryen and Hardy are both spectral presences that are difficult to exorcise entirely; Dud cannot just 'shake off the past' (*MC* p. 382) as attested by his belief in 'a childish story about his father being some great Welsh nobleman, who claimed to be descended from Sir Pellenore' (*MC* pp. 128–29). However troubled and uneasy Dud may feel about his 'hunched-up progenitor', he is compelled to read in Uryen an exaggerated version of his own perverse preconceptions.

Ultimately, Powys is less interested in positing a matriarchal cult based on the worship of 'Demeter' (*MC* p. 370), than he is in showing how the excavated 'finds' function as beguiling symbols of subconscious impulses: 'that staring stone head, that headless torso, that shapeless beast-form, though interpreted so differently by all of them, were still at work in the secret places of their minds' (*MC* p. 387). Such fragments make Dud 'feel as if there were abysses of dark notions within him whose nature he hesitated to plumb' (*MC* p. 123). This 'antiquity worship' (*MC* p. 375) creates an esoteric mystery: on the one hand 'these diggings for dead idols' (*MC* p. 355) inspire Dud in his odyssey for fresh sensation; on the other, such vestiges incite moments of grotesque farce as an Irish terrier advances towards the bench on which a 'Discovery' reposes and proceeds 'in all calmness to relieve nature' (*MC* p. 375). The dog urinates on Uryen's unfathomably ancient relic.

Uryen avers that the 'three-horned bull' was crafted by a 'people possessed of secrets of life that Aryan science has destroyed' (*MC* p. 254). Based on the presence of the 'other world' in Celtic mythology, Uryen contends that there exists a 'living entity [. . .] that'll survive death and burial' (*MC* p. 236). This idea should reverberate powerfully with Dud's capacity as an inveterate ghost-seer, but he will not underscore his father's fervent perspective. In trying to distance himself from his father's 'nebulous talk' of a 'mystic Past, more magical than any possible Present' (*MC* p. 236), Dud ironically promotes the first article of Uryen's recondite creed. Uryen invests as full-bloodedly in his private inner myth as Dud does in the irradiating potency of his own aesthetic agenda, which resuscitates Mary Channing as a lingering rebuke to the prohibitive and paranoid culture which executed her. Morine Krissdöttir is alert to Powys's Magus-like figures and concludes that 'Dud's Platonic philosophy is [. . .] echoed in Uryen's teachings, but in a magical form' (Krissdöttir, 1980, p. 114). When he quarrels with Uryen at Maiden Castle, he is dismayed to register that he has 'become like his father even in the act of denouncing him' (*MC* p. 149). Both value mysteries of identity once the coolly rational and disciplinary traits of selfhood are stripped away. Dud even parrots his father's imprecations on the tattered culture of 'mad scientists' who 'torture animals in their laboratories for what they call "knowledge" just as the Romans did for what they called "pleasure"' (*MC* p. 347).

Dud's anxious attempts to grapple with his patriarchal inheritance and especially the dark gods which emanate from the prehistoric earthwork are charged with a teasing awareness of D. H. Lawrence's savage pilgrimage. In the discarded drafts of *Maiden Castle*, Dud is responsive to Lawrence's artistic vision as part of an emphatic, even wild eclecticism that embraces the dauntingly highbrow as well as the cheerfully trashy and vacuous: 'He never discussed religion. He even refrained from telling people what they ought, as intellectual persons, to read. He sold Miss Braddon with as much gusto as Miss Stein and Egdar Wallace with as much aplomb as D. H. Lawrence' (qtd. in Hughes, 1984/1985, p. 16). In the 1932 collection of essays on *Sex in the Arts* Powys canvasses Lawrence's attempt to break through, like Uryen, the 'trappings of our bourgeois civilization'

(Powys, 1985, pp. 52–54). That Powys refers to Lawrence's 'dark gods' six times in this essay (Hughes, 1984/1985, p. 16) reflects a strong engagement with his predecessor's yearning to uncover the chthonic fusion of knowing, feeling and seeing. This aspiration partially imbues Dud's aesthetic resolve to plunge 'like a diver into the mystery of the old town about him' (*MC* p. 485). For all Lawrence's 'feverish and frantic gravity' however, Powys finds this campaign rashly conceived and peculiarly problematic:

> We have all made the mistake – in fact, it is one of the ways in which posterity will recognize our generation – of assuming that this eminently moral way of being libidinous ex cathedra is the same thing as being what we are accustomed to call 'pagan'. Nothing could be farther from the truth. Anything less 'pagan' than the feverish and frantic gravity with which Lawrence goes to work to transform his 'dark gods' into a New Religion could hardly be imagined. (Powys, 1985, p. 54)

Powys construes Lawrence's 'pagan' pose as too consciously cultivated and geared towards disrupting orthodox proprieties for its own sake. Powys's mordant emphasis on Lawrence's 'New Religion' indicates that his precursor's fierce gusto would have been better channelled into fashioning a frank, gracious and affectionate acceptance of human frailties rather than in trying to transcend them. Powys even parodies Lawrence's 'New Religion' with its veneration of the crusading hyper-masculine archetype by showing Wizzie's 'submission to' Uryen's dark 'spell' (*MC* p. 339), which mischievously recalls Alvina Houghton's 'worship' of the obtuse yet domineering 'Dark Master' Ciccio in *The Lost Girl* (1920).

For Powys, Lawrence's 'dark gods', encouraging the fulfilment of the 'natural animal' in the self, represents a rigid humourless credo, and a politically conservative one at that. A 'New Religion' in Lawrence's leadership fiction of the 1920s merely re-brands a tired and traditional hierarchy in which the imperious husband-lover is accorded absolute sway. Powys crafts *Maiden Castle* as a necessary corrective to Lawrence's strident attitudinizing. Uryen's search for the 'gods of Mai-Dun' (*MC* p. 250) which have been vanquished but whose 'Power' remains largely untapped is impelled by vexed, thwarted or smothered sensual appetites. This is in striking contrast to Mary Butts's female fertility figure in the next chapter, who revels in her own status as an 'infidel' and 'unchaste' priestess (*AR* p. 174). Uryen's credentials as a genuinely constructive hierophant and campaigner for 'progressing backwards' are made to seem increasingly hollow as nonplussed wandering and feckless wondering become basic facts of his diurnal existence.

> You must know, lad, that there are secrets only revealed by magic. I don't mean physical magic; I mean *spiritual* magic. And this kind only comes when the emotion of love-hate gathers to a point that's terrible. And you must know too that it only comes when the passion remains sterile. Any fulfilment

dissipates its power. Nothing but unfulfilled love, love turned to hate, can beat hard enough upon the barrier of life, can beat hard enough what separates us from the secret till it breaks through! (*MC* p. 248)

This passage is notable for its stress not just on the acolyte's cleansing discomfort, but more accurately on the need for ritual self-immolation in an incult milieu. Uryen remarks: 'I become convinced, not from any revelation, you understand, but because of this *necessity* I'm under of bearing the pain of the world' (*MC* p. 251). Uryen, for all his belief in a new 'heathen' fusion of disabused wisdom and intuition, secured by revering an august 'turf metropolis' (*MC* p. 256), is unaware that his own rhetoric strays into the orthodox Judeo-Christian terrain of insight clinched through stoical self-abnegation. It is this discipline that Dud must also learn through his disillusioning experiences with Wizzie, who eventually leaves him to embark upon a new narrative in North America.

Powys's conception of Wessex in *Maiden Castle* is comparable to the region defined by archaeologist Barry Cunliffe as

[A] curious, in-between, place where things are not always as they seem – a zone of merging and mixing. At various stages in history it was a place where principal actors like Arthur, Alfred and the Duke of Monmouth could vanish and reappear: a place of safety where time could be bided [. . .] it is a liminal zone where all things are possible. (Cunliffe, 2006, p. 11)

Cunliffe discusses the region as 'a kaleidoscope of fragments', a 'rag-quilt of discarded scraps of landscape giving rise to an amazing variety of ecozones each with its own highly distinctive character' (2006, p. 12). This concept of busy 'mixing' and 'merging', could not offer a more pointed contrast to the seditious pastoral fiction of Mary Butts, which mobilizes an increasingly harsh rhetoric of racial purity to offset the stealthy 'insidious creep' of a 'democratic enemy' (Butts, 'Warning', 1998a, p. 270) as signalled by the hordes of visitors that flock to the excavations in *Maiden Castle*. Whereas Cunliffe acclaims Wessex for its dizzying multiplicity and blurring of racial and social boundaries, Mary Butts promotes a single national narrative that stifles or abominates hybrid voices or 'in-between' identities. When Uryen extols 'the mysterious secret' of his 'race' (*MC* p. 467), he captures the 'Power of the Underworld' as potentially amenable to all, promising 'a real movement of imaginative art, at once modern and mystical' (*GR* p. 966). For Mary Butts on the other hand, the chthonic is only savoured by members of a patrician 'elect'. Unlike T. F. Powys's novel *Innocent Birds* (1926) the Dorset downs in Butts's literary milieu are not 'high enough to keep out the vulgar' (qtd. in Wright, 1996, p. 134). So she invents a clannish and extremely insular fellowship whose lives are dedicated to reconfiguring Wessex as a 'walled garden' (*AR* p. 43).

Chapter 5

The Return of the Nativist

Trespassers Beware

I know no part of England where the earlier people have left their mark so indelibly as in Wessex [. . .] the abundance of historic and prehistoric remains, and the possibility of 'stories' are not the chief charm of the west country [. . .] There is generally that magic about it which Mr. Matthew Arnold attributes to the Celts.

([Anon.], 'Good-Bye to Wessex', 1871a, p. 354)

This contributor to *London Society* canvasses what Matthew Arnold termed in 1867 the unearthly spiritual charisma of the 'Celts' and how that genius infuses the 'magic' of Wessex, a 'land where the air is charged with that subtle kind of ozone which predisposes (if it does not force) you to receive impressions from outward nature. [. . .One] gets into an Arthurian state of mind, and forgets the nineteenth century' (p. 354). In 1931, Mary Butts also renders a magical 'part of England' as an inimitable topographical text, rich in Celtic and Arthurian resonance and etched 'indelibly' with the scars of the arcane, the atavistic and the antiquated:

We both came from the same part of England, the short turf & chalk hills which are like nothing else on earth. They sprawl across counties, & our history & the history of man written on them in flint & bronze & leaf & grey stone. Written on very short grass full of small black & white snail-shells. A dry country of immense earth-works & monstrous pictures done on the chalk stripped of its grass. From Avebury [in Wiltshire] to Stone Cliff [in Sussex] it is the same, sprawled across a kingdom, the history of England open. Also its secret history in letters too large to read. (*Journals* p. 360)

In this tribute to her friend the artist Christopher Wood (1901–1930), Mary Butts remembers a 'kingdom' whose lineaments contain a past that is recoverable, redemptive and 'open': 'immense earth-works' and other concrete survivals of ancient occupation. Alongside the 'visible' and non-fungible vista, Butts adumbrates more recondite historical annals opaque to outsiders, about which one 'finds it difficult to judge how much to say' (*CC* p. 179). Like John Cowper Powys, she offers a highly idiosyncratic view of 'County History' (*AR* p. 6), unearthing 'the psychic chemistry of religious cults far older than Christianity' (*GR* p. 165). Here are archetypal *numina* of vegetation, weather conditions and seasonal fluctuation – akin to the 'soul-secrets' (*SH* p. 45) described in *The Story of My Heart* – whose fateful potency causes the gamekeeper to react with deep unease in Richard Jefferies's rural sociology:

> The idea of a park is associated with peace and pleasure, yet even here there is one spot where the passions of men have left their mark. [. . .] the gamekeeper, like most persons with little book-learning and who take their impressions from nature, is somewhat superstitious, and regards this place as 'unkid' – i.e. weird, uncanny. (Jefferies, 1978, p. 51)

Jefferies implies that the gamekeeper's fraught perception of 'uncanny' nooks, of something 'inexplicable in the dark and desolate places' (1978, p. 17) is an index of mental frailty. However, Butts validates these revelations of intransigent otherness in the vicinity of park, lake and spinney as 'great mystical' experience that 'cannot be told directly' (*Journals* p. 449). Her *Journals* testify to the sheer 'difficulty [. . .]' of writing down these conceptions that constantly occur, yet *always* on the borderlands of the mind' (p. 467).

This Wessex borderland – 'shadowy earth [. . .] lit with wild hyacinths' (*AR* p. 139) – is defined by encrypted, particularized and 'uncanny' reverberations; as well as the threat posed by the invasive, homogenizing incursions of 'gaping tourists' (*AWM* p. 8): 'there is a Neolithic earthwork in the south of England. It is better not to say where. The fewer people who pollute that holy and delectable ground the better' ('Ghosties', p. 349). 'Mystical' derives from the Greek verb *myein*, signifying 'to close' and more specifically, 'to close one's eyes'. With regard to the pre-Christian mystery cults that Butts references repeatedly in her published writings, the term specifies those symbolic ceremonials and local cultural productions about which adepts 'keep their mouths shut' (*CC* p. 52). *Death of Felicity Taverner* establishes that 'silence is a most effective part of courage' (*DFT* p. 233). Only those anointed by 'the feudal touch' (*AR* p. 140) access 'the almost limitless store of information consecutive cultures had imprinted on' the literal 'soil' (Deuel, 1971, p. 53). For Butts, 'mystical' embraces 'an act that belongs to more than one plane of existence' (*GR* p. 196); it is also 'the truth which cannot be told' (*AR* p. 104) about '[o]ne of the least known places in England' (*DFT* p. 249).

That Butts reinvents her Wessex homeland as a precious magical script is unsurprising given how the possession of, and by, arcane volumes energizes her novels, short stories and memoirs. Young Mary's reluctant entanglement in the burning of her father's rare book collection in *The Crystal Cabinet* becomes its core traumatic event (*CC* pp. 99–100), and evokes John Milton's

famous warning about the ambiguous and volatile potencies released by the
printed page:

> For books are not absolutely dead things, but do contain a potency of life in
> them to be as active as that soul whose progeny they are; nay they do preserve
> as in a vial the purest efficacy and extraction of that living intellect that bred
> them. I know they are as lively and as vigorously productive as those fabulous
> dragon's teeth; and being sown up and down, may chance to spring up armed
> men. (Milton, 1957, p. 720)

'Though books, as Milton says, may be the embalming of mighty spirits', according to John Cowper Powys, 'they are also the resurrection of rebellious,
reactionary, fantastical, and wicked spirits!' (qtd. in Moran, 1990, pp. 181–92)
Mary Butts seizes upon these complex connotations: the Book of Ashe in
Ashe of Rings incorporates 'a section in cipher, which, so far, no one has read'
(*AR* p. 13); Vanna Ashe's 'papyrus fragments' reflect their owner's ostenta-
tiously 'odd learning' (*AR* p. 60); Mr. Tracy's antiquarian catalogue of 'the
mass-cups' stirs 'violent imaginations'(*AWM* p. 86) in *Armed with Madness*; the
precise content of Felicity's 'personal papers' (*DFT* p. 259) is one of myriad
darkly inscrutable mysteries in *Death of Felicity Taverner*. These runic and elliptical
texts, such as the 'forbidden' tomes (*GR* p. 94) garnered by Owen Evans in
A Glastonbury Romance, are measured against the 'flood, cheap or costly, of
"books about bits of England", sentimentalities, whimsical descriptions, scraps
of folk-lore' which Butts excoriates in her 1933 article 'Our Native Land'.

In pointed contrast to the popular guides of the 1920s, such as F. J. Harvey
Darton's *The Marches of Wessex* (1922), C. E. Vulliamy's *Unknown Cornwall* (1925)
and Donald Maxwell's *Unknown Dorset* (1927), all of which mingle pseudo-
scientific and sentimental tropes to project a 'green world' (*AWM* p. 23)
haunted by history for the casual day-tripping 'trespasser' (*AWM* p. 131), Butts
enshrines an obscure geography as if it were a foreign and faded parchment,
whose 'special rhythmic secret' (*GR* p. 186) baffles even the forensic eye of an
experienced ethnographer. David Matless calibrates this cagey, even paranoid
facet of Butts's oeuvre as the 'sense of claiming a special place while pulling
up the drawbridge to keep others out' (Matless, 2008, pp. 335–38). Indeed,
palpable vestiges cut out of 'chalk', 'flint' and 'bronze' comprise her fictional
monuments to a charmed locality, watered by 'the streams of England' (*DFT*
p. 339), that is precariously perched on the brink of extinction; defaced by
the baleful avatars of 'an abandoned age' (Butts, 'Hesiod', 1932a, p. 113).
In *Ashe of Rings* for instance, Butts finesses a symbolic struggle between those
who safeguard the 'earth-works' (*AR* p. 50) and other forgotten fragments of
prehistoric peoples – a covert clique who designate themselves the 'Eumolpidae'
(*AR* p. 20), the sacred family of priests charged with preserving the Eleusinian
Mysteries – and those pollutants who abrade an area which may be of '*neolithic
origins, used by the Romans; a refuge for Celt and then for Saxon, a place of legend*'

(*AR* p. 6). Anthony Ashe cautions that 'once one starts disturbing old things, one raises something one did not know was there to be disturbed' (*AR* p. 18).

In some respects, Mary Butts evinces an orthodox bourgeois endorsement of the 'west country' as a region of metaphysical insight, 'ghostly tamperings' (*AR* p. 28) and comfortless grandeur; as Patrick Wright, Jane Garrity and Matless variously note, it is *within*, but not necessarily *of* England. Philip Crang argues that 'there is more potential in regional imaginations that [. . .] are less about the imagined – the picturing of an order, an answer to our questions, a map of our locations – than about the imaginary – a figure of the possible, a question kept open, a terrain to explore' (Crang, 1997, p. 162). However, Butts's writing cannot brook the notion of her Wessex as a timeworn terrain 'kept open'; only her venturesome female protagonists in whom runs 'the most ancient blood in England' (*CC* p. 163), grasp a historically sedimented district because these women '[breathe] naturally a different air' (*CC* p. 163). The narrator of *A Glastonbury Romance* remarks that there 'is doubtless in certain old' families an 'instinct of ethos-preservation, suspicious of the menace of mixed bloods' (*GR* p. 699). Butts amplifies this concept by showing that her fertility figures are entrusted with the solemn mission of thwarting 'people from the world outside, [. . .] people in vulgar clothes, on motorcycles, in Ford cars' (*AWM* p. 41).

Butts's 'spiky pastoralism' (Esty, 2004, p. 19) defiantly proclaims then a dissident difference: her sense of embattled exclusivity and sardonic *separateness* (*CC* p. 4) underscores the 'mystical' as an intricate historical and cultural category. 'As in art and love', Butts remarks in her review of Vera Brittain's Great War memoir *Testament of Youth*, 'magic qualities are notoriously dangerous to deal with – and in their danger is their delight, and their capacity to confound the most virtuous schemes of men' ('It was like that', 1933, p. 44). This 'awareness' she delineates in a 1934 *London Mercury* essay on 'The Art of Montague James'. She mulls over the 'essence' of this writer's craft as 'a sudden, appalling shock of visibility'. Like James, Butts believes that she extracts an analogous 'essence' from the '[r]ough, barrow-haunted places' of her homeland (*AWM* p. 128):

> Everyone who has lived much out of doors feels something of what he tells. Not by association with tradition, but by a direct kind of awareness, an impact on the senses – and something more than the senses. It can be a recurrent, almost an overwhelming, experience. Much ancient bogey-lore was a rationalization of it. (Butts, 1934a, pp. 307–17)

Picus also intuits this overwhelming 'impact on the senses' in *Death of Felicity Taverner*: the numinous, the inspirational and irrational, by their very resistance to the clipped precision of expository discourse, disinters a deeper truth: '[y]ou can get a first in Greats or fly around the crater of Vesuvius, but what you depend on for your private life is your degree in witch-doctoring' (*DFT* p. 179). Butts's abiding fascination with a 'direct kind of awareness' is inextricably linked with her 20-acre family estate, Salterns. In her writing 'the wind-lulled quiet of Salterns' (*CC* p. 17), the 'utmost expanse of Poole Harbour and the Purbeck

Hills' (*CC* p. 63), 'the secrets of Badbury Rings' (the remains of an early Iron Age citadel near her natal home), as well as the fishing village of Sennen Cove near Land's End in her final years, all vouchsafe a cluster of coordinates from which to take our bearings on her 'version' of Wessex as a 'wild' west country.

In *The Crystal Cabinet* Butts adumbrates a 'magic map' of this region:

A perception arose which I tried to tell – to make clear – to myself by saying that this coast I knew so well, bay by bay, cape by cape, could be seen double. That there were two versions of it. Or that it had an existence in two worlds at once. (A double aspect of a place that has been described once in a story by Mr Metcalfe called 'The Bad Lands.')

There ran the coast, and that was what you saw on a map; what you landed on, quay or shingle. Places at the same time, from sea or on shore, with another aspect or identity. (*CC* p. 136)

This 'chart' (*CC* p. 137) discloses the *numina* of the coastal terrain; what lies beyond the lip of the apprehensible. It is oddly appropriate that Butts articulates this abstruse perception by invoking the now largely forgotten macabre stories of John Metcalfe (1891–1965).[1] No doubt Butts would have endorsed L. P. Hartley's 1925 assessment of Metcalfe's narratives, which expose our trust in human self-sufficiency as not only illusory but as a brittle fiction: 'to enjoy the final *frisson* of their horror, one must be capable of a sustained diffused panic'. Many of Metcalfe's tales depict fraught excursions into the 'Bad Lands' of the subconscious mind and 'the weak places of the nerves' (Hartley, 1925, pp. 123–24). Butts elaborates this map 'to show what those places "really" were' (*CC* p. 137) in her December 1933 review, 'Magic of Person and Place', which commends the American archaeologist Hugh O'Neil Hencken's study of *West Cornwall*. Butts extends her anthropological concept of 'mana' which her 1932 preservationist pamphlet *Traps for Unbelievers* highlights as 'the non-moral, beautiful, subtle energy in man and in everything else, on which the virtue of everything depends' ('Traps', 1932, p. 328). By designating 'mana' as 'non-moral', Butts implies that it is a teaching 'above race, based on the mysticism common to all mankind'; an intuition 'shared with Christ and Plato, and the supreme mystics from Glastonbury to Persia' ('Vision of Asia', 1932–1933, p. 224). However, her statement partially shrouds a vexed component of this ostensibly wide-ranging, boundary-breaking entity in her fiction: its discon-certing association with the 'white heat' of 'a hierarchized universe' (*CC* p. 258), Anglo-Saxon supremacy and racial cleansing.[2] Indeed, there are '*classes* of mystics as there are of artists, or in any of the great intuitive faculties of man' ('Visions of Asia', p. 224; my italics). Hencken's 'scientific precision' persuades Butts that he is '[b]orn, not made' (*AR* p. 73): among the initiates who compre-hend the 'temenos, a primordial sacred space' (Lansing, 1995, p. xix).

Within this cartography, according to Butts, the blessed minority excavate not only a fund of resilient racial memory, but also 'a kind of implicit design, as though there lay behind it, maimed and exceedingly strange, a ritual dance, as old as time or man' (Butts, 'Aristophanes', 1933a, p. 152). This formulation not only smothers the sense of Englishness as irretrievably mixed and muddled, as a synthetic product of multifarious historical and cultural factors, but also negates the vivid panoramic vistas of ancient civilization vouchsafed by the comparative anthropology that Butts read with avid curiosity throughout her life. Hers is a reactionary mythic modernism according to David Matless; one in which an austere conception of social engineering merges with an occult spirituality to signify the rustic 'earth' as 'one growing stillness, of innumerable separate tranquilities, for ever moving, for ever at rest' (*AWM* p. 92).

In the first full-length critical study of Mary Butts's corpus, Roslyn Reso Foy explicates this imaginative mapping of Wessex – demarcating boundaries, territorial possessions, and topographical curiosities – as one evincing a staunch commitment to 'the beauty and wonder of nature', overseen by a valiant 'feminine archetype', such as Scylla Taverner in *Armed with Madness*, who calls up 'a heritage that offers a universe at once organic, sacred and whole'.[3] However, Butts's conception of the 'west country' and the 'very human Earth goddess' synonymous with it are far more problematic than Foy's monograph implies (Foy, 2000, p. 65). Foy underestimates how Butts radically refurbishes Hardy's literary milieu as a rugged 'Grail country' to revile those deracinated 'foreign' figures who vandalize 'an old rural constituency' (*CC* p. 245). So in her *Journals* she recounts 'the horrors done to Salisbury Plain [. . .] Hoardings & vile villas & petrol-stations, & that most beastly sight, the rotting bodies of cars' (p. 451). This rhetoric apes the strength of feeling imbuing the 1929 campaign, endorsed by Arnold Bennett and Rebecca West, to prevent the 'submergence' of Stonehenge 'under the rising tide of bungalows' (Bennett et al., 1929, p. 23). The 'sacred nature' that Foy locates in Butts's affirmation of her natal home is not as winsomely idyllic, inclusive or 'open' as it initially appears. Butts's enterprise is rooted in a barely concealed eugenic prejudice which ordains that only the *English* scion of landed aristocracy can savour 'an epiphany of supernatural patterning' (Lansing, 1995, p. xix) in a secluded corner of Wessex that Hardy saw undergoing severe social and economic upheaval at the end of the nineteenth century. Patrick Wright avers that Hardy's novels 'strain to describe a landscape [. . .] abstracted by an increasingly mechanised and capitalised agriculture', while in Butts's fiction 'there is no longer any closely experienced country life to recount' (Wright, 1985, p. 107).

At the end of her preservationist tract *Warning to Hikers*, Butts illustrates how her homeland offers an 'experience of reality' which acts as a cultural curb to the desultory urban visitors targeted by *Death of Felicity Taverner*: 'out-of-town by rapid transit from the slums; young, heavy-haunched and over breasted women, wearing a terrible parody of country clothes' (*DFT* p. 201):

For once they have taken one step across the line of protection, the belt of urban needs and values each of them carry strapped tight about them, they will find themselves in a world as tricky and uncertain, as full of strangeness, as any wood near Athens. No friendly greenwood, fixed by poets; no wise gnome-tapped mountain; no gracious sea. *The dragon-green, the luminous, the dark, serpent-haunted.* Will they face it? When the Sirens are back at their business, sisters of the Harpies, the Snatchers? When the tripper-steamer – her bows to the sun – turns into the boat called Millions-of-Years? Quiet in the woods. They can be very quiet when a wind from nowhere lifts in the tree-tops and through the pine-needles, clashing the noise of a harp runs down the trunks into the earth. *And no birds sing.* (Butts, 'Warning', 1998a, pp. 294–95)

Her crystallization of this 'country of the Sanc Grail' (*DFT* p. 300) reveals a 'dark, serpent-haunted' hinterland of sinisterly sentient mythic 'potencies who are watching man' (*AR* p. 136), rather than the cozy pastoral swains and fey nymphs deployed by poetasters from the 'rising tides of villadom' (Crawford, 1933, p. 291). That Butts ends with a quotation from Keats's 'La Belle Dame Sans Merci' implies a retreat into a flippant and facile residual Romanticism. However, there is a more urgent purpose at work: Butts reclaims an admired poetic precursor to salvage a shared sense of the chthonic as female, feral and 'full of danger' (Butts, 'Warning', 1998, p. 269); this 'daimon' makes the 'spine crawl' (*AR* p. 45) and raises 'insoluble terrors' (*AR* p. 46) in those who, like Clarence Day from *Armed with Madness* come up against 'a flawless barrier' (*CC* p. 163), because they are 'not intuitively tuned' to 'the vast spaces under the star-blazing sky' (*AWM* p. 128). As David Matless remarks, if 'both dragon green and classical allusion are, by implication, unknown to hikers, nature knowledge' and classical erudition 'might yet combine to repel them, creating, in the divine sense, Panic' (Matless, 2008, p. 349).

In *Cultural Geography* Mike Crang posits that a quest for 'authentic national cultural identity often results in efforts to reconstruct a lost national ethos as though it were some secret inheritance or that cultural identity were a matter of recovering some forgotten or "hidden music"' (Crang, 1998, p. 166). On a cursory inquiry Butts defines this 'secret inheritance' as the native imagination: an ingenuous pride in a heritage of homely things that fosters ardent regional affiliation, local accountability and unstinting community service. However, the 'sensibility' Butts valorizes in her highly strung fables of the democratic tide 'flooding the tranquillity of English rural life' (*CC* p. 112) is far removed from any generous or 'common' interest: the 'most ancient blood in England' (*CC* p. 163), cyclical patterns of land-holding and esoteric 'knowledge' (*AR* p. 100) coalesce to form a vehement *nativism* (Garrity, 2003; Wright, 1985).

Butts's abiding preoccupation with the 'intruder' who dares to 'step across the line of protection' into an enclave of 'earthworks and barrows' (*AWM* p. 13) functions as a stringent reappraisal of Hardy's regional tapestry. In some of his most acclaimed novels, Hardy charts how a native countryman's romantic and professional aspirations are tragically derailed by the meddling of a predacious 'foreign' interloper. Sergeant Frank Troy in *Far from the Madding Crowd*; the entrepreneurial Scot Donald Farfrae in *The Mayor of Casterbridge* and Edred Fitzpiers in *The Woodlanders* are all memorable examples of the 'stranger' who infiltrates a bucolic hinterland and 'unmans' a primitive fertility figure, like Gabriel Oak, Michael Henchard and Giles Winterborne, whose powers of guaranteeing organic plenitude for the community are no longer operant. In *Tess of the d'Urbervilles*, the eponymous protagonist's encounter with the effete outsider Angel Clare augurs the collapse of an entire province once rich in folklore survivals. Butts records re-reading Hardy's *Tess* in her journal of 16 August 1921 and it is this narrative of irretrievable dissolution that she seeks to correct in her own trilogy of 'Wessex Novels'.

Vanna in *Ashe of Rings* (1925), Scylla in *Armed with Madness* (1928) and Felicity in *Death of Felicity Taverner* (1932) all seek in the 'Grail' myth an antidote to 'this leprosy on the face of our land' (*CC* p. 93).[4] As Jane Garrity argues, a daughter's 'claim' to an ancestral habitation in *Ashe of Rings* and the *Taverner Novels* is ratified by demonstrating how a cultural 'fantasy of Englishness' is anchored in 'patriotic' reverence for the moral benefits of 'reproduction', alongside a profoundly 'insular' definition of 'racial and cultural homogeneity' (Garrity, 2003, pp. 188–93). In Butts's fiction, 'celebrating pride of race' (Butts, 'Hesiod', 1932a, p. 113) blurs into a punitive and prohibitive ideology that dreads 'the sullen, chained, savage look that comes over country-places once man comes to defile them' (*DFT* p. 343). This 'intolerance' towards outsiders would, according to her friend Bryher [Winifred Ellermann] in 1937, not only appear 'reckless' or 'incomprehensible' to middlebrow reviewers, but would make 'easy fame impossible' (Bryher, 1937, p. 160). Far from having 'obstructions removed, revealing a landscape that had always been there' (*AWM* p. 78), Butts underpins existing physical and racial 'boundaries of the Sacred Wood' (*DFT* p. 343) to keep the unwary out. Alongside this 'intolerance' however, and what deserves more measured scrutiny, is a unique archaeological alertness to space and place. Glenway Wescott remarked in his review of Butts's short story collection *Speed the Plough* for *The Dial* in 1923:

> This moody, haughty mind, essentially religious, collects no drawing-room symbols; but gathers exactly the sense of ploughs, blades and blood. It is rich in the scholarship of a golden bough, of a stamen of wood twelve feet long hung with a fox-pelt and feathers, of a dark grail. Strictly contemporary experience is lit by an antique fiery light; life an 'infernal saga [. . .] coming up-to-date'. The racial memory, the animal memory, has been strangely extended; and memory is the identifiable soul. (Wescott, 1923, pp. 282–84)

This 'moody, haughty mind' strives to recoup her birthplace as a locus of patrician verve; managing and monitoring a grandly historicized English past to offset an 'urban' evil (*DFT* p. 302) carried on the 'brown sea of London's mud' (*AR* p. 88).

'[D]istinction of race or class' (*CC* p. 254) is evidenced by lifelong fidelity to the natal homestead and a maverick self-assurance which resists the dictates of a 'democratic enemy' ('Warning', 1998, p. 270). In her posthumously published autobiography *The Crystal Cabinet*, drafted retrospectively from 1935 to 1937, Butts delineates the formative experiences that gave rise to this exclusionary sense of regional belonging. She positions herself as a snubbed but precocious child whose enjoyment of the social and cultural blessings of an 'only slightly sub-aristocratic home' (Wright, 1985, p. 104), is irredeemably tainted by the death of a much-loved, indulgent father and her mother's subsequent remarriage. The narrative arc of *The Crystal Cabinet*, which resonates through much of her non-historical fiction, is a canny reprogramming of countless mid-Victorian potboilers in which a seemingly 'united family' (*AR* p. 21) is vitiated by the sudden eruption of aberrant sexual passion. Among the 'sufferings' of her 'age' Butts highlights the extensive abrasion of kinship bonds, supplanted family obligations and especially the tragedy of the 'aristo-crat who knows only the aristoi are worth having, & yet seeing the people it was his business to help coming to destroy him' (*Journals* p. 412). The social unit that is chiefly responsible for determining the location of prestige and the means of reckoning descent in Butts's oeuvre – the patrician clan ruled by a 'stainless gentleman' (*AR* p. 33) – is not only bedevilled from without by a burgeoning open-air movement of hikers, sightseers and rambling clubs. The 'tribe', a supposedly stalwart and durable social institution, is plagued from within by psychic and emotional vicissitudes; or even a catastrophic want of 'nice judgement' (*DFT* p. 279). A 'fever runs in these people' (*AR* p. 46) which leads to an 'irregular situation' such as a 'mercenary marriage' (*AR* p. 117), even 'adultery' (*AR* pp. 32–33). The dearth of 'proper mothers who comfort their children' (*AR* p. 183) or an imprudent alliance debases the illustrious currency of 'caste'. '[S]heer bad character' may 'run in families' (*DFT* p. 314): Melitta in *Ashe of Rings* is an 'insect trespassing' (*AR* p. 27); Judy is a 'filthy' demon (*AR* p. 119) and a 'microcosm' of 'war' (*AR* p. 67); while the 'infernal bully' Aunt Julia is a 'Taverner only' by matrimony and twists 'family-life' into a disreputable 'forcing-bed for the Oedipus complex' (*DFT* p. 171).

In *The Crystal Cabinet*, Butts pinpoints in her antecedents the traits most likely to expose metropolitan modernity itself as a 'hideous unreality' (Massingham, 1988, p. 68): a thin veneer beneath which something richer and more robust flows. This is 'a secret common to the blood. A secret concerned with time and very little with death, with what perhaps medieval philosophers called *aevum*, the link between time and eternity' (*CC*, p. 15). Again Butts prioritizes the 'secret' in her rendering of Salterns, an estate which resembles E. B. Tylor's definition of an anthropological 'survival', an object carried along the waves of time to reside, incongruously, beside more modish habits, manners and styling. Tylor's 'survival' is essentially a moribund, dysfunctional or embarrassing relic, much like the dissolute and 'sinister antique' (*AWM* p. 83) Mr Tracy in *Armed with Madness*: 'something built by centuries of experience, and now no longer in flower' (*AWM* p. 74). By contrast, Butts envisages her lush estate – with its lawns, terrace and orchard – as a repository of vital energy or '*aevum*' by which an aesthetic of yearly remembrances, 'big magics' and revenants counteracts 'the formally democratic rationality of the liberal marketplace' (Patterson, 2001, p. 187). She sees herself as a member of that coterie which Ezra Pound celebrated in 1914: decisively disdainful of the average and the 'general'. For Pound aristocratic cachet, once synonymous with inherited political privilege, now becomes a benchmark of aesthetic excellence:

> The artist has no longer any belief or suspicion that the mass, the half edu-cated simpering general [. . .] can in any way share his delights [. . .] The aristocracy of the arts is ready again for its service. Modern civilization has bred a race with brains like those of rabbits, and we who are the heirs of witch-doctors and voodoo, we artists who have been so long the despised, are about to take control. (Pound, 1914, pp. 67–68)

Pound's slyly sardonic reference to the 'artist' as heir of 'witch-doctors and voodoo' is suggestive. Butts's own ineffable comprehension of regional lore which inheres in 'a certain hardihood of race' (*CC* p. 211), imbues her 'approach to the Grail' (*CC* p. 134) and forms the dramatic centrepiece of *Armed with Madness*. In *The Crystal Cabinet* Butts recalls that as a child the 'real Grail [. . .] was the most wonderful thing to think about in the world' (*CC* p. 33). *Armed with Madness* repositions the Grail 'as an object of mythic longing', the goal of a gruelling 'personal quest that gains greater poignancy [. . .] after World War I' (Anderson, 2007, p. 246).

Rewriting the Grail Quest

> An excursion down the well to clean out the dead hedgehogs had led to a discovery. An odd cup of some greenish stone had been found, rather like pea-soup carnelian. [. . .] 'You're done in this country if your well gives out. Wait till ours does'. Carston was not interested. This might interfere with his making love to Scylla, which he had decided was to be his expression of a suc-cessful visit. [. . .]
>
> Then Ross produced the cup suddenly, out of his pocket, and handed it round. Carston said:
>
> 'That means nothing to me'.
>
> 'Been cut by hand', said Felix. 'Is there a kind of opaque flint glass? Keltic twiddles, I think, very worn round the rim'.
>
> A good deal was told Carston, casually, about Kelts and Saxons and Romans and early Christianity; things completely over so far as he knew [. . .]
>
> Then Ross said, roughly and softly, as though he was loving something:
>
> 'The thing was that we fished it out with a spear'.
>
> (*AWM* pp. 15–16)

The key archaeological 'event' in *Armed with Madness* is the unexpected 'discovery' of a small 'glass dish' that might be the chalice of the 'Sanc Grail' (*AWM* p. 25).

The salvaging of this ambiguous artefact from the bottom of an unusable well coincides with the arrival of an American guest in South Dorset, Dudley Carston, who struggles to register the sheer magnitude of this find 'that had been lost out of the world' (*AWM* p. 79). Though the expatriate Carston has 'a great sensibility to take impressions' it is invariably 'in relation to people' rather than 'scenery' (*AWM* p. 12). Indeed, he is more exercised by the chance of seducing his insouciant English hostess, Scylla Taverner, than by the palpable actuality of the Grail as a religious remnant, or its evolution into a multifaceted secular symbol in the modern imagination. He judges the intricately stratified past of 'Kelts and Saxons and Romans' to be 'over'; a frivolous distraction, utterly irrelevant and divorced from the exigencies of the present. That Carston appears profoundly 'out of touch' during this episode is inextricably enmeshed with his status as a naïve newcomer who lacks 'belief' in a 'possible sanctity' (*AWM* p. 62), embodied by the Grail itself. As Butts remarks in a January 1936 review, this trinket is tied to historically embedded identity as 'the very spring of our culture, as Milton knew, the "matter of Britain" *in excelsis*' ('Parzival', 1936, p. 57). Yet the only past that Carston esteems in the initial exchanges is the dainty heritage of 'Hardy's country', which signals a reductive reading of the Wessex Novels as a repository of quaint, inoffensive rustic lore.

> [Scylla] reminded herself of the pleasure it would be to show a stranger their land, as they knew it, equivocal, exquisite. From what she had observed of Americans, almost certain to be new. [. . .]
>
>   'God! What a beautiful place', [Carston] said. When 'beautiful' is said, exactly and honestly, there is contact, or there should be. Then, 'This is the England we think of. Hardy's country, isn't it?' (*AWM* p. 11)

As Scylla reflects, Carston is prone to 'slightly overdoing the beauty business' (*AWM* p. 11). He converts the particularities of his immediate milieu into a trite sylvan topos, a standard of commodified bucolic charm. This is what Butts calls 'the curse of the whimsical, the curse that has part of its origin' in 'urban immaturities' (Butts, 'Two Blind Mice', 1934e, p. 255). Indeed, the 'England' that Carston conjures up is a 'prettified' site (*AWM* p. 8) of sub-Wordsworthian pantheism. When he gazes at 'a chart of the coast' soon after his arrival, he reveals a sensibility that knows only how to consume, rather than commune. Unfortunately, according to Butts, Carston as an 'American boy, very polished' (*AWM* p. 30) is, like his countrymen 'arriving here without root or memories of any kind in this land' ('Americans on England', 1936, p. 13). Americans are 'bad players' at 'the sacred game' (*AWM* p. 43) in *Armed with Madness* because instead of seeing beauty as an inevitable result of common use and traditional agriculture, they praise countryside as picturesque scenery. Against the counterfeit and callow urban pastoralism of retinal sensation which Carston personifies, Butts's novel canvasses a 'pilgrimage' (*AWM* p. 81) through a more visceral version of 'Hardy's country', to unearth magical 'old patterns' which 'repeat themselves' (*AWM* p. 16) in striking ways. This vision debunks the disciples of Hardy who secured modest commercial success in the early years of the twentieth century, such as M. E. Francis, in titles such as *Fiander's Widow* (1901) and *Hardy on the Hill* (1909). Orme Agnus also focused on Dorset villages though with less recourse to Francis's Arcadian excesses: *Jan Oxber* (1900); *Love in Our Village* (1900); *Sarah Tuldon* (1903) and *The Root* (1905). Butts details her approach, which transcends an insatiable 'thirst for antiquities' (*AWM* p. 63), in a journal entry for September 1927:

> Carry on from the last, *Armed with Madness*. Which might well have been called 'the Waste Land'. Eliot always anticipates my titles! Re-reading Weston's *From Ritual to Romance*. A fruitful book, cf. Eliot, & as Jane Harrison & Frazer are to me. (Eliot and I are working on a parallel.) (*Journals* pp. 263–64)

While Butts grants that 'T. S. E is now one of the Guardians of the Sanc Grail', claiming his 'work' has had a 'profound effect' on her 'generation' (*Journals* p. 444), and even quotes his 'Rhapsody on a Windy Night' in *Armed with Madness* ('Prepare for life, / The last twist of the knife' [p. 36]), she counteracts his stricken sense of social and cultural severance (Kroll, 1999, pp. 159–73). In sharp contrast to '[g]ood old Freud' (*AR* p. 183) and especially Eliot's thesis that the nebulous, wayward confusion of the savage mentality was beyond our civilized ken, Butts intuits a 'mystical' mindset to which 'knowledge of the Grail belongs' (Butts, 'Parzival', 1936b, p. 57). This firm 'conviction' evinces 'a factual quality of which not even the rising tide of fashionable psychology could dissuade' her (*CC* p. 137). Indeed, her heroine Scylla Taverner displays a different mode of seeing in which 'we are spectators of a situation which is the mask for another situation [. . .] in a remote age', a 'world that is outside time' (*AR* p. 44). This evokes Butts's own recondite conception of history, 'a kind of ambidextrous time sense; in certain states I will confuse my analysis of the present into immediate past & immediate future, & use them interchangeably' (*Journals* p. 372). Butts signifies in her journal entries that her commitment to imaginative archaeology, prioritizing terms like *mana* and *tabu*, functions as a credible and consoling alternative to Eliot's *The Waste Land*, whose myriad 'austerities' (*CC* p. 18) signals an unavailing mood of intractable loss and deprivation.

Armed with Madness dramatizes, through the movements of Scylla's clique of friends, the 'procreative' facets of the spiritual Grail quest in Wessex, connecting it to Jane Ellen Harrison's discussion of 'ritual practice' and natural cycles (Garrity, 2003, p. 187). Scylla fulfils the role of the 'female spirit of life' (*AWM* p. 30), a resuscitating influence who posits 'a new value, a different way of apprehending everything' (*AWM* p. 9); that throws into bold relief what Butts judged as Eliot's 'peculiarly' undernourished 'genius', and its reliance on stunted or fractured images of femininity (*Journals* p. 444; Kroll, 1999). In *Armed with Madness*, Scylla's coterie apprehends the same 'great torment'

(*AR* p. 78) that *The Waste Land* evokes and dissects, but they extricate themselves from the metropolitan hub which Scylla belittles as a mere 'lumber-room to be foraged for junk, rubbish, white elephants' (*AWM* p. 114). Only among the chalk downlands of Dorset can Scylla inaugurate a 'game' imbued with sacramental suggestiveness.

Scylla and the other questing knights comprise the fortunate few who unravel these arcane mysteries – what Patrick Wright calls 'special people in special places' (1985, p. 96). Scylla is a modern 'enchantress', 'translating' the natural world 'into herself: into sea: into sky. Sky back again into wood, flesh and sea' (*AWM* pp. 67–68). She reveres 'old standards' (*AWM* p. 121); what Lydia's 'gigolo' spouse Philip disavows as vapid 'fancy words' (*AWM* p. 121) in fact divulge fields of thought which enshrine the precepts of a more chivalric era. 'Man is continually making a highly selective picture out of favourite points in the past,' according to Butts in her 1932 article 'The Herschel Chronicle'. 'Some moment or epoch or group of persons takes his imagination, and he at once begins to turn such data as he has into a work of art, rejecting and selecting and arranging, until he arrives at a satisfactory composition' ('Herschel Chronicle', 1933, p. 252). It is precisely this tactic which informs her renovation of primitive and medieval fertility myth in *Armed with Madness*.

By having Scylla and her modish clique re-enact a venerable rite, Butts aligns them with 'a new point of view' (*AR* p. 225) that blends instinctual and emotional perception, unlike the purely rationalist rigour which dominates the verbal texture of Eliot's *Waste Land* (Kroll, 1999; Garrity, 2003, pp. 188–220). *Armed with Madness* applauds the aristocratic 'finer orders' who 'see more deeply into the structure of reality', looking beyond Eliot's 'cold water' which is 'by no means the entire answer' (*CC* p. 264). What is most striking about this Wessex as a 'place for magical rites' is how it recalls D. H. Lawrence's conception of the west country in *Kangaroo* (1923). Lawrence renders the Cornish moors as an 'altar' upon which primitive blood-sacrifices have been staged. His vivid imagery invites comparison with Butts's view in *Armed with Madness* of a locus where crops are 'blood-bright' (*AWM* p. 41). In her 1932 *Bookman* article 'On Gardens', Butts reflected:

> [I]t would seem that in gardens there is all that we have of a nature religion left to us. Once we worshipped, feared and propitiated, but also adored everything there is out of doors. The classic religions show it and the cults of our ancestors. When Christianity turned out the gods, it kept the garden; left a hole in the wall for patron saints to creep in [. . .] and though on the whole it stripped the orchard, the grove, the sea with its fish of their potencies, Our Lady was fond of flowers [. . .] that which has been part of the divine dress is made of such stuff as can always be put on again. (Butts, 'On Gardens', 1932b, p. 40)

Armed with Madness gives the 'flowers' more destabilizing connotations, an act of resistance to Christianity's persistent domestication and dilution of the 'great outdoors'. So in the novel lawns are 'stuck with yuccas and tree-fuchsias, dripping season in, season out, with bells the colour of blood' (*AWM* p. 3); Clarence notices 'a blood-mist of poppies on the stony earth' (*AWM* p. 126). On one level, the ravaged expanse of Flanders fields in 1915 has been transposed to a rustic retreat 'smeared with futility' (*AR* p. 98), so as to dramatize the war-veteran's complex and subtle suffering. However, Butts also signals that her Wessex is saturated with the irrefutable evidence of ethnic and national descent: 'blood' implies pedigree and pure 'breeding' (Garrity, 2003, pp. 200–15). Through this imagery Butts examines the social and cultural formation of modernity so as to reinstate her secret – the formidable 'affective power' of what Ian Patterson terms 'the old gods' – to the 'impersonal forces' that the sociologist Max Weber, at the same time, was exposing to the 'light' of sustained rational scrutiny (Patterson, 2001, pp. 183–90). *The Crystal Cabinet* bolsters this conception of a chalky south Dorset coastline whose 'signatures' bespeak a Caucasian racial provenance: 'the white Salterns walls' (*CC* p. 258) are 'the physical expression of a supernatural quality' (*CC* p. 35); narrow 'paths of pure white sand' stretch across the furzy heath (*CC* p. 8); the sea has 'a ravening fury of whiteness [. . .] thundering at the roots of the bones of the earth' (*CC* p. 26); and 'the Purbeck cliffs' blaze 'their fierce white' (*CC* p. 120).

This single-minded insistence on the 'clean' colours of local landmarks (*AWM* p. 7), such as the 'white cup' and 'cradle' of Rings (*AR* p. 189), intimates the genetic superiority of the indigenous elect in Butts's oeuvre: the 'moon's white' in *Ashe of Rings* connotes Vanna's irradiative and prodigal fecundity: 'a great egg at the point of cracking, so smooth, so blank' (*AR* p. 36). It is surely no accident that the 'business' of the Grail 'cup' in *Armed with Madness* evokes the citation 'Lighten our Darkness' (*AWM* pp. 138, 147) from the Book of Common Prayer, in particular the Collect for Aid against Perils, which echoes like a mantra throughout the text (Garrity, 2003, p. 24). For Lawrence by contrast in the 'Cornwall' section of *Kangaroo* atavistic immersion is figured as an engulfing, irresistible yet fertile darkness; a magisterial rejection of that 'old, white light, much older than the sun' (*AR* p. 159). Similarly, Powys's *Maiden Castle* affirms Uryen Quirm, the redoubtable 'Black Man' (*MC* p. 343), with his 'great dark countenance' (*MC* p. 369), as the mystical priest of Dorchester. Butts's edgier, more 'equivocal' Grail country, with its uneasy associations of eugenic prestige and hereditary fitness, validated by 'mana', stymies the town-bred interloper's endeavours to enframe Wessex as if it were a painting of landscaped tranquillity for mass delectation.

Like Powys in *A Glastonbury Romance*, Butts depicts the Grail cup as the result of intricate and evolving assignations of meaning, bridging Judeo-Christian and Hellenic discourses (Garrity, 2003, pp. 208–21). She expresses her mystical theories in her 1933 review of *The Later Life of Wordsworth*: through the elusive Grail 'Paganism and Christianity met and were fused at that *white heat* which alone puts an antithetic good into men's possession' ('The Real Wordsworth', 1933, p. 1448; my italics). Is the recovered artefact in *Armed with Madness* an 'early Church vessel', divulging a 'fine, mysterious, almost sacred fable'

(*AWM* p. 132), or an absurd theatrical prop in a bogus ceremonial? The curio's 'probable origin' (*AWM* p. 132) is of less interest to Butts than its slippery status as an enticing absence; forcing its owners to react with 'courage and imagination' (*AWM* p. 44). The essential 'value' (*AWM* p. 132) of this receptacle is determined chiefly by what the loyal neophyte pours into it; the apparently 'holy' cup has held innumerable 'lowly' residues over time: human spittle, whisky-and-soda (*AWM* p. 37) and cigarette ash 'in a Cairo club' (*AWM* p. 140).

Like Felicity Taverner in the 'sequel' to *Armed with Madness*, the Grail object offers an incessantly contested 'space', a 'set of symbols' (*AR* p. 20) or chain of associations which connote the heady excitements as well as grave spiritual perils of storytelling; indeed, the narrative 'escalates through variously authored acts' of 'describing the background of the cup' (Rives, 2005, p. 613). Does the 'inconclusive' jade vessel boast 'impressive antiquity' (*AWM* p. 61) as 'part of a crusader's loot' (*AWM* p. 132)? Or would experts at the 'British Museum' (*AWM* p. 131) classify it as an Indian Rajah's poison cup, gathering over centuries myriad accretions of 'uncanny' import (*AWM* p. 61), as empires rise up and founder? That this artefact may be a mere bagatelle, a vulgar 'cocktail shaker' (*AWM* p. 115), or a 'question mark to the question we can none of us answer' (*AWM* p. 137) is hardly a cause for despair in the novel; rather it proclaims the immense 'fertility' of a chalice which occasions a plethora of tantalizing distractions, 'far-fetched' fantasies (*AWM* p. 131) and feats of 'personal invention' (*AWM* p. 132) during the 'Freud game' (*AWM* p. 29). Unlike the grimy Tollerdown well from which it is retrieved, or the 'empty cisterns' in Eliot's *The Waste Land*, the 'dumb circle of pale green' (*AWM* p. 123) does not 'dry up'; it is inexhaustible in its capability to trigger impromptu speculations, heterodox reveries and thought-adventures about its 'pedigree' and provenance (*AWM* p. 131).

That Scylla is appointed 'damsel of the Sanc Grail' (*AWM* p. 44) is no surprise since she is, like the cup, 'mischief-making' (*AWM* p. 131). In the second chapter Scylla, 'in a quicksilver mirror, [. . .] saw the men come in' (*AWM* p. 7). This does not imply petty vanity or smug self-regard but rather her status as a 'point of reflection' (*AWM* p. 15); a sassy and versatile 'actor' who cannot be trapped in any one subject position – this is the only 'fact' (*AWM* p. 132) to bear in mind. That she negotiates among the roles and masks socially ascribed to her underlines her adroitness in crafting fresh personae of her own, restlessly revising conventional categories. She is delineated as a 'fancy-girl' (*AWM* p. 144) with 'strong appetites' (*AWM* p. 9) and a 'hypothetical virginity' (*AWM* p. 132). To the impetuous Dudley Carston she seems 'lovely and mad' (*AWM* p.14), as well as overly familiar with the louche and gamey tics of 'erotic conversation' (*AWM* p. 32). This 'slender, cousinly bitch' (*AWM* p. 128) and 'witch' (*AWM* p. 10) infuriates Clarence by situating herself artfully against numerous backdrops, targeting scenarios that will display her to flattering effect, feigning affective and sexual availability (Garrity, 2003; Foy, 2000, p. 65). Scylla's 'openness' is 'deceptive' (*AWM* p. 14), however. Like Butt's own childhood reminiscences, her testimony 'is full' of arch tergiversation, perplexing 'gaps' and conundrums (*CC* p. 165) which are underscored by grammatical omissions and strategic feints: auxiliary verbs, connectives and relatives are dispensed with at decisive junctures; a fondness for abstract nouns and definite articles placed against indefinite nouns transmits a veiled urgency. The gnomic, teasing narrative viewpoint oscillates between free indirect discourse, first-person interior monologue and beguiling passages of omniscient third-person narration (Rainey, 1998, p. 16). Such rhetorical and perceptual 'knight's moves' permit Scylla's cousin Felicity Taverner to appear at once spotlessly 'chaste' (*DFT* p. 172) and the epitome of alluring vulnerability. A 'fast woman' (*AR* p. 33) whose impudent daring contributed to a 'scandalous' reputation (*DFT* p. 183), Felicity kept diaries that betrayed 'erotic' expertise (*DFT* p. 260), 'disgraceful knowledge' (*DFT* p. 323) and seditious 'ways of looking at things' which had 'nothing to do with Christianity' (*AR* p. 20). As Butts remarks of the queenly priestess Olympias in *The Macedonian*, who is by turns 'the loveliest of sacred mothers' and a raging 'termagant', some 'essential significance lay just below the surface, slipping to and fro beneath the level of another medium, like fish' (1994, p. 19). When Hardy designates Tess Durbeyfield as a 'Pure Woman', caustically misapplying the lexicon of Christian respectability in the provocative subtitle to his most feted novel, it is meant as a mutinous challenge to those ruthlessly repressive attitudes that Mary Butts assails through Scylla and Felicity Taverner, such as those voiced by the National Vigilance Association, which appealed, as Jane Garrity notes, for sexual abstinence as a woman's solemn 'patriotic' responsibility (Garrity, 2003, p. 223). *Tess* explicitly aligns the female form with the resplendent Blackmore Vale, while Butts disparages any inference that the 'purity' of her natal habitation can be conserved by the exercise of demure 'lady-like' decorum. Scylla, like Felicity, is a complex exemplar of the 'vigorous, flesh-eating Saxon woman' (*AR* p. 41), who has benefited from the shelter afforded by the possession of private property as well as the economic sway of vested interests to resist the democratic tide. Scylla's witchery, at times 'cold, cruel, and insolent' (*AWM* p. 117) thus comprises a calculated affront to the stern regulation and 'fetishizing' of 'female chastity' (Garrity, 2003, pp. 217–20).

Scylla is a vivacious – and voracious – modern illusionist whose manoeuvres with, and around, the young men of her bohemian set discloses her gift for improvising selfhood in a standardizing 'machine' culture (*AWM* p. 90). While she embodies from one angle the clichéd association of exuberant femininity and profuse elemental nature – 'the wood and the woman' are 'interchangeable' after all (*AWM* p. 12); '[n]aked, the enormous space, the rough earth dressed her' (*AWM* p. 5) – she is also a sophisticated cosmopolite who grasps only too well her friend Lydia's graceless and facile 'London' manners. Whereas canonical accounts of the Grail saga acclaim an extrovert and crusading 'virility' (*AWM* p. 55), *Armed with Madness* asserts the centrality of a female priestess, as 'strong as a tree-cat' (*AWM* p. 144); an intriguer with 'formidable wits' (*AWM* p. 117), who adumbrates 'a state of consciousness unique' (*AWM* p. 140). This is, quite deliberately, a novel unencumbered by hidebound conceptions of 'a REAL MAN' (*AWM* p. 121). Scylla is the 'living cup' (*AWM* p. 38) – the force and figure that taps the primal, perennial energies of Wessex so as to deter impostors, thus returning 'England' to its rightful, indigenous, patrician inheritors (*Journals* p. 62).

Jane Garrity, in her trenchant analysis of the racial politics imbuing interwar British women's writing, argues that without the 'serene courage' (*AWM* p. 137) of this female fertility figure, an 'authentic' Wessex cannot survive, let alone thrive (Garrity, 2003, pp. 191–225). This key concept is reinforced by the sexual imagery of the Grail, and the novel attaches symbolic weight to the 'spear', which was first employed by Picus (who inaugurates the search) to 'fish' the 'odd cup' out of the well (*AWM* pp. 15–16). While the Grail cup overflows with multifarious meanings and applications, its association with 'white is right' Englishness never suggests a convertible ethnic currency in Butts's unforgiving fictional scheme.

This punitive agenda is discernible not only in the treatment of the querulous American expatriate Dudley Carston, who pays little heed to the 'magic' of ancestral legacies, but also in the demonizing of Clarence, a black homosexual veteran of the Great War whose supposed deficiencies are measured against Scylla, a young woman with blonde 'moon-fair hair' (*AWM* p. 145), and her more temperate Caucasian companions (*AWM* p. 14). Having 'seen war' (*AWM* p. 26) at its most wantonly destructive, Clarence suffers from what we would term nowadays post-traumatic stress disorder: '[s]omething had broken in him' (*AWM* p. 27).[5] His attempts to maintain rational clarity among his would-be friends in and near Gault House are undermined by 'frightful emotion' (*AWM* p. 63), even sadistic 'fury' (Foy, 2000, p. 69; Garrity, 2003, p. 212). While Scylla's palpable presence harmonizes with a Wessex 'full of echoes and overtones' (*CC* p. 109), the account of Clarence's physique ('close-set eyes and a walk affected to hide his strength') is filtered through the prism of fantasies about racial deterioration: his body 'branded with shrapnel and bullet and bayonet thrust' (*AWM* p. 128).[6] Feeling 'raw', 'ill-adjusted' and 'uneasy' (*AWM* pp. 26, 35), Clarence fails to cultivate a rapport with many of Scylla's allies, such as the 'better bred' Ross and Picus Tracy, whose 'colour' was 'drawn from the moon's palette, steel gilt and pale' (*AWM* p. 14). Elizabeth Anderson argues that

> As a shell-shocked veteran, Clarence provides a focus for the distress caused by the pervasive effect of World War I, from which neither Butts nor her characters can escape. Physically, mentally and spiritually wounded, he contains destruction on behalf of them all. Clarence figures the wounded Fisher King of the Grail legend. (Anderson, 2007, p. 251)

Scylla's strenuous policing of the 'keltic border' (*Journals* p.127) in *Armed with Madness* entails the prevention of further intimacies between Clarence and the mercurial, flirtatious Picus. As Vanna tells Serge in *Ashe of Rings,* in the 'world [. . .] the normal aim of its creatures, is towards birth or making things' (*AR* p. 148). However, this '[t]ruth isn't everyone's breakfast egg' (*AWM* p. 20), and Butts's definition of generative sexuality seems anchored in an imperious female principle which does not countenance the black gay man's 'unfruitful' and hysterical compulsions (*AWM* p. 132), signifying 'desire pushed out of vigour and proportion into a monstrous order of insanity' (*AR* p. 70). To a distraught Clarence, 'for each question that is answered' concerning the Grail legend, 'a fresh one drops out, like eggs out of a hen' (*AR* p. 170). Consumed by 'desolation and rage against Scylla' (*AWM* p. 129), Clarence is a 'frustrated hen' who has no 'eggs to lay' (*AWM* pp. 111, 87) and underscores Roslyn Reso Foy's thesis that he both articulates and exemplifies the 'depravity and plight of the external world' (2001, p. 63). In marked contrast, the blithe heterosexual 'warriors' Picus and Scylla validate 'the passage of rebirth' (*AR* p. 83) and so receive the 'natural' rewards of a resplendent milieu which Hardy shows in *The Woodlanders* as defined by a venerable past of fertility ritual, sanctifying the 'up-thrust of trunk and root, of bulb and seed' (*CC* p. 258). Given Scylla's status as 'a different egg' and Picus's flair for 'riding and blowing birds' eggs'(*AWM* p. 19), this couple is best situated, Butts implies, to prosecute the august and challenging 'business' of the Grail 'cup' (*AWM* pp. 138, 147). As Jane Garrity shows, the Grail is a vibrant 'reminder' (*AWM* p. 21) that Clarence's 'non-procreative sexuality', merged with his 'tortured' psyche (*AWM* p. 35), disqualifies him from unbridled access to the sacred game, which is played 'straight' (*DFT* p. 169) by Scylla and her boisterous 'Parish bunch'. The uncompromising severity of this message seems all the starker in a novel which exploits the protean 'flux' of the Grail cup (Garrity, 2003, p. 214) to highlight salutary discrepancies between the 'perpetual motion' (*AWM* p. 88) of a standard historiography, with its linear narratives and chronological divisions, and the delicate equipoise and cyclical patterns synonymous with visionary romance conventions.

Through the 'complicated, violent' adventure of the jade cup, *Armed with Madness* attributes a bracing political value to the 'play' of riddling ambivalences (*AWM* p. 95). However, the 'introvert' Clarence, 'born at the end of old civilisations' (*AR* p. 149), personifies the grievous pitfalls, and not the invigorating instabilities, of being 'undecided sexually' (Foy, 2000, p. 63). His blackness, 'race sadism' (*AWM* p. 153) and 'abnormal' sexual proclivity (*AR* p. 149) are associated with a covetous 'rage' that seizes him 'by the throat' and 'crawl[s] over him' (*AWM* p. 128). So the 'story of the cup', instead of becoming a boon or a 'holy wonder' (Baldick, 2004, p. 231), collapses into unspeakable 'horror' (*AWM* p. 128). For Clarence, the only way to shatter the cup's curse is to hurl it, and his nonchalant tormentor Scylla, back into the gloomy chthonic realm, a 'vent hole for infernal powers' (*AR* p. 70): 'down the well, where the cup came' is the 'best place for you' (*AWM* p. 144). Clarence's demented and homicidal impulse lends a malignant resonance to the citation from Exod. 22.18, *Thou shalt not suffer a witch to live* (*AWM* p. 55).

Ultimately – and disappointingly – *Armed with Madness* promulgates a firm 'faith' (*AWM* p. 70) in the elegant 'beauty' of heterosexual 'passion' (*AWM* p. 54), an orthodox 'section of erotics' (*AR* p. 148) which is trumpeted by countless Victorian novelists: Scylla's 'proper business' is 'to marry' and 'establish herself' (*AWM* p. 116). At the finale she and Picus speak with 'one voice' (*AWM* p. 65) in their stewardship of the lonely downs (*AWM* p. 8). That this 'trance of love' (*AWM* p. 59) promises 'a space full of clear forms and veritable issues' (*AWM* p. 153) reflects Butts's investment in 'mysteries of harmony' (*AWM* p. 117), founded upon being 'the same thing' (*AWM* p. 58) in terms of rearing, temperamental bias and ethnic makeup. Racial accord guarantees 'a foretaste of Paradise' (*AR* p. 144) and is reiterated by Vanna Ashe's 'milk-white nudity' (*AR* p. 170) as well as the light-skinned Scylla's indifferent grace (*AWM* p. 5) – a poise which 'broods' scenarios until 'they hatch' (*AWM* p. 20). Both young women are ardent followers of what Jane Garrity terms the 'procreative earth goddess' (2003, p. 214) whose 'female instincts' (*AWM* p. 84) foster civility rather than overweening pride, 'falsehood' or 'malice' (*AWM* p. 89). This goddess is a version of Hardy's 'votive sisterhood' (p. 19) in *Tess of the d'Urbervilles*. However, Hardy angrily debunks this ritualized interaction through the Marlott 'club-walking' or 'Cerealia' to show how pagan fertility worship based on sex and magic has been almost entirely deposed by a joyless Christian creed whose central tenets, as underscored by *Jude the Obscure*, disseminates a profound mistrust of biological imperatives. In Hardy's 1890s fiction, the female creatrix is irremediably atrophied, and a once sacred ceremonial welcoming the return of overflowing ripeness to the earth after the arid winter months becomes a 'crude exposure to public scrutiny' (*Tess*, 1988, p. 20). Hardy is no longer bullish that by manipulating tone or perspective he can delineate the moralities and social verities of his cultural heritage so as to leaven their corrosive impact. Jane Harrison's anthropological concept of 'woman' as 'the primeval Lawgiver' (1926, p. 132) cannot find a home in this jaundiced artistic vision.

Armed with Madness, on the other hand, reinstates Scylla's aesthetic and biological prodigality. Butts evinces a tenacious enthusiasm for the links between the ancient shaman and the audacious modern 'witch' who experiments with 'irrational fear' (*AWM* p. 16) to attain cathartic liberation. Yet Clarence, like other inveterate 'enemies of the rose' (*AWM* p. 42), lacks 'sound instinct' (*AWM* p. 131), and is impervious to this teaching. Locked in a 'deadly grey land' of 'infinite suffering' on the 'black heath' (*AWM* p. 65), he has little hope of securing Scylla's 'state of enlarged being' (*CC* p. 189), as Jane Garrity explains:

> Through the depiction of Clarence, Butts exposes her belief that authentic Englishness is synonymous with racial purity [. . .] Unabsorbed by the community, he is [. . .] irredeemable not just because he is homosexual and suffers from emasculating shellshock, but because he is racially Other. (Garrity, 2003, p. 212)

Garrity's sense of Clarence as an 'irredeemable' contaminant is complicated by Scylla's compassion after his psychotic episode, in which he exalts 'torture through hysteria' (*AR* p. 117). Whereas Carston, in no mood to make 'excuses' for the war-veteran's murderous act, hurls abuse at the 'self-pitying, self-centred [. . .] son of a bitch' (*AWM* p. 158), Scylla solaces Clarence. Though she cannot 'save his reputation for sanity' (*AWM* p. 156), she stops him from committing suicide over 'the cliff edge': 'Scylla jumped off the divan and with her hand at his side, ran out to him' (*AWM* pp. 157–58). Indeed her relationship with Clarence carries a piquant and elliptical charge in the closing pages: 'He took Scylla's hand, remained a moment in her embrace' (*AWM* p. 160). Even after her quasi-crucifixion ordeal, Scylla remains the undaunted 'leader' whose attitude to the 'pain-racked' Clarence (*AWM* p. 139) is not simply reminiscent of a mother's forgiving indulgence towards a petulant child:

> 'Look', she said, and pulled off the handkerchief that tied her shoulder – 'and my head is cut and my side. It was partly my fault that Lydia wrote to you. Go on carving while we talk'.
>
> He did as she told him. Carston watched them. Like an idyll: a young lover making a present for his sweetheart, sitting on her bed. A harrow of wild geese with their necks out at flight. A border of fish.
>
> 'It ought to be set. Can you work in silver, Clarence? We might melt down that atrocious salver – '
>
> Insufferable to be hushed like this. He preferred Carston glaring at him, wondering if he should get the gun. Picus came in. (*AWM* p. 158)

Is it Carston who jealously reads into the spectacle of Clarence and Scylla together a romantic 'idyll'? Scylla recalls 'how once in London she had come to him straight back from Spain, and he had lifted her up and carried her over the threshold, so glad he had been to see her' (*AWM* p. 143). That such moments remain 'delicately indefinite' (*AWM* p. 41) in the text is of a piece with Clarence's fate. He may resolve to 'hide' at Tambourne, under the watchful gaze of the kindly 'old parson', or seek out 'Picus's father' (*AWM* p. 158). That Clarence is effectively marooned in a region of terrible ambiguity, where 'there are no easy answers' (*AWM* p. 139), does not harmonize with the hints that his ruthless treatment of Scylla (he behaves like 'Apollo, or a roman official with an early Christian' [*AWM* p. 154]) has engendered 'ecstasy' and 'vision' (*AR* p. 117) – a healing bond among the 'magic ring' of the other Grail questing 'knights' (*AWM* p. 140). This 'moment of sacrifice' according to Jennifer Kroll, 'seems to trigger a sort of restoration of harmony among the friends', signifying that Clarence plays a more decisive role in the narrative ritual than critical orthodoxy permits (Kroll, 1999, p. 169).

What remains clear, however, is that while the other characters enact modern modes of ceremonial observance and retain a whit of dignified self-command – the incorrigible trickster Picus even achieves 'an assurance like maturity' (*AWM* p. 153) – Clarence cannot traverse the 'keltic border' and remain unscathed. So the 'agony' (*AWM* p. 91) he feels is difficult to dilute or transmute into an enabling positive; he is haunted by the 'phantoms' of his own febrile devising (*AWM* p. 89), scalded 'by the spiritual adventure he had not been equal to' (*AWM* p. 157). Yet Scylla continues to register Clarence as a serious romantic rival. Even after Picus has 'given her all he had', where 'love and saga were mixed', Scylla wonders whether Picus will bring Clarence to Gault House: 'I have no business to be glad that Clarence does not know, nor ask if he will be taken here. I came first'. (*AWM* pp. 57–60)

The key irony here is that Clarence considers himself Picus's 'first' lover. What does it mean to be 'first' in a narrative which records – and relishes – a dizzying succession of fickle 'erotic triangulations' (Garrity, 2003, p. 214)? Like the Grail legend and 'Clarence's bowl', this 'finale' (*AWM* p. 91) derails glib critical constructions and defers absolute rest. Each character's testimony is 'as open to revision as research in the electromagnetic field' (*AWM* p. 141):

> There had been an apple once. There had been an apple tree. When it gave no more apples, it had made fire, and a slice of its trunk had become a bowl cut into birds. The bowl unless it was turned into fire again, would stop growing and last forever. Things that came out of time, and were stopped, could be made over into another sort of time. (*AWM* p. 159)

The 'apple' impishly alludes to Scylla's standing as a brazen, risk-taking Eve who opens dangerous 'doors every sane person knows are better shut' (*AWM* p. 101). Scylla is also affiliated with 'Iduna' (*AWM* p. 114), the Norse chthonic goddess and wife of Bragi, deity of poetic eloquence (Garrity, 2003). Iduna stored golden 'apples' (*AWM* p. 114) in a box which the gods consumed to keep themselves young and spry. One of Vanna Ashe's treasured possessions is a 'golden apple' (*AR* p. 76) and Scylla's cousin Felicity ('*like a sweet apple*' [*DFT* p. 169]) is identified as a hierophant because she 'was always off, robbing some heavenly orchard and sharing the spoil' (*DFT* p. 169). The Taverner clan, as a sign of its lofty 'breeding', prefers 'apples before tinned peaches' (*DFT* p. 300). Against these mythic associations of magically preserved youth and arrested development is the ceaseless flux of 'time', 'made over' into a different form of temporality – an 'intermezzo' (*AR* p. 62) too oblique to specify and too remote to seize. However, it does facilitate another 'fine story to pick over' (*AWM* p. 159) in the shape of *Death of Felicity Taverner*. Though as Anne Armstrong concedes in her 1932 *Saturday Review* piece, the internal organic logic of its narrative is one of those secret codes that proliferate in Mary Butts's corpus: '[i]t would be easier to say what Miss Mary Butts' novel is not than to describe what it is' (Armstrong, 1932, p. 673).

An Alternative 'Historie' of Albion?

Miss Mary Butts will have no truck with the reader. The atmosphere of her *Death of Felicity Taverner* is tense and resistant, with almost a personal hostility to intruders. An individual idiom at once awkward and forbidding, a sense of beauty linked to the sinister, and absorption in the *solidarity* of her material (which the reader's sympathies are never allowed to pierce through) – these qualities are as uneasy of access as they are rare in fiction. Miss Butts stands by herself.

(Stonier, 1933, pp. 133–34)

G. W. Stonier's 1933 review of *Death of Felicity Taverner* accentuates the 'tense' and 'resistant' ambience that also infuses its prequel. Stonier pinpoints the 'personal hostility to intruders' which is a crucial facet of Butts's dialectic of modernity. Responding to the vandalizing interference of town-bred invaders, Scylla Taverner in the later novel compiles a prodigious antiquarian archive:

> Scylla's passion [. . .] was – spending if necessary her life over it – to leave behind her the full chronicle of their part of England, tell its 'historie' with the candour and curiosity, the research and imagination and what today might pass for credulity of a parish Herodotus. There was material there, for ten miles round about them, which had not been touched; not only manor rolls and church registers or the traditions which get themselves tourist-books. She had access to sources, histories of houses, histories of families, to memories that were like visions, to visions which seemed to have to do with memory. To her the people talked, the young as well as the old; and there were times when the trees and stones and turf were not dumb, and she had their speech [. . .] She did not know how she knew, Kilmeny's daughter, only what it looked like – the speechless sight of it – her thread to the use of the historic imagination, Ariadne to no Minotaur in the country of the Sanc Grail. (*DFT*, pp. 299–300)

Scylla's elaborate book project renders and ratifies 'that most perfect instrument for social or for solitary life, the English country-house' (*CC* p. 112). Although her younger brother Felix is designated as 'the family's professional chronicler' (*DFT* p. 168) at the outset of the novel, it is Scylla who assumes – and revels in – the daunting task of recording the Taverners' 'blood-link' (*DFT* p. 174) to the 'old part of oldest England' (*DFT* p. 340). This enterprise evokes the sedulous amateur antiquarianism of John Hutchins, Thomas Hardy's favourite local historian. Hutchins's *History and Antiquities of the County of Dorset* – imbued by a farrago of intellectual pursuits such as archaeology, ecclesiology, heraldry, genealogy, botany, folklore, the etymology of place-names – consecrates the imposing 'houses' and great 'families' of this region. Hardy's Napoleonic romance, *The Trumpet-Major* (1880) refers puckishly to Hutchins's opus as 'the excellent county history', whose third edition lavishly details individual sites, excavations and discoveries by 'pioneer archaeologists' (Douch, 1978, p. 123). Hutchins construed Scylla's homeland as a key focus for anthropological enquiry: 'the advantages of its situation, fertility of its soil, rare productions, the many remains of antiquity with which it abounds [. . .] well deserves an Historian' (Hutchins, 1861, I, p. vii).

Hutchins's brash and breathless eclecticism informs Scylla's approach to illustrating Wessex manners and mores – moving through orthodox religion, musty parish registers, pagan revivals, and the occult – that mocks any effort to discern a coherent methodology in it.

Scylla's diligent exercise of 'the historic imagination' (*DFT* p. 300), sifting national, diocesan, county, borough, family and parish records for relevant data, affirms on one level the sheer topographical diversity of 'Taverner-land' and how nature's 'pattern was repeated in' the august clan, 'the stuff of a country made into man' (*DFT* p. 339). For the Taverners, the sacred turf is 'strictly of their flesh' to the extent that 'leaf and air and water had nourished their bodies' (*DFT* pp. 258–59). The ominous import of this imagery is accentuated when it emerges that Felicity's vindictive spouse, the Russian half-Jewish entrepreneur Nicholas Kralin, pours his 'creative desire' and 'dry terrible power' into reducing this well-irrigated 'garden' of Wessex into a 'desert' with 'a few bones about' (*DFT* p. 242).[7]

Scylla's 'full chronicle' of the tribe's 'bit of England' (*DFT* p. 258) cannot be dismissed as self-conscious nostalgia then; nor does it epitomize the stereotypical antiquarian's omnivorous appetite for the miscellaneous and anecdotal. In her 1933 review 'The Isles of Greece' Butts avers that the 'magic of names is the most powerful of all the magic of words' (1933, p. 505). This implies that Scylla advocates a set of activities which keeps the 'memory' of her cousin Felicity's 'name' and 'blood' untarnished (*DFT* p. 282). In this project the woman is not just a part of regional heritage; she is a sharer in, and munificent contributor to its legends. Through her opus the Taverner 'name' safeguards the entrancing 'essences' which 'attach themselves to old houses' (*CC* p. 142). Scylla's 'historie' is rooted in a concept of clannish estate culture as a rich repository of 'heathen' lore (*AR* p. 16) that illumines not only minute manifestations of power in a secluded district, but also draws attention to a 'national' destiny (*Journals* p. 467). Scylla amasses a compendium of data from primary, unwritten sources, making use of oral testimony; she does not merely extrapolate or crystallize the regional mosaic: she *produces* the Taverner past as a heady, intoxicating spell. She foregrounds 'many of the supernatural occurrences' so 'crudely questioned by scoffing historians' (*GR* p. 370), whose tightly circumscribed research promotes hackneyed modes of visual and mental cartography. Scylla's notion of patrician caste is kudos made concrete by elaborate architecture and manicured lawns; but more crucially a fund of moral and mystical solace between 'intervals of violence' (*DFT* p. 228), based on the cultural assumption that 'the countryside is full of places with permanent spiritual characteristics' (Lowerson, 1992, p. 171).

What remains peculiarly problematic in *Death of Felicity Taverner* is how awkwardly Scylla's project sits with the actual condition of the aristocratic clan as a noble enclave battling the curse of 'foreigners'. Butts's depiction of Julia Taverner, a 'country-woman by instinct' (*DFT* p. 229) does not showcase so much the heroic 'vitality of a dying stock' (*CC* p. 162) or a resilient 'great gentry' (*DFT* p. 196), but rather a ferocious epitome of parental bungling and insolence. This matriarch, with 'a decidedly corrupt horror' of 'the processes of sex' (*CC* p. 173), presides over a 'once wide' patrician enclosure (*DFT* p. 230). Her 'energies and habits of domination' had found an 'outlet' in her 'generous preoccupation with the beauty of England', a 'passion' for 'its antiquities and local characteristics, especially in her own land' (*DFT* p. 285). Yet this 'generous' trait clashes with the troubling 'question marks' raised by the clan's coat-of-arms – a 'snake with its tail in its mouth' (*DFT* p. 200).[8] This 'curious addition' implies that a tribe formerly 'used to its own way and to war' has 'run to seed' (*DFT* p. 201). The regimented symmetries that once governed diurnal existence have been supplanted by parlous eruptions of hormonal caprice; the 'stock' is 'played out' (*DFT* p. 230) and locked into a historic loop of grotesque error – blighting its own offspring with 'vicious' Victorian 'refinements' (*CC* p. 45) in an ambience of crumbling luxury (Garrity, 2003; Foy, 2000, p. 83).

That Scylla's delineation of this 'country of the Sanc Grail' is inextricably intermingled with Arthurian romance signals Butts's keen responsiveness to the Cornish terrain around Tintagel which was, according to E. Havers Rutherford in 1926, 'the centre of his kingdom': 'the hard facts of history are clothed in the colours of old romance'. This country 'is geographically more vague than the ancient Kingdom of Wessex, which Hardy has brought out of the shadowy past' (Rutherford, 1926, p. 651). As Simon Trezise notes, Tintagel Castle may be partly construed as 'a monument to invention', especially the literary skills of the twelfth-century cleric, Geoffrey of Monmouth, who professed to have received the story from a Welsh book given to him by a fellow arch-deacon (Trezise, 2000, p. 65). In 1824, the poet Parson Robert Stephen Hawker (1803–1875), imitating a 'medieval' register, called the Holy Grail a 'Sangraal' and conceived Arthur in 'a specifically Cornish context', renaming Tintagel 'Dundagel'. He had, as Trezise explains, notable 'success' in putting his unique stamp on the 'legend' (p. 64). Alfred Lord Tennyson sought to exploit the poetic resonance of Hawker's 'version' of the name in his *Idylls of the King* and Hardy invokes it in his third published novel *A Pair of Blue Eyes* (1873), which depicts the topographical lineaments of West Cornwall (Trezise, 2000, p. 65).

Scylla's techniques as parish archivist and caretaker of a disappearing Dorset are more imaginatively promiscuous than what John Cowper Powys illustrates in *A Glastonbury Romance*. Scylla lauds the energizing and peerless superiority of the 'tribe' (*DFT* p. 252) not by focusing exclusively on the glorious public activities of men in the realm of national power and warfare. Rather she disinters women's unofficial and 'secret folk-knowledge' (*CC* p. 264) – tangible tokens of which are absent from the sepulchral 'museum' that repels the young Wizzie in Powys's *Maiden Castle*. As Richard Jefferies observed in 1867 when undertaking his own antiquarian endeavours, a complex and worthwhile history imbues 'the daily life' of those 'not distinguished as having performed' any role in a seamless story of dauntless masculine heroism (qtd. in Chandler, 1996, p. 21). Scylla herself, revolting against the male curator's so-called rational principles and scientific savvy, does 'not know how she knew' (*DFT* p. 300) about the subliminal fault-lines in women's undervalued and misconstrued private domestic lives. Scylla adumbrates a concept of historical 'truth' that is amenable to intensive, searching and self-referential critique. In this respect, her more gender-aware, formally experimental archive canvasses the meanings and long-term social effects of women's omission or erasure from an antiquarian tradition which invariably charts 'the dusty actualities of men' (*CC* p. 163). Scylla's 'summary' of an archaic megalithic culture surpasses 'terms of start and finish' (*CC* p. 264) as well as the taxonomic shortcomings of comparative folklorists; her corpus is within, yet simultaneously outside published documents. So her enterprise is a brash declaration of independence and resists ready classification; she gleefully stalls the glib, conclusive historical narrative by lauding fecund female unreason over settled forensic scrutiny, metaphysical trance over material remains, historically smothered cadences over illustrious public feats. Scylla's 'clairvoyance' outstrips the 'archaeology' (*CC* p. 264) which had reaped such abundant returns on the sites of ancient Mycenaean and Minoan shores in the final years of the nineteenth century (Hodgen, 1936, p. 117). In her intrepid pursuit of physical and visual contexts for biographical oral evidence 'the bizarre' becomes 'her hunting-ground' and 'the exotic her pack' (*DFT* p. 253).

In a journal entry for 1 October 1929, Butts posits that the crusading artist-seer, such as the 'stern young goddess' Scylla (*DFT* p. 252) or Olympias in *The Macedonian* whose 'passionate sureness [. . .] blew to tatters the decencies of thought' (1994, p. 18), is better placed to grasp the mythic mutuality of diverse traditions than James Frazer's school of comparative ethnography. '[A]s for our anthropologists – they will write up the facts of every belief in every quarter of the globe; but even the best of them, Frazer hardly, gives one the least idea, the least suggestion of the passion, the emotion that made men behave like that' (*Journals* p. 324). All truth about the past must be relative, and the only way to inscribe history is through 'a set of subjective tools and filters' (Stout, 2008, p. 3); so why shouldn't art 'take over the anthropologist's material' (*Journals* pp. 324–25)? Butts felt that this process was already under way in Naomi Mitchison's historical romance *The Corn King and Spring Queen* which she reviewed positively in 1931 as a 'story told in the setting of classic civilisation and a reconstruction of antique psychology and ways of life':

> To-day, because of archaeology and *The Golden Bough*, most of all because Hellenism has been a preoccupation with our race, there are promises that this kind of story telling, with its extraordinary possibilities, is coming into full use. (Butts, 'Antiquity', 1931, p. 137)

While she acknowledges *The Golden Bough* as a signal influence on her generation, Butts is deeply suspicious of Frazer's followers recording 'the facts' as a mode of imaginative imperialism that conveniently forgets how all raw data and values are subjective hypotheses determined by historical and cultural conditioning. The apparently neutral, fastidious and elegantly understated cadences of empirical analysis in *The Golden Bough*, which had sought to free its readership from the unwholesome strictures and narrow piety of a Christian creed, is itself an unwieldy weapon of disciplinary control. Through Scylla's expansive 'chronicle' of the Grail country Butts supplies an alternative lens through which to magnify the sedimented folds of Wessex history. The excavated artefacts located by Mortimer Wheeler and his team do not contain the same esoteric pleasures and politically subversive brio as the vague voices of 'trees and stones and turf' (*DFT* p. 300).

Scylla, the 'ash-fair tree-tall young woman' (*AWM* p. 12) and her uncanny 'translations' of the 'interminable conversations' of 'trees' (*AWM* p. 180), evokes Hardy's muted tribute to Marty South in *The Woodlanders*. Marty's quasi-mystical correspondence with her sheltered locale is figured in terms of how she 'reads' the 'hieroglyphs' of a 'wondrous world of sap and leaves' as if it were 'ordinary writing' (pp. 248–49). Although, in Butts's opinion, 'Christianity [. . .] had taken away from women their priestesshood' (*Journals* p. 422) Scylla, through her combination of rapt immersion and 'detached scrutiny' (*CC* p. 112), still has access to neglected topographical nooks – *Born to see strange sights, Things invisible* (*DFT* p. 224). This privilege stresses 'the equivocal nature of the contact between visible and invisible, the natural order and the supernatural' (*CC* p. 265). Scylla's gift partakes of, yet finally transcends, the artist Paul Nash's conception of 'Unseen Landscapes' as summarized in his 1938 article for *Country Life*: the regions he has in mind 'are not part of the unseen world in a psychic sense, nor are they part of the Unconscious. They belong to the world that lies, visibly, about us. They are unseen merely because they are not perceived; only in that way can they be regarded as invisible' (Nash, 1938, p. 526).

Given her ability to comprehend phantasmal presences, as well as to illustrate the subtle delicacy and fleeting variations of the Sacred Wood surrounding her home, Scylla overhauls the stale, male and musty image of the amateur antiquarian that Hardy lampoons in *A Pair of Blue Eyes* through Parson Swancourt, a character of mincing narrow-mindedness who slavishly traces lines of influence and descent. In her 1932 review 'This England' Butts deplores the type of 'county history reduced to guide-book size' which tells 'either too little or too much'. She upholds rather a 'hint of that personal point of view' which refuses to coerce the cumbersome mass of uncovered materials into classificatory crispness. Scylla's freewheeling verve, which treasures the legendary encrustations upon the 'true', may render history wildly 'inaccurate' and tendentious; yet also makes it eminently 'readable' and rewarding ('This England', 1932, p. 276). The versatile and combative Scylla attains what Butts construes as the most vital aspects of the bucolic chronicler: her 'style is pure evocation, as though, absent-mindedly' one 'were walking in and out of England's pasts' – mischievously improvising around investigative methodologies and consistencies of viewpoint:

> Scylla's chronicle had grown, story of a site, of a name on a grave, the lowdown [. . .] of a ghost, a family or a village; the story of what happened [. . .] in the nation-breeding doings, plain or secret, of part of an english shire. (*DFT* p. 301)

In this 'shire', Felicity's antecedents practised 'tribal hunting' (*DFT* p. 230) so as to defend English 'race-solidarity' (*DFT* p. 272). Scylla's preoccupation with the 'nation-breeding doings' of a secluded 'part' of Wessex (*DFT* p. 301) seems like petty provinciality or a veiled articulation of sectarian animus. Yet she recalibrates this myopic tendency to affirm traditional roots which reach back into an eerie past of spectral visitations ('the low-down' of a 'ghost'). She possesses that untrammelled mode of inquiry which, according to Butts in her 1932 review 'Rome', is most 'precious': awareness not of 'tombs, temples, palaces and great works of art or pride – not where they ended, but where they were begun and carried out. The places where the makers of a national tradition, its statesmen and artists and inventors and lovers lived before the world had got to hear about them – it is here that the inner knowledge of a land begins' (p. 254). This 'inner knowledge', emerging from modest beginnings, imbues Scylla's reaction to 'Stone End':

> At Stone End were there any more stories about the stone? It wasn't a devil's nine-pin. Archaeologists did not connect it with sacrifice or the sun. It was a local stone, the wrong kind really for Stonehenge. Nobody carved their names on it. It wasn't a tryst. It was just there, and the real village dodged away from it along the valley. It was said vaguely, to be unlucky. They said that it had brought about the ruin of the family who had lived in the tudor house. [. . .] she thought that just as some trees have character and personality, so also have rocks. If one has had time to know them, a very long time. (*DFT* p. 333)

The stubborn frigidity of this 'local stone', far removed from the stately and imposing glamour of 'temples' or 'palaces', piques Scylla's antiquarian imagination because of its primal ability to confuse and defy the scientific excavators who cannot ascertain the site's basic function or symbolic significance. Nor can the native population personalize or domesticate the shrine; because of its resemblance to a petrified archaic priest the 'real village' skirts around it nervously, all too aware of its malevolent potential. Like the Roman Ring in *The Mayor of Casterbridge*, no trysts take place in the vicinity. What strikes Scylla is the holy stone's formidable power of negation, its marked 'hostility to the warmth of reality' (Massingham, 1988, p. 47). To estimate its 'character', or whether it was ever associated with a strenuous faith that practised a cult of the dead, requires a commitment to haunted history: '[i]t is easy to gape at summaries of national existence, but one may go away stunned rather than enlightened; while for the actual understanding of its splendours, patience is necessary' (Butts, 'Rome', 1932c, p. 254).

With 'patience' and highly individualized excursions into the sphere of paranormal phenomena, Scylla pieces together the slivers of local lore which irradiate forsaken or traduced facets of 'national existence'. This 'story of high merit' (*DFT* p. 221) effectively reverses the historical actualities of 'an enormous' and irreparable 'loss' (*CC* p. 155) – a landed class betrayed, demoralized and dethroned by the chaotic forces of petit-bourgeois, 'urban culture' with its 'butcher-coloured scum of little houses' (*CC* p. 112). Against this detritus of the paltry, the transient and the superficial Scylla cherishes dialectal survivals which

> have a patina to them by which [. . .] to convey [. . .] familiarity, delight and something like profundity. Things said in their right order, which [. . .] is the receipt for story-telling. In this case the story of a stream, told in fragments, quotations from a parish register, an old song, the look of a tree, swans preening, a door that stared at [her], a place where it was good to pray. Fragments which some process of style has fused into one. [. . .] All about the dead, it is full of the sense of them, living, a quiet mysterious pottering in and out, a criss-cross of leaf-shade and bars of sunlight among ghosts. (Butts, 'This England', 1932d, p. 278)

Butts contrasts the 'scum' of standardized units of suburban housing, forming along recently laid arterial roads, with the countless generations of gentility that 'patina' implies, accrediting the venerable and the trinity of ethics, beauty and utility. Similarly, when Rudyard Kipling documents the artefacts discovered in the 'mud' while cleaning out an old pond as 'pearly with the patina of centuries' (Kipling, 1937, p. 186) he ordains the fathomless 'depth' and enduring rhythms of Nature against the inescapable dreariness and headlong rush of a mongrel modernity, epitomized by bourgeois day-trippers visiting the south coast via train, bus and motorcar. Butts measures the lichen-stained walls of remote farmhouses, with their inherent harmonies of hue, line and fitness to the turf, against the 'insipid' and flimsy crust of prefabricated bungalows: 'life that for ages lay on the hill-side, weathering [. . .] charged in some places with magic and always with wisdom' (*DFT* p. 302). As H. J. Massingham avers, the rustic homestead is not only an organic composition of frugality and grace, but also converts into a vernacular idiom 'the hidden history of the earth'; such a dwelling epitomizes 'a better handbook of geology than any printed text. It is not only a guide to the strata underlying it but an exposition of their qualities, texture, capacities and natural vegetation' (Massingham, 1988, p. 65). Butts's archaeological and philological 'dig' unearths a supernatural concord of time and space evidenced by the poignant ordinariness of tributes scratched into 'a parish register', to the 'profundity' of oracular incantation (things 'said in their right order'), as well as unimaginably ancient fragments 'outside our range' (*DFT* p. 170). The 'look of a tree', 'a door that stared' signifies an elliptical ripple across the bare solitudes of the 'shire', whose permutation of shape, curve and colour skirts, like Felicity Taverner herself, 'divine simplification' (*DFT* p. 187).

Scylla's exacting undertaking reflects the novel's puckish deployment of literary tropes and conventions synonymous with the contemporary craze for 'detective' fiction (*DFT* p. 221). Butts weaves around Felicity's disappearance an atypical country 'house-mystery' (*CC* p. 141), concerning 'a woman who was a miracle' – inspiring the other questing knights in their odyssey for an 'incalculable enlargement of human power' (*DFT* p. 200). To excavate fully the secret history of Wessex, Scylla must play the roving amateur sleuth; indeed as

O. G. S. Crawford averred in 1921, the 'practice of making deductions from material evidence is not peculiar to archaeology. It is the method of Sherlock Holmes, of the military intelligence officer and of the student of living primitive races' (1921, pp. 41–42). Scylla uncovers the circumstances surrounding Felicity's demise, given that her cousin personified the regal 'beauty of England' (*DFT* p. 285): 'the hills were her body laid-down, and "Felicity" was said, over and over again, in each bud and leaf' (*DFT* p. 191). Scylla pores over 'each bud and leaf' as if it were a crime scene, disclosing half-obliterated 'letters of earth and stone, of bank and ditch, of foliage and crop' (Randall, 1934, p. 5). This evocation prompts comparison with the former war artist Donald Maxwell's *A Detective in Kent: Landscape Clues to the Discovery of Lost Seas* (1929): the 'detection of crime by means of observation, deduction, and reconstruction of motive is a thing already built up into a science. That there could be such a thing as the science of reading landscape for the unravelling of its history has not occurred to very many' (qtd. in Hauser, 2007, p. 48). It does occur to Butts, however, who situates Scylla as a highly proficient 'reader' who divines the hidden events of regional lore and makes the mute traces speak because she accepts that 'there are depths beyond depths in the simplest scene' (Hoskins, 1949, p. vi). The brisk 'business' of an orthodox 1930s detective plot, such as Nicholas Blake's *A Question of Proof* (1935) and *Thou Shell of Death* (1936), is to 'bring order, proportion, light into what is happening. That where there has been falsehood and muddle, there shall be knowing and clearness' (*DFT* p. 254). Instead of deciphering and unpicking, with calm balanced lucidity, a tortuous tangle of family secrets, Butts's allegorical 'whodunit' (Buchanan, 2003, p. 380) offers 'equivocal' testimony, richly variegated yet full of intentional 'omissions' (*DFT* p. 168). Indeed she concludes with a 'version of the truth' (*DFT* p. 168) that is also enshrined in Scylla's antiquarian opus: data that can be critically examined as mutable, ever-shifting and prone to subtle indirections.

   Death of Felicity Taverner delineates a murder that must remain submerged, a sacrificial slaughter to dispel the contagion that menaces the 'sun-worked bases of the chalk downs' (*DFT* p. 312). The target of ritual sacrifice is a Russian Bolshevik Jew Nicholas Kralin, Felicity's spouse who hopes to overturn a culture of bloodlines and archaic inherited privilege by transmuting the elegant terraces of 'Taverner-land' into a dismal and derelict waste, or a 'public lavatory' (*DFT* p. 229); purchasing the surrounding land for a hotel, holiday bungalows and a golf course. In her review 'This England' Butts asks, '[h]ow far have we begun to breed a new type of man with a new type of consciousness, and, if we have, what is he like; and do we like him, and what will we do with him and he with us?' (1932, p. 276) She is referring specifically to the interwar hiker, but the unease also extends to the unabashedly dissolute Kralin, a 'mechanical evil' whose milieu of unlovely abstractions sharply contrasts with the lush images of unkempt profusion tied to Felicity's ghost.

   Like the sacred chalice in *Armed with Madness*, Felicity is a beguiling vacancy – a 'container' for others' repressed yearnings, thwarted ambitions and flickering intuitions. She is something 'other' than what 'she initially seems to be' (Garrity, 2003, p. 221; Foy, 2000, pp. 78–83). Indeed, Jane Garrity argues persuasively that the object that 'had been lost out of the world' (*AWM* p. 79) is Felicity herself, a 'metonymic Holy Grail' to the 'extent' that she is voiceless, submerged, inchoate; a permeable yet forceful symbol of regional pride (Garrity, 2003, p. 215). That Felicity personifies a Grail vessel is lent further resonance since her surname not only connotes 'one who keeps a tavern' but also one who drinks or partakes of 'intoxicating substances' (Wagstaff, 1995, p. 230). Through Felicity's 'passion' and 'death' we glimpse 'some uncharted place' which lies 'east of the sun, west of the moon' (*DFT* p. 181). According to Butts in 1933, the Grail is 'an incident, *a not yet exhausted event*, in the most secret, passionate and truthful part of the spiritual history of man' ('The sanc grail', p. 73; my italics). Just as gossip and malicious innuendo circulates about the circumstances surrounding Felicity's death so

> theories have arisen in which the Sword, the Lance, the Cup appear as vegetation spirits, as wish-fulfilments, as phalloi or as solar myths. While how many have attempted to explain why these objects [. . .] should continue to haunt men's souls, in a way at once matter-of-fact and infinitely remote, as though a star were at the same time a source of food. (Butts, 'The sanc grail', 1933i, p. 73)

Felicity is 'at once matter-of-fact and infinitely remote' – 'the shadow of a shade' according to Anne Armstrong's 1932 book review (p. 674). The making of this goddess involves a 'perception not easy to discuss for lack of terms', and even elaborate figurative strategies do not divulge the shrouded recesses of her being: '[i]f a crystal became a white narcissus, you'd have something like her' (*DFT*, p. 169).

Though Felicity embodies purity of perception and Taverner 'high-mindedness', it is through the 'impure', hybridized and dubious 'suburban' repertoire of genre fiction (detective yarn, espionage thriller, Gothic melodrama) that we glimpse the dead woman's mysteriously enigmatic, Grail-like temperament. According to the narrator, Felicity seemed to emerge 'out of Paradise' and comforted 'people who could not find their way [back] in' (*DFT* p. 180). What these 'clues' indicate is the sense of dexterous, hot-tempered multiplicity imbuing Butts's idea of 'the State of Girlhood' ('The girl through the ages', 1933, p. 110), as the spectral Felicity drifts between semantic categories without ever being trammelled by one oppressive 'frame', such as the image of glossy opulence that Felix conveys: 'it seemed as though great houses had been built to display her' (*DFT* p. 169).

Is Felicity an embellished spectacle, a 'miracle of grace' (*DFT* p. 217) and merciful 'guardian-angel' (*DFT* p. 277) who, though dead, evinces a compelling interest in the living; or a savage 'Errinys' (*DFT* p. 209) – the 'angry one' of Greek mythology, a chthonic deity grimly seeking retributive justice? Felicity

'was a woman made for a particular kind of love, a love that [. . .] [r]ecognises
no God with her for priestess' (*DFT* p. 188). Felicity's tendency to define and
dominate the 'frame', rather than vice versa 'celebrat[es] pride of race' (Butts,
'Hesiod', 1932a, p. 113) and forewarns those 'traitors' who would auction off
'the body' of Wessex 'to the Jews' (*DFT* p. 346).

Brutal Mystifications

As Patrick Wright argues, *Death of Felicity Taverner* is not merely 'innocent pastoral' drifting into 'unfortunate but occasional contact with unsavory attitudes';
rather the Jew is 'actively given a meaning which is culturally *necessary* to the
valued England which he contaminates' (1985, pp. 84–120). In other words,
'territorial nationalism' validates itself through the 'strangling' (*DFT* p. 346)
of that which assails it: namely the 'town-bred' fabricated man Kralin (*DFT*
pp. 302–303), the speculative capitalist who profits by acts of flagrant dissimula-
tion against the Taverners who aspire to be 'lovers of truth' (*DFT* p. 257). This
is borne out by Butts's strident emphasis on Kralin as a 'case history': washed up
on the Wessex coast from the 'under-tow of the world's tides', who speaks for
demonized social minorities 'of mixed or exiles' upbringing' (*DFT* p. 314). For
Butts, the 'secret of classical antiquity – Roman or Greek – is that at that period
men bred right' ('The grandeur of Rome', 1934, p. 119). Kralin subverts this
correct breeding since he is of 'fallen, uncertain or bastard origin', of 'no fixed
caste or situation' (*DFT* p. 314). Maren Tova Linett proposes that Butts's novel
is an 'extreme instance in modern British fiction' whose 'antisemitism is overt
and powerful': 'Jewishness for Butts represents an actively destructive force,
robbing rural England' of 'tradition' and innocence (Linett, 2007, pp. 82–83).

But 'rural England' does not have 'innocence' to start with in this portentous
narrative, given the manifold troubles which beset the Taverner clan: Adrian,
Felicity's egotistical brother has made 'a wilderness of his life' by 'cutting away'
his 'own roots' and discarding his 'mana-objects' (*DFT* p. 235). Julia Taverner is
guilty of 'malicious collusion with Kralin against her own daughter' by throwing
him 'a few Taverner scalps' (*DFT* p. 253) in 'appeasement' (Garrity, 2003, p. 222).
Armed with Madness construes the lack of 'fixed situation' as a piquant positive
among the nomadic Grail knights, eroding the rigidity of boundaries that
surround analytic categories of selfhood such as race, ethnicity and gender,
affirming their pliancy. Felicity and Scylla each personifies a dissident and
redemptive femininity that thrives on variability and unending fluctuation.[9]
Kralin, we might argue, is equally protean and 'inconclusive' (*DFT* p. 213); yet
it is one of the sequel's most glaring inconsistencies that his canny adaptability
and indolent swagger in a region to which he is foreign are presented solely in
terms of corrosive cynicism: 'Kralin governed his soul by refusing to admit even
immediate truth under any passionate form, to whom the soul's nakedness was
no more than one of a series of masks' (*DFT* p. 217). His legerdemain – recasting
sensuous local attachments as a studied cultural performance or carefully

rehearsed artifice – sickens Scylla and the other 'lovers of truth' (*DFT* p. 257). In their obsession with recognizing, recounting and construing the minute particularities of place – the 'nation-breeding doings' of only a 'modest part' of Wessex (*DFT* p. 301) – the Taverners cannot stomach fakery, subterfuge or 'imitations of anything' (*DFT* p. 301). The socio-economic historian William Cunningham's 1897 text *Alien Immigrants to England* contends that over time 'English sympathy for fugitive strangers had come to be deeply rooted and widely spread'. Reflecting on the recent influx of East European Jewish refugees and political exiles seeking a safe haven in Britain, Cunningham averred:

> The isolation of our country and the character of our people have been so marked, that we have been able to receive all sorts of strangers from abroad and to assimilate them; for they have not remained as separate elements, or only for a brief period, as the duration of cities and communities goes: they have been absorbed into our national life. (Cunningham, 1897, pp. 260, 270)

Death of Felicity Taverner reviles this 'liberal tradition' (Young, 2008, p. 175) by refusing to 'assimilate' Kralin into its coherent and patterned fictional milieu. For Butts, the Jew's profound indeterminacy operates as a 'new agony let loose in the world' (*DFT* p. 245); he is 'the opposite of those who carry the Sanc-Grail' (*CC* p. 105) given his ignoble association with a working-class mass democracy spreading across Western Europe in the fallout from the Bolshevik insurgency. For George Eliot, as for Butts, racial and cultural intermingling would be 'a calamity to the English', dissolving 'all sense of boundaries' and narrow 'limits' (Young, 2008, p. 179); the worst case scenario is to 'undergo a premature fusion with immigrants of alien blood' (Eliot, 1878, p.186). This is why the violent rite of purging at the novel's close is depicted as 'a bath, a purification' or a 'taking-back, in a profound sense, into caste' (*DFT* p. 229). *Death of Felicity Taverner* shows that 'Kralin is a Jew' (*DFT* p. 284) because of inescapably tainted 'blood'. Jane Garrity demonstrates that this portrayal of Kralin as a 'master in his vileness' (*DFT* p. 281) should be interpreted 'within the context of the early twentieth-century scientific discourse of racial anti-Semitism, which attributed the Jew's difference not to religious practice but to eternal and immutable hereditary characteristics' (Garrity, 2003, p. 226). Ian Patterson indicates that the iconography of anti-Semitism and anti-Bolshevism moulds many literary genres in the 1930s, from detective fiction to John Buchan's imperial romances, to the writings of Virginia Woolf (who like Butts had a Jewish husband). In Dorothy Richardson's *Pilgrimage*, Miriam castigates the 'Jew' Bernard Mendizabal as 'another of those foreigners who care for nothing in England' – a reaction that implies the racial and cultural integrity of her 'homeland' has been sullied by the 'infiltration' of sinister trespassers (1980, p. 343).

As the epitome of an 'untraditional part of humanity' who has emerged from the ranks of 'crooks, cranks' and 'criminals' (*DFT* p. 314), Kralin is determined to commercialize Wessex, cluttering the 'Sacred Wood' (*DFT* p. 359) with 'greasy papers' (*DFT* p. 343).[10] This financial adventurer has honed his skills of chicanery by absorbing 'abstractions of machinery, an abstract of the cerebral life of towns' (*DFT* p. 300). From the 'towns' Kralin has adopted the modish teachings and slick certainties of 'fashionable psychology' (*DFT* p. 246), though Butts herself is not above using these ostensibly trite and trivializing terms when depicting the complexes and repressions which beset the Taverner 'tribe'. To G. W. Stonier, 'Kralin is not so much a spoiling business man as that most powerful of adversaries – the genuine idealistic nihilist. He is out to destroy all positive ideals and emotions, any beauty or truth that has become sacred. He is, in short, a spirit of evil' (1933, pp. 133–34). That Butts employs the character of Kralin to illustrate a myth of capitalist modernity as externally imposed, conveniently occludes the fact that England, this 'exquisite part of the earth' (*DFT* p. 258) was 'the prototype industrial nation, the first state of the modern period' (Platt, 2001, p. 52).

In a novel that suggests at times a proto-fascist pastoral obsessed with 'unadulterated' citizenship, it is surprising that Butts shows the gay Russian refugee Boris (who also features in *Armed with Madness*) as conversant, like his antiquarian hostess Scylla, with the recondite lore of witch-doctoring. Since *Armed with Madness* remorselessly fixes the homosexual Clarence as a tormented 'stranger' unable to savour the 'ancient sap' and 'tang of living earth' (*CC* p. 205), we expect Boris to be a similarly 'lost' and nonplussed entity in 'very queer country' (*DFT* p. 247).[11] However, even the 'original bitch' Julia Taverner is struck by Boris's regal poise, as implied by her 'quotation' from Rudyard Kipling's poem 'The Ballad of East and West': 'he trod some kind of heather "like a buck in spring," and "looked like a lance"' (*DFT* p. 235). Picus employed Clarence's 'spear' to salvage the Grail cup from the unusable well in *Armed with Madness*; Boris in the later novel actually *personifies* the 'spear-touch' (*CC* p. 106), allowing him to 'raise' and propitiate 'the ghost of Felicity' (*DFT* p. 244). Whereas Clarence is denigrated because he fears Scylla's procreative sexuality, Boris, though an outsider from 'the remote east' (*AWM* p. 161) holds 'the key to some private [. . .] paradise' because he divines the acute 'intellectual passions' (*DFT* p. 252) of which Felicity is votary. Indeed, *Death of Felicity Taverner* goes to great lengths to illustrate 'the poet's quality' of 'finesse' in Boris (*DFT* pp. 233, 209), even though 'Kralin and he were partly of the same race' (*DFT* p. 284). Boris is of 'pure blood', a high-born 'country-house brat' (*AWM* p. 162) of irreproachable 'upbringing' (*DFT* p. 311) and alert to the 'ambience' of the 'magic ring' (*DFT* p. 232). Boris's grasp of the patrician English family's impotent fury at Kralin's 'evil version of the magic secret' – the 'formula of Not-Being' (*DFT* p. 242) – stems from an unshakable conviction that the lowly 'Jew' (*DFT* p. 217) has defiled his own well-appointed Russian heritage: 'These people's people had peddled fairings at the back-door of his chateau' (*DFT* p. 202).

Through the 'enchanted' Boris's 'intuitive speciality' (*DFT* p. 200), Wessex is effectively liberated from Kralin's pernicious influence. In her 1932 review 'This England' Butts asks, has 'any country-side' been 'described as England has been? Where have natural varieties been so dwelt on, distinguished [. . .]

and adored? What country has its Pan visible in such a variety of shapes, the god putting on one mask in Lincolnshire, another in Dorset [. . .] In most countries is the answer; but in what other lands are there such altars to him [. . .?]' (pp. 274–80) 'Taverner-land' boasts an array of such 'altars', and lends the image of Felix's alternative 'map' of Dorset an especial force:

> [Scylla] told Boris what they had been doing, the enquiries they had made among the estate agents, and the map Felix had drawn to show exactly what part of the downs and the valley Kralin intended to buy. He had bought nothing yet, but Felix's map of his intentions showed their world nearly all gone red, and for the names of old bee-pastures, the words 'golf-links', 'bungalows' and 'shops'. (*DFT* p. 337)

Kralin, the Taverners' 'Nemesis' (*DFT* p. 319), has vampiric lineaments ('an unspeakable face, with cheeks drawn in, and his teeth sticking out below his lip' [*DFT* p. 316]), and his commercial empire will turn the lush green world blood 'red'. Boris suspects Kralin to be a 'Red agent' (*DFT* p. 314) and Felix's 'map' implies the sheer 'terror' of a Bolshevik conspiracy, 'running in and out of Europe's cities' and carrying its 'small iced wind' into Wessex (*DFT* p. 316). Boris, the victim of a Red Revolution in his own natal district, becomes the unlikely guardian of and worshipper at the threatened shrines of Scylla's Sacred Wood. Though an opportunistic 'outlaw' (*DFT* p. 271) in this eerily becalmed territory, and believing himself free of 'antisemitic' prejudice ('pogroms in theory he abhorred' [*DFT* p. 312]) he nevertheless devises and prosecutes the racial purging of 'Hardy's country' and rehabilitates the Taverners' 'whole family history' (*DFT* p. 350).

Boris safeguards the 'right formality' of 'a national tradition' by willingly playing 'executioner' (*DFT* p. 358): he entices Kralin to a 'secret place' boasting 'a small cove which the cliffs hide' (*DFT* p. 353). Here is a tide-bound grotto that Boris claims could be transformed into a tourist trap, so piquing Kralin's 'profitless desire for cash' (*DFT* p. 186). If Felicity haunts this lonely tomb as womb, then it is to show that the earth-goddess, in addition to providing succour to her stalwart devotees, also exacts a gruesome revenge upon those who 'wound and torture and bleed her to death' (*DFT* p. 171). Boris's ritualistic slaying of Kralin enables the Taverners' threadbare reputation, and more importantly their largely unvisited 'piece of pure pastoral' (*DFT* p. 354) to endure. Although Julia wrongly accused the young Felicity of being vulgar, vicious and 'dirty at home' (*DFT* p. 321), it is Kralin who is 'a dirty piece of work' (*DFT* p. 345) and so prompts Boris's 'ethnic cleansing' of the estate. This resolution punctures the traditional country-house mystery plot with mordant gusto. Instead of depicting how 'things which are hid are fated to become known' (*GR* p. 192) through the painstaking exercise of inductive acuity, Butts shows the concealment of a corpse by a figure who forswears the 'ferocious reasoning' (*DFT* p. 241) and chilly 'abstraction' of Kralin's inner-city 'curse'

(*DFT* p. 302) in favour of a visceral re-staging of primeval 'ritual' (Garrity, 2003, p. 229). The denouement to this idiosyncratic 'detective story of high merit' (*DFT* p. 221) offers a 'transaction' on another plane of existence, which operates as a cultural disincentive to 'town-bred' speculators (*DFT* p. 303).

Scylla Taverner in *Armed with Madness* and Felicity each face a ceremonial martyrdom: '[i]t was as if it had been decided on' that they were 'to be crucified' (*DFT* p. 226). However, unlike the brutally unjust 'sacrifice' of Tess Durbeyfield in Hardy's novel, the crucifixion narrative in Butts's imaginative scheme does not deliver the death-stroke to any lingering pagan mythology, such as veneration of 'Good mother-magic' (*DFT* p. 309). In explicating 'the antiquities' of her 'native land' (*DFT* p. 235), Butts wishes to 're-enter greek religion & carry on where Jane Harrison left off' (*Journals* p. 346). Roslyn Reso Foy affirms Butts's 'search for an authentic divine heritage that she believed lived within' (Foy, 1998, p. 183) the 'intelligent gentry of England' (*CC* p. 183). Yet Butts's art, so insouciant in arrogating 'the anthropologist's material', finesses an oppositional polemic, a feverish 'house-saga' (*DFT* p. 168) reliant upon prohibitive and Anti-Semitic categories of Englishness.

In the closing pages of her memoir *The Crystal Cabinet*, Butts mulls over that quality which in her 'blood' and her 'training' came out of 'the very stuff of England'. Her conviction is that local customs and cults represent a form of private property, 'spiritual specialities' (*DFT* p. 296) which are 'inviolate' (*CC* p. 262). This is far from the 'discovery of a transcendent power' that Christopher Wagstaff locates in her oeuvre, 'underlying and unifying the plurality of psyches, attitudes and egos encountered in everyday life' (Wagstaff, 1995, p. xii). Butts's paranoid conception of Wessex is all the more unsettling when set against her historical novel *The Macedonian*, in which Alexander receives a vision of the Holy Spirit, prompting him to imagine a dazzling cross-pollination of races, creeds and social codes: 'He wants to make the earth and its various peoples plastic, interpenetrated, one with the other, capable of exchange of resources and excellences' (p. 104). Butts's sacred geography of Wessex, in which past and present mysteriously interpenetrate, is by contrast a 'forbidden thing', or 'only allowed under the utmost safeguards' (*CC* p. 194) to those who exalt it as revealed faith rather than as empirical proof. Her 'knowledge of house and breed' (*CC* p. 262), evinces what is 'unpurchasable' and 'untouchable' in her brave Grail knights (*DFT* p. 254). Ultimately, her 'obscurities of personality' (*CC* p. 259) are grounded in a hostile formulation of Anglo-Saxon pride and bygone benisons which stigmatizes the curious 'outsider' (*AWM* p. 115) as the harbinger of ecological and spiritual infection, bringing with him 'pockets of poisoned air' (*DFT* p. 225). Such sectarian rancour chafes against, and obviates Butts's lively interest in a national terrain which discloses potentially reconciling symbols of 'deep-buried race memories' (*GR* p. 93) – the seedbed of a common culture replete with personal and political resonances.

Chapter 6

Conclusion

One part of 'Country' is an appreciation of a remote part of England – remote in the sense that no one knows anything about it. A place that is a small complete country in itself. (There are many such. Near here lies a few miles of hill and moor as whole, as unknown, as strange as anything at the Antipodes. A pocket of earth, complete image in itself of some idea in the divine Mind.)
(Butts, 'Review of H.J. Massingham's *Country*', 1934d, p. 189)

A 'small complete country in itself': this is Wessex as covert and prized possession, a magically charged 'pocket of earth', that Mary Butts discerns in Thomas Hardy's fiction, and of which she speaks with prejudiced pride. *The Return of the Native* and *The Mayor of Casterbridge* are both shaped by Hardy's personal obsession with the mysteries and challenges linked to the provenance of religion, and the genetic relationship of that institution to aesthetic experimentation, language, myth, matrimony and philosophy. By focusing on E. B. Tylor's doctrine of 'survivals', as well as the anthropological motif of the infiltration of communities from the outside, Hardy canvasses with especial intensity the notion of refurbishing a lost collective identity. His readiness to conjure the threadbare remnants of time – ranging from concrete Neolithic landmarks such as Maumbury Ring to the ancestral estate crusted with centuries of domestic discord – expresses an abiding interest in remaking the parochial past; rendering it coterminous with the modern moment as well as a foretaste of the future. Even when the novels show that the cultural construction of place is tied to images of moribund or tainted relics, Hardy savours the incongruities which arise from a persistent focus on the overlapping strata of Wessex history. The 'survivals' modify his viewpoint of contemporary manners and he encourages his audience to extract the multifaceted connotations of the bizarrely comic juxtapositions which result.

Hardy often registers the presence of the past with a cagey ambivalence of tone, querying the utility of fossil fragments that belong to a forgotten yesterday. By contrast, Richard Jefferies in *The Story of My Heart* articulates a fierce commitment to an atavistic actuality which might solace victims of the jaded, listless disarray that, he avers, is synonymous with metropolitan modernity. Jefferies openly declares his lack of faith in the 'science[s] of modern times'

(*SH* p. 85) – the very intellectual disciplines that had made the antique and the arcane vivid and enticing to a late-Victorian readership. Jefferies is withering about the efficacy of anthropological dogma to surmount the historical record's glaring gaps, and to push back dated scrutiny to an earlier epoch for which other documentary clues were rare, too mangled or simply nonexistent. Instead, Jefferies favours the cultivation of 'soul-life' which invites detailed comparison with Hardy's perception of animistic Wessex soil and the pathetic fallacy in *The Return of the Native*. In order to arrive at a fuller picture of the pasts imbuing his Wiltshire homeland in *The Story of My Heart*, Jefferies must temper, even 'exorcise' his own once enthralled and avid interest in antiquarian and ethnographic discourses. As his dystopian fable *After London* demonstrates, with its innovative deployment of the 'scientific imagination', such an exorcism is impossible for him to attain. *After London* is keenly alert to the mystical possibilities of sites such as the White Horse Vale and Stonehenge.

Stonehenge also looms large in the early chapters of John Cowper Powys's *A Glastonbury Romance*. Like Jefferies and Hardy, Powys makes Wessex 'novel' again by revisiting imaginatively the loci of purported historical and cultural beginnings. In *A Glastonbury Romance* it is the notion of an arduous Grail quest that grounds the various antiquarian enquiries of this intricately plotted narrative; in *Maiden Castle*, Powys radically rewrites *The Mayor of Casterbridge*, to indicate how a prehistoric earthwork triggers startling, even life-changing, 'intensity of vision' (*AR* p. 116). Powys is notoriously difficult to 'pin down' and we look in vain for a coherent or programmatic perspective on the Grail and the recondite energies emanating from Mai-Dun; this is his notable strength as he permits vexed interpretations of heroic histories and cultural legacies to proliferate. Mary Butts mobilizes her archaeological passion for a more monolithic purpose: she retools the religious discourses of election and predestination, sacrifice and redemption to position her chosen few as fearsome exemplars of inbred distinction and genetic descent. Indeed, her 'anti-modern modernism' (Matless, 2008, p. 336) is a far cry from Powys's often puckish delight in protean inconsistencies and quietly humane awareness of the motley pilgrims and interlopers who flock to the ancient shrine of Glastonbury.

Mary Butts, focusing chiefly upon interpersonal and anthropological relationships, is entranced by how 'life' conceals 'something at the bottom of the [Grail] cup' (*AR* p. 104). Her *Taverner Novels* supply an idiosyncratic assessment of a salvaged artefact – the 'symbol of the very condition of symbol-making' (Duncan, 2003, p. 90) – which carries a range of resonances concerning the 'family's good name' (*AR* p. 107), sexuality, race and ethnicity. On a cursory reading it appears she is motivated by the same facet of Grail lore as Powys: the recovery of a chalice whose capacity to evade crisp classification is boundless. This enterprise is part of Butts's 'science of mysticism' (*Journals* pp. 131–33) whose nurturing 'potency' (*AR* p. 104) is underpinned by her fascination with the Cambridge Ritualists. Butts's *Journals* hail Jane Ellen Harrison's ability to conceptualize the shadowy past not as inaccessibly alien, but rather as a vibrant actuality which bolsters urgent personal and cultural imperatives, lending sobering gravitas 'to a new form of society' (*AR* p. 103). The 'primitive', for acolytes of Frazer and Freud, signified a volatile force menacing to diurnal routine and which 'still lay stratigraphically embedded in the human psyche' (Stout, 2008, p. 106). Butts *re-brands* the primitive by finessing Harrison's thesis that the female fertility figure, or 'enchantress' (*AR* p. 6) possesses 'values pure' (*AR* p. 100); these qualities resist the dreariest repercussions of the matrimonial contract, with its alteration in property rights and the status of women (Garrity, 2003). Butts's figure of mutinous ambition and 'adorable courage' (*AR* p. 94) prompts us to unpick normative national myths and the exact location of authority in advanced culture. The priestess, in her tireless 'search for the Grail' (*Journals* p. 264), unmoors the clan from the stuffy conception that patriarchal family mores should be universally construed as the undying and fixed foundation of civil society.

In order to validate her vision of a 'great goddess', the 'type of all things which a woman is or may become' (*AR* p. 13), Butts refines an increasingly strident rhetoric that stresses discernible social differences and a deterministic credo of 'blood' immune to comparative scrutiny or logical criticism. In the 1930s Mortimer Wheeler stressed the educative function of archaeology which promulgates

> a new, and, in our crowded land, much needed respect for the traditions which, in one form or another, make up so much of the fabric and beauty of the English landscape. Archaeology, in this applied sense, then becomes something more than a science or a cultural luxury; it takes upon itself incidentally a steadying social function which is not negligible in these days of easy destruction. (Qtd. in Stout, 2008, p. 228)

In Butts's writing the growing public fascination with Wheeler's excavations was the very antithesis of 'steadying'. Partisan and divisive chauvinism infuses her rendering of a liberal, rational yet profoundly placeless 'democratic enemy' that wages a war of attrition against dynastic defenders of numinous geography. The obscure ceremonials of a propertied elite outstrip 'conventional hocus pocus' (*AR* p. 13) and 'dilettante devil-worship' (*AR* p. 137) by punctiliously managing historical memory. Richard Jefferies's idea, in *The Gamekeeper at Home*, of nondescript 'roughs from the towns', delighted 'at the chance of penetrating into the secret recesses of woods' (Jefferies, 1978, p. 41) presages Butts's regression to a resentful and hectoring tribalism that vetoes any dissent, brooks few qualms and certifies a family saga by mandating racial uniformity over disciplined variety or daunting complexity.

Through the retrieval of the jade vessel in *Armed with Madness* she shows an artefact which epitomizes not only the down-land turf's natural plenitude and human culture's inherited wealth but also a spiritual and moral charisma that divulges an abiding abhorrence of the trespasser. In *A Glastonbury Romance*

John Crow wonders 'if there were some residual secret of human experience' that the Grail's rooted mythology discloses; he concludes it is 'human imperfection' (*GR* p. 507) for which the holy chalice allows. However, the highly defined and distinctly powerful aesthetic of Mary Butts extirpates 'imperfections', symbolized by the myopic sentimentality of interlopers and the tacky paraphernalia of cultural tourism. She remakes herself as the exclusively ordained and irreducibly unique guardian of the 'maternalized primitive' (Garrity, 2003, pp. 188–241); her encrypted catechism, '[s]ecret wisdom laughing in its sleeve' (*AR* p. 174), actuates 'the lost dimension' of history in 'an environment apparently bent on' excising it altogether (Hauser, 2007, p. 199). Indeed Butts's selective myth of ethno-cultural provenance and 'sturdy feudal tradition' (1994, p. 19) is tied to an imaginary Wessex of elemental fastness in which 'social stratification is as comfortable, and as time-tested, as its archaeological and historical strata' (Hauser, 2007, p. 203). The policing of this exalted district, coded as a 'quintessence of privacy' (*AR* p. 9), sanctions outbursts of bellicose bigotry and xenophobia against 'outsider[s]' (*AR* p. 109) whose outlook is doggedly anti-archaeological; revelling in the evanescent, the shallow and the makeshift. Mary Butts reprograms primitive vegetation rituals to reinforce rather than reconcile racial difference; where individuals 'of solid worth are permitted to despise the vulgar' day-trippers who abrade ancient Roman roads and despoil the natural accretions of time they claim to revere in the 'sacred south' (*GR* p. 507). Ultimately, her commemorative campaign, with its want of 'redeeming humour' (Kalnins, 2004, p. 331) and hierarchical creed of patrician links revamped as mystical largesse, is fatally weakened by a 'crude theory of eugenics' (*AR* p. 86) as well as a failure to decouple the paranoid from the parochial.

Notes

Chapter 1

1 John Cowper Powys's 'Wessex Novels' are *Wood and Stone* (1915); *Ducdame* (1925); *Wolf Solent* (1929); *A Glastonbury Romance* (1933); *Weymouth Sands* (1934); and *Maiden Castle* (1936).

2 Of the recent studies on Butts's fictional and autobiographical writings, Jane Garrity's is the most thoroughly attuned to how *Armed with Madness* and *Death of Felicity Taverner* seek 'to overhaul legalistic or legislative entitlement to cultural inheritance' with a 'mystical ownership' of Wessex, one that provides a 'racial' link between the initiated daughter's 'Saxon sturdiness of blood' and England's stratified geographical heritage. Because of their 'metonymic relation' to, and rapt communion with, the elemental rhythms of a south Dorset locale, Butts's female fertility figures, all descendants of eugenic design, not only have 'natural' rights of inheritance to this time-crusted terrain, but that the spiritual and material wellbeing of 'the nation' is furthered through their 'heroic agency' (Garrity, 2003, pp. 188–241).

Chapter 2

1 Kevin Z. Moore's resourceful reading of this pivotal scene demonstrates Fitzpiers's 'blindness' to the 'virulence' of the elm-tree totem which 'inadvertently kills' Old South. In this scheme, Fitzpiers exists 'in ironic relation' to his own provenance as 'a member' of an 'ancient local family' whose name is associated with 'the most traditional of English trees': the Fitzpierses of Oakbury-Fitzpiers (Bate, 1999, p. 553). His 'determined rationality', as well as decadent aestheticism 'supersedes tradition' and demands the inauguration of a fresh method of doing things: the worthless 'lumber' of 'old faiths' that have fallen into pernicious 'superstition' must be 'cleared away' (Moore, 1990, pp. 107–59). Indeed, Fitzpiers's capacity for 'woodland enjoyment and appreciation' stems from the 'established difference' between himself and those he observes. He 'dreads and avoids any familiarity' with the woods, which he finds alternately either 'revolting or stultifying' (Moore, 1990, pp. 113–27). It is appropriate that this figure should marry Grace Melbury, a 'sentimental tourist' in her own homeland. Fitzpiers is also a 'sensation-seeking tourist' who effectively 'kills off' what he should conserve by his 'excessive reasoning' upon the intricate 'mechanisms' and 'agencies' of the aberrant, the 'inspirational' and the 'irrational' (Moore, 1990, p. 112–25). 'By having the tree removed', Moore contends, 'Fitzpiers "modernizes" South's

view by showing him the very vacancy he has sought to conceal. [. . .] When the object of his affection' is felled, the 'startling appearance of the vacant sky fills him with the very horror of disconnection he has been at pains to repress in and through a romantic fantasy. [. . .] It is not an increment of independence he achieves by his resolution to worship the tree, but rather an intensified dependency' which leads to the erosion 'of his entire woodland line of descent' (Moore, 1990, pp. 118–20). Moore's analysis of Old South's arborial paranoia positions *The Woodlanders* as a chronicle of 'romantic severance' in which 'Nurse Nature' no longer has the capacity to 'heal a wounded spirit'. Old South 'is alienated from his life-supporting woodland labour, and, ultimately, from his life in the Hintock community because of his fixation'. Indeed, the felling of the totem-elm enacts the notion of 'dissociating traditional affiliation' and the 'institution' of 'artificial liaisons in their place'. This narrative arc begins with Barber Percomb's cutting of Marty South's 'chestnut hair' which is swiftly converted into a 'saleable artefact' to protect Mrs Charmond from the withering effects of age – the daughter 'tempted by material necessity' to vend her 'natural adornment' to 'support an ailing parent' (Moore, 1990, pp. 113–25).

Chapter 3

¹ Gideon Mantell was among the most popular geological lecturers in Victorian England. His major books on earth science include *The Fossils of the South Downs* (1822), *Illustrations of the Geology of Sussex* (1827), *The Geology of the South-East of England* (1833), *The Wonders of Geology* (1838), *Medals of Creation* (1844), and *Petrifactions and Their Teachings* (1851).

Chapter 4

¹ Malcolm Jones explicates the reference to a picture of 'Nobody' in Shakespeare's *The Tempest* (3.2. 124), which alludes to a grotesquely comic 'joke picture' popular in 'the first decade of the seventeenth century': 'A pun available only in English, this Nobody is depicted with *no body*, i.e. as a head on legs'. See Jones (2002, p. 357).
² I am greatly indebted to W. J. Keith's detailed analysis of this archaeological context; especially his insights into how *Maiden Castle* weaves into its imaginative fabric the rival hypotheses of Mortimer Wheeler and H. J. Massingham.

Chapter 5

¹ See Metcalfe (1998). On 'the uncanny power of Mr. Metcalfe's short stories' see Hartley (1928).
² Jane Garrity's *Step-Daughters of England* presents a convincing case for how 'mana' – what Harrison called an 'unseen power lying behind the visible universe' (1962, p. 68) – carries unmistakable 'connotations' of 'heterosexual

propriety' in Butts's fictional framework. Garrity notes that in *Armed with Madness* the concept is invoked 'three times': by Ross, who alludes to 'the law of kinds' by thinking of 'the brickness of a brick' (*AWM* p. 92); and twice by Scylla, whose remarks 'recall Butts's conservatism on the issue elsewhere' (Garrity, 2003, p. 214). 'Scylla's first reference to the law of kinds alludes to heterosexuality by invoking the notion of gender opposition' (Garrity, 2003, p. 214): 'Chaucer who loved everything for what it was. A sword for being a sword, or a horse. And they for what they were, the "gentle girls and boys"' (*AWM* p. 68). This reference recalls Butts's childhood memory of 'handling rare and delicate things' in *The Crystal Cabinet*: 'A joy of the senses [. . .] their life communicating itself as Chaucer says, "accordynge to its kynde"' (*CC* p. 156). Scylla's second allusion simply 'reiterates the essence of what mana is': 'Each thing *accordynge to its* kynde' (*AWM* p. 69) which Aristotle also explicates in *The Macedonian*: 'the qualities that are in one thing and not in another, and how each thing has the virtue proper to it, according to its kind' (Butts, 1994, p. 12). Scylla's two observations 'immediately follow her sexual encounter with Picus under Gault Cliff' (Garrity, 2003, p. 214), an 'interlude' described as being 'as much of a creation as any growth in nature' (*AWM* p. 68). See also Bilsing (2005, p. 61); Blaser (1995, pp. 159–221); Foy (2000, pp. 65–67).

3   Concerning the rhetorical manoeuvres by which Butts 'hypostatises' the link between patrician lineage 'sanctioned by myth' and numinous 'geography' see Garrity (2003, pp. 188–241); Foy (2000, pp. 51–71); Blaser (1995, pp. 159–88). Both Garrity and Foy explore in detail how Butts's heroines are versions of 'the redemptive earth goddess', even figures of 'genealogical and national continuation' (Foy, 2000, p. 86); implying an essentialized conception of the female body as a wellspring of racial replenishment. Olympias from *The Macedonian* and Cleopatra are other signal examples of Butts's 'biologically determined' protagonists who operate as 'dynastic defender[s]' (Armstrong, 2005, p. 76). See also Bilsing (2005, pp. 61–73); Foy (1998, pp. 183–191); Gariepy (1988, pp. 69–109); Garrity (2003, p. 191); Rives (2005, pp. 607–27).

4   Ian Patterson demonstrates that Butts's 'natural aristocracy' of female fertility figures, who all claim robust ancestral ties to a rustic retreat which is both motherland and plentiful spiritual archive, also underpins the aesthetic of W. B. Yeats, for whom the imaginative and bucolic domains are 'closely correspondent', rather than simply 'analogical or parallel'. Yeats's figure of 'instrumental consumption', according to Patterson, as the 'type' of all those haplessly ensnared in 'the cycles of commodity capitalism', reveals a notable cluster of concerns imbuing the *Taverner Novels* (Patterson, 2001, pp. 183–90).

5   Clarence's status as a shell-shocked non-Caucasian, consumed by 'gay self-hatred' (Rainey, 1998, p. 16), throws into high relief the quasi-crucifixion episode in *Armed with Madness*. The loss of 'his set-piece' and 'jewel' (*AWM* p. 87) Picus to Scylla reduces Clarence to a jealous and vindictive frenzy (*AWM* p. 128). He strikes Scylla with a stone flint and ties her to a clay statue of her beau, then ritualistically pierces her with crude arrows and nearly kills her (Garrity, 2003, pp. 212–14; Rainey, 1998, p. 16). The terms in which this pitiless act is couched highlights, according to Garrity, Scylla's riddling status as 'eroticised spectacle', her body 'indistinguishable' from the greenish clay statue pricked with white feathers that Clarence has moulded (Garrity, 2003, p. 212): '[An arrow] ripped

the skin on her shoulder and entered the clay' (*AWM*, p. 145). The critic Robin Blaser also canvasses whether this 'quasi-crucifixion' of a fertility deity shows Butts prioritizing the close affiliations between the 'mystic primordial state' and the unguarded rapture of the 'artist's sensibility', which creates 'a graph of life in its sequences' (*Journals* p. 300). Jane Ellen Harrison explicates this link when she contends that aesthetic experiment, like ceremonial observance, harnesses arcane and fitful emotional promptings (Blaser, 1995, pp. 219–23). This would situate Scylla as hazardous contaminant and Clarence the saintly and virtuous agent of redemptive release, a view lent credibility given the ominous Homeric and 'mythic associations of her Christian name'. But Clarence is actually the tortured malefactor for seeking her 'expulsion' (Garrity, 2003, pp. 210–13). Butts maintains in her preservationist pamphlet *Warning to Hikers* that these rites occasionally manifest imbecilic illogic, even profound 'ill-health of the soul'. That Clarence is decried as 'a martyred ass' (*AWM* p. 24) intimates his acute vulnerability to the psychic 'grinding and tearing' (*AWM* p. 129) of atavistic derangement and sadistic cruelty (Garrity, 2003, pp. 212–14). On the significance of 'ritual martyrdom' in Butts's oeuvre and how it unflinchingly confronts an 'order which exists outside subjective time and space' see also Foy (2000, p. 9); Barbara Wagstaff (1995, p. 224–42).

6 For a more positive reading of Clarence's role, which complicates his supposed status as luckless 'outsider or scapegoat for racist reasons', see Anderson (2007, pp. 245–56).

7 Ian Patterson highlights that Kralin's name not only evokes 'Stalin' but also suggests the 'proletarianized mass democracy' *crawling* across the borders of Western Europe in the 'chaotic aftermath' of the Russian Revolution. Kralin is not merely 'coded' as the emissary of demonized 'Jewish entrepreneurship' or some 'covert conspiracy' (Garrity 2003): this metropolitan blackmailer is a 'shapeless entity' and 'limitlessly self-interested' (Patterson, 1998, pp. 126–40). To the Taverners 'Kralin becomes a murderer' because he is incapable of appreciating Felicity or her land (T. M., 1932, p. 7). Patrick Wright argues that the 'preservation of rural England' depends upon the 'murder' of the Jew, an act that Boris carries out with 'grim satisfaction' (Wright, 1996, pp. 88–9). Wright proposes that Kralin is 'to an extent formed after the image of John Rodker, the Jewish writer and leftist publisher who was also the father' of Butts's daughter (Wright, 1985, p. 123). On Kralin as 'a mana-less product' of 'a new agony let loose in the world' (*DFT* p. 245) see Garrity (2003, pp. 225–34); Linett (2007, p. 82); Rose (1999, p. 84); Barbara Wagstaff (1995, p. 238).

8 On the symbolism of the Taverner coat-of-arms as an image of 'gruesome self-devouring' and, more crucially, as a scalding insight into the 'psychopathologies' of the 'hereditary alliance' see Garrity (2003, pp. 215–24).

9 As Jane Garrity contends, because *Armed with Madness* 'is a series of shifting erotic triangulations (Picus-Clarence-Scylla; Scylla-Lydia-Philip; Carston-Picus-Scylla; Felix-Boris-Ross), it is difficult to enshrine any dyad as definitively stable' (2003, p. 214). See also Buchanan (2003, pp. 360–88).

10 See Blaser (1995, pp. 220–22); Foy (2000, pp. 6–9); Garrity (2003, pp. 226–30); Patterson (1998, pp. 128–36).

11 Recent commentary on Butts's oeuvre has interrogated the 'queer miracle' (*DFT* p. 336) of Boris Polteratsky's apparent readiness to offset Kralin's 'crass

commercialism' (Foy, 2000, p. 83). That a gay Anglophile Russian émigré should assume the mantle of 'determined, ruthless soldier' (Barbara Wagstaff, 1995, p. 239), protecting the Taverners' 'quiet land-cup with its sacred wood' (Barbara Wagstaff, 1995, p. 236) from the deleterious schemes of his fellow countryman seems at odds with the novel's shrill insistence upon indigenous English roots (Garrity, 2003, p. 231). Whereas the homosexual in *Armed with Madness* is sketched as a ghoulish threat to the novel's validation of reproductive splendour, Boris does not permit his own predilections to dilute or derail Felicity's 'mother-magic' (*DFT* p. 309). He pledges to save the Taverners by joining their 'magic ring' (*DFT* p. 232), effecting a timely 'katharsis' (*DFT* p. 198) which expunges the 'Grey Thing' of Kralin from the sumptuous green milieu of south Dorset (Garrity, 2003, p. 230). Boris 'succumbs' to what he believes is 'the sincerity of the Taverners' (Foy, 2000, p. 83), thus underwriting Jane Harrison's concept of matriarchy as the deep respect for tribal togetherness, ritual ceremony, racial pride and its continuance. Boris's actions illustrate how 'the seekers find the Grail – but only within a material category, the land and the local pattern of culture which is preserved being merely a representation of Felicity herself' (Adeane, 1951, p. 26). Like the Taverners, Boris has been unjustly severed from his own ancestral clan; and he 'blames' Kralin's rapacious 'Jewishness' for this 'dispossession' (Garrity, 2003, pp. 215–34). Butts indicates that during his 13 years of drifting around the major capitals of Western Europe, penniless and disconsolate, in search of the next fleeting frisson – a 'pilgrimage to nowhere' (*DFT* p. 304) – it is Boris's 'blood' and 'scrupulous' rearing which 'had kept him alive' (*DFT* p. 311). On this character's marked and intriguing 'similarities' to his gay forerunner (also named Boris) in Butts's epistolary novella *Imaginary Letters*, who 'claims patrician and hieratic descent', see Garrity (2006b, pp. 233–51).

Bibliography

Abdoo, Sherlyn (1984), 'Woman as grail in T.S. Eliot's *The Waste Land*', *Centennial Review*, vol. 28, 48–60.

Adeane, Louis (1951), 'Mary Butts', *World Review: New Series*, vol. 33, 23–27.

Allen, Grant (1885), 'Review of *After London; or Wild England*', *The Academy*, vol. 676, 271.

Allen, J. Romilly (1884), 'The past, present, and future of archaeology', *Archaeologia Cambrensis*, vol. 1, no. 3, 240.

Anderson, Elizabeth (2007), '"The knight's move": fluidity of identity and meaning in Mary Butts's *Armed with Madness*', *Women: A Cultural Review*, vol. 18, no. 3, 245–56.

[Anon] (1865), 'Archaeological institute', *Gentleman's Magazine*, vol. 2, 199.

— (1866a), 'Archaic anthropology', *The Reader*, vol. 7, no. 203, 941.

— (1905), 'Book review – *After London*', *Saturday Review*, no. 1751, 1237.

— (1885a), 'Chronicles of English counties: Dorset', *All the Year Round*, vol. 36, 352.

— (1868a), 'Dust', *The Quiver*, vol. 3, no. 144, 630.

— (1866b), 'Dust ho!', *Good Words*, vol. 7, 645.

— (1909a), 'Earthwork of England', *Dublin Review*, no. 144, 404.

— (1893a), 'Excavations in Bokerly Dyke and Wansdyke', *Archaeologia Cambrensis*, vol. 10, no. 37, 73.

— (1878), 'The gamekeeper at home', *Saturday Review*, vol. 46, 187–88.

— (1856), 'The geological observer', *London Quarterly Review*, vol. 7, no. 13, 71.

— (1869a), 'Geological time', *North British Review*, vol. 50, no. 100, 406.

— (1871a), 'Good-bye to Wessex', *London Society: An Illustrated Magazine of Light and Amusing Literature for the Hours of Relaxation*, vol. 19, no. 112, 354.

— (1880a), 'A hedgerow philosopher', *The Examiner*, no. 3787, 1022–23.

— (1871b), 'History and biography', *Westminster Review*, vol. 40, no. 1, 271.

— (1894), 'The Kaim of Kimprunes', *The Speaker*, vol. 9, 560.

— (1849a), 'Layard's Nineveh', *Fraser's Magazine*, vol. 39, no. 232, 446.

— (1866c), 'Lubbock's *Prehistoric Times*', *Archaeologia Cambrensis*, vol. 12, no. 47, 379.

— (1851), 'Lyell – on *Life and its Successive Development*', *Quarterly Review*, vol. 89, 412–51.

— (1862a), 'The Mythology of Polynesia', *Westminster Review*, vol. 21, no. 2, 308.

— (1924), 'Nature and archaeology', *Saturday Review*, vol. 138, no. 3592, 220.

— (1908), 'Notes on current events', *The British Architect*, vol. 58, 220.

— (1887a), 'Obituary Charles Warne F. S. A', *The Antiquary*, vol. 15, 134.

— (1880b), 'Old Rural Songs and Customs', *The Antiquary*, vol. 2, 245.

— (1850), 'On the influence of archaeology on architecture', *Archaeologia Cambrensis*, vol. 1, no. 3, 162.

— (1869b), 'Pre-historic England', *Quarterly Review,* vol. 100, 396–424.

— (1879a), 'Pre-historic records', *Chamber's Journal of Popular Literature, Science and Arts,* no. 834, 805.

— (1870a), '*Prehistoric Times, as Illustrated by Ancient Remains, and the Manners and Customs of Savages*', *Quarterly Review,* vol. 128, no. 256, 436.

— (1872), 'The present phase of prehistoric archaeology', *British Quarterly Review,* vol. 112, 443.

— (1874), 'Primitive man: Tylor and Lubbock', *Quarterly Review,* vol. 137, 70.

— (1857), 'Proposed monuments to the two Wiltshire antiquaries, Aubrey and Britton', *Gentleman's Magazine,* vol. 84, 203.

— (1864a), 'The races of the old world', *National Review,* vol. 36, 455.

— (1885b), 'The reader', *The Graphic,* no. 807, 499.

— (1885c), 'Review of *After London*', *The Pall Mall Gazette,* no. 6264, 31.

— (1885d), 'Review of *After London; or, Wild England*', *Athenaeum,* no. 2998, 463.

— (1885e), 'Review of *After London, or Wild England*', *British Quarterly Review,* vol. 82, no. 163, 197–98.

— (1888), 'Review of *The Eulogy of Richard Jefferies* by Walter Besant', *The Pall Mall Gazette,* no. 7386, 45–46.

— (1862b), 'Review of Hutchins's *History of Dorset*', *Quarterly Review,* vol. 3, no. 222, 285.

— (1884), 'Review of *The Life of the Fields*', *The Pall Mall Gazette,* no. 6024, 23–24.

— (1849b), 'Review of *Nineveh and Its Remains* by Austen Henry Layard', *Athenaeum,* vol. 87, 45.

— (1849c), 'Review of *Nineveh and Its Remains*, by Austen Henry Layard', *Westminster and Foreign Quarterly Review,* vol. 51, 290–334.

— (1868b), 'Review of *The Pedigree of the English*', *London Review,* vol. 16, no. 412, 518–19.

— (1870b), 'Review of *Prehistoric Times, as Illustrated by Ancient Remains, and the Manners and Customs of Savages*', *Quarterly Review,* vol. 128, no. 256, 432.

— (1928), 'Review of *Spring Darkness*', *The Bookman,* vol. 74, no. 442, 230.

— (1902), 'Review of *The Story of My Heart*', *The Academy and Literature,* no. 1594, 554.

— (1879b), 'Review of *The Return of the Native*', *New Quarterly Magazine,* vol. 11, no. 22, 237.

— (1909b), 'Richard Jefferies', *Edinburgh Review,* vol. 210, no. 429, 223–29

— (1889a), 'Richard Jefferies', *London Quarterly Review,* vol. 11, no. 142, 228.

— (1893b), 'Richard Jefferies', *Wiltshire Archaeological and Natural History Society,* vol. 27, 69–99.

— (1887b), 'Richard Jefferies, and the open air', *National Review,* vol. 10, no. 56, 245.

— (1889b), 'Richard Jefferies's late essays', *The Pall Mall Gazette,* no. 7454, 34–35.

— (1859), 'The scouring of the white horse', *The Eclectic Review,* vol. 1, 111.

— (1869c), 'Survival of instincts', *Saturday Review,* vol. 28, no. 730, 536.

— (1864b), 'Through Berks', *Temple Bar,* vol. 11, 52.

— (1926), 'Very early Britons', *Saturday Review,* vol. 142, no. 3701, 383–84.

Archer, H.G. (1903), 'White horses', *Good Words,* vol. 44, 187.

Armstrong, Anne (1932), 'New novels', *The Saturday Review,* vol. 154, no. 4026, 673.

Armstrong, Tim (2005), *Modernism.* Cambridge: Polity.

Ashe, Geoffrey (1932), *Mythology of the British Isles.* London: Methuen.

Austin, Linda M. (2007), 'Aesthetic embarrassment: the reversion to the picturesque in nineteenth-century English tourism', *English Literary History,* vol. 74, no. 3, 629–53.

Baldick, Chris (2004), *The Modern Movement: Volume 10. 1910–1940.* Oxford: Oxford University Press.

Bann, Stephen (1999), 'Preface', in Myrone and Peltz (eds.), *Producing the Past,* Aldershot, UK: Ashgate, xvii–xxiii.

Barber, Richard (2004), *The Holy Grail: Imagination and Belief.* Cambridge, MA: Harvard University Press.

Bate, Jonathan (1999), 'Culture and environment: from Austen to Hardy', *New Literary History,* vol. 30, no. 3, 541–60.

Bayley, John (1985), 'Review of *Wolf Solent*', *New York Review of Books,* reprinted in *Wolf Solent.* London and New York: Harper and Row, 1–10.

Beer, Gillian (1983), *Darwin's Plots: Evolutionary Narrative in Darwin, George Eliot and Nineteenth-Century Fiction.* London: Routledge.

Belloc, Hilaire (1904), *The Old Road.* London: Constable.

Bender, Barbara, ed. (1993), *Landscape: Politics and Perspectives.* Oxford: Berg.

Bennett, Arnold et al. (1929), 'Stonehenge: letter signed by nine prominent authors', *The Times,* 23 March, 23.

Bennett, Tony (1995), *The Birth of the Museum.* London: Routledge.

Benson, Chris (1871), 'The holy grail', *Powder Magazine,* vol. 56, 95.

Bettey, J.H. (1994), 'Dorset', in C.R.J. Currie and C.P. Lewis (eds.), *English County Histories: A Guide,* Dover: Alan Sutton, 125–31.

Bilsing, Tracy (2005), '"Rosalba and all the Kirchner tribe": Mary Butts' "Speed the Plough" and the regenerative image of the feminine', *Essays in Arts and Sciences,* vol. 34, no. 1, 61–73.

Birch, B.P. (1981), 'Wessex, Hardy and the nature novelists', *Transactions of the Institute of British Geographers,* vol. 6, no. 3, 348–58.

Björk Lennart, ed. (1985), *The Literary Notebooks of Thomas Hardy,* 2 vols. London: Macmillan.

Blaser, Robin (1995), '"Here lies the woodpecker who was Zeus"', in Christopher Wagstaff (ed.), *A Sacred Quest,* New York: McPherson & Co., 159–223.

Blind, Karl (1885), 'Dr. Schliemann's discovery at Tiryns and his plans for Krete', *Time,* vol. 12, no. 2, 143.

Bloch, M. (1962), *Feudal Society,* trans. L. Manyon, 2 vols. London: Routledge & Kegan Paul.

Blondel, Nathalie (1997), *Scenes from the Life: A Biography of Mary Butts.* New York: McPherson.

Blunden, Edmund (1932), *The Face of England.* London: Allen.

Bottrell, William (1880), *Traditions and Hearthside Stories: Third Series.* Penzance, Cornwall: Stipney.

Bowden, Mark (1991), *Pitt Rivers.* Cambridge: Cambridge University Press.

Brayshay, Mark, ed. (1996), *Topographical Writers in South-West England.* Exeter: University of Exeter Press.

Brewster, David (1853), 'Review of *Discoveries in the Ruins of Nineveh and Babylon,* by Austen Henry Layard', *North British Review,* vol. 19, 136–58.

Bryher (1937), 'Recognition not farewell', *Life & Letters To-Day,* vol. 17, no. 9, 160.

Buchanan, Bradley W. (2003), 'Armed with questions: Mary Butts's sacred interrogative', *Twentieth-Century Literature*, vol. 49, no. 3, 360–87.

Buckman, James (1877), 'Preface', *Proceedings of the Dorset Natural History and Antiquarian Field Club*, vol. 1, ix–x.

Burdett, Osbert (1935), 'Fiction', *The English Review*, no. 46, 237.

Burne, Charlotte Sophie (1911), 'The essential unity of folk-lore', *Folk-lore*, vol. 22, 16–21.

Butts, Mary (1936a), 'Americans on England: pilgrims of the past', *The Sunday Times*, 13.

— (1931), 'Antiquity', *The Bookman*, vol. 81, no. 482, 137.

— (1933a), 'Aristophanes, the laughing philosopher', *The Bookman*, vol. 84, no. 501, 152.

— (1934a), 'The Art of Montague James', *The London Mercury*, vol. 29, no. 172, 306–17.

— (1998a), *'Ashe of Rings' and Other Writings: 'Ashe of Rings', 'Imaginary Letters', 'Warning to Hikers', 'Traps for Unbelievers', 'Ghosties and Ghoulies'*. New York: McPherson.

— (1998b), 'Bloomsbury', *Modernism/Modernity*, vol. 5, no. 2, 343–58.

— (1993), *The Crystal Cabinet: My Childhood at Salterns*. Manchester: Carcanet.

— (1933b), 'The girl through the ages', *The Bookman*, vol. 84, no. 500, 110.

— (1934b), 'The grandeur of Rome', *The Bookman*, vol. 86, no. 512, 119.

— (1933c), 'The Herschel chronicle', *The Bookman*, vol. 85, no. 507, 252–53.

— (1932a), 'Hesiod, an Hellenic prophet', *The Bookman*, vol. 83, no. 494, 113–14.

— (1933d), 'The isles of Greece', *The Bookman*, vol. 85, no. 507, 505.

— (1933e), 'It was like that', *The Bookman*, vol. 85, no. 505, 44.

— (2002), *The Journals of Mary Butts*, ed. Nathalie Blondel. New Haven, CT: Yale University Press.

— (1994), *'The Macedonian' and 'Scenes from the Life of Cleopatra'*. New York: McPherson.

— (1933f), 'Magic of person and place', *The Bookman*, vol. 85, no. 507, 141–43.

— (1932b), 'On gardens: gardens and gardening', *The Bookman*, vol. 82, no. 487, 40.

— (1933g), 'Our native land', *The Bookman*, vol. 84, no. 503, 252.

— (1936b), 'Parzival', *Time and Tide*, vol. 17, no. 2, 57–58.

— (1934c), 'The past lives again', *The Bookman*, vol. 86, no. 511, 44–45.

— (1933h), 'The real Wordsworth, review of *The Later Life of Wordsworth*, by Edith Batho', *Time and Tide*, vol. 14, no. 28, 1446–48.

— (1934d), 'Review of H.J. Massingham's *Country*', *Bookman*, vol. 86, no. 511, 189.

— (1932c), 'Rome: of the Renaissance and Today', *The Bookman*, vol. 83, no. 495, 254.

— (1995), *A Sacred Quest: The Life and Writings of Mary Butts*, ed. Christopher Wagstaff. New York: McPherson.

— (1933i), 'The sanc grail', *The Bookman*, vol. 84, no. 499, 72–74.

— (1992), *The Taverner Novels: 'Armed with Madness' and 'Death of Felicity Taverner'*. New York: McPherson.

— (1932d), 'This England', *The Bookman*, vol. 83, no. 495, 274–80.

— (1934e), 'Two blind mice', *The Bookman*, vol. 86, no. 515, 255.

— (1932–1933), 'Vision of Asia', *The Bookman*, vol. 83, no. 495, 223–25.

Calderwood, H. (1871), 'Review of *Primitive Culture*', *Contemporary Review*, vol. 19, 212–15.

Cambridge, O.P. (1887), 'In memoriam Rev. William Barnes', *Proceedings of the Dorset Natural History and Antiquarian Field Club*, vol. 8, xx–vii.

Casagrande, Peter (1999), *Hardy's Influence on the Modern Novel*. London: Macmillan.

Cavaliero, Glen (1973), *John Cowper Powys: Novelist*. Oxford: Oxford University Press.

Chamberlayne, Edward (1671), *Angliae Notitia; or, The Present State of England*, 5th edn. 2 vols. London: Smith.

Chandler, John (1996), 'An uncomfortable antiquary: Richard Jefferies and Victorian local history', *Richard Jefferies Society Journal*, vol. 5, 14–24.

Clarke, C. (2002), 'Richard Jefferies and Thomas Hardy: parallel lives', *Richard Jefferies Society Journal*, vol. 11, 17–20.

Clarke, Graham, ed. (1993), *Thomas Hardy: Critical Assessments. Vol. III*. London: Helm.

Clifford, James (1997), *The Predicament of Culture: Twentieth-Century Ethnography, Literature and Art*. Cambridge, MA: Harvard University Press.

Clutton-Brock, A. (1905), 'A neglected romance', *The Speaker*, vol. 45, 108–109.

Coates, C.A. (1982), *John Cowper Powys in Search of a Landscape*. London: Macmillan.

Collett, Anthony (1926), *The Changing Face of England*. London: Nisbet.

Collins, H.P. (1966), *John Cowper Powys: Old Earth-Man*. London: Barrie and Rockliff.

Coombes, H. (1980), 'Chronicles of country life', *Books and Bookmen*, vol. 25, no. 7, 65.

Corbett, David Peters, Ysanne Holt, Fiona Russell, eds. (2002), *The Geographies of Englishness: Landscape and the National Past 1880–1940*. New Haven, CT: Yale University Press.

Crang, Mike (1998), *Cultural Geography*. London: Routledge.

Crang, Philip (1997), 'Regional imaginations: an afterword', in Ella Westland (ed.), *The Cultural Construction of Cornwall*, Exeter: Patton Press, 154–65.

Crawford, O.G.S. (1927), 'Editorial Notes', *Antiquity*, vol. 1, no. 1, 1–4.

— (1921), *Man and His Past*. London: Milford.

— (1924), 'The Origin of Civilization', *Edinburgh Review*, vol. 239, 101–116.

— (1955), *Said and Done*. London: Phoenix House.

— (1933j), 'Some recent air discoveries', *Antiquity*, vol. 7, no. 27, 291.

Crawfurd, Oswald (1898), 'Richard Jefferies: field-naturalist and litterateur', *The Idler*, vol. 13, no. 3, 292.

Crolley, George (1850), 'Review of *Nineveh and Its Remains* by Austin Henry Layard', *Dublin Review*, vol. 28, 354–98.

Cubitt, Geoffrey, ed. (1998), *Imagining Nations*. Manchester: Manchester University Press.

Cucullu, Lois (1998), 'Shepherds in the parlour: Forster's apostles, pagans, and native sons', *Novel: A Forum on Fiction*, vol. 32, no. 1, 19–50.

Cunnington, Robert H. (1975), *From Antiquary to Archaeologist: A Biography of William Cunnigton 1754–1810*. London: Shire.

Cunliffe, Barry (1993), *Wessex to A.D. 1000*. London: Routledge.

— (2006), 'What manner of place is this?', in Barry Cunliffe (ed.), *The West: England's Landscape Volume 4*, London: Collins, 11–12.

Cunningham, William (1897), *Alien Immigrants to England*. London: Swan.

Daniel, Glyn and Renfrew Colin (1986), *The Idea of Prehistory*. Edinburgh: Edinburgh University Press.

Daniels, Stephen (1998), 'Mapping national identities: the culture of cartography, with particular reference to the Ordnance Survey', in Cubitt (ed.), *Imagining Nations*. Manchester: Manchester University Press, 112–31.

Dartnell, George E. (1893), 'Richard Jefferies', *Wiltshire Archaeological and Natural History Society*, vol. 27, 69–99.

Darton, F.J. Harvey (1922), *The Marches of Wessex: A Chronicle of England*. London: Nisbet.

Darvill, Timothy (1996), *Prehistoric Britain from the Air: A Study of Space, Time and Society*. Cambridge: Cambridge University Press.

Davenport Adams, W.H. (1872), *Life in the Primeval World, (founded on Meunier's 'Les Animaux d'Autrefois')*. London: T. Nelson & Sons.

De Lange, Attie (2008), *Literary Landscapes: From Modernism to Postcolonialism*. London: Palgrave.

Defoe, Daniel (1927), *Tour through England and Wales*, 2 vols. London: Everyman.

Deuel, Leo (1971), *Flights into Yesterday: The Story of Aerial Archaeology*. London: Macmillan.

Douch, Robert (1978), 'John Hutchins', in Jack Simmons (ed.), *English County Historians*. Wakefield, England: EP Publishing, 113–60.

Du Maurier, Daphne (1972), *Vanishing Cornwall*. Harmondsworth, Middlesex: Penguin.

Duke of Argyll (1869), *Primeval Man: An Examination of Some Recent Speculations*. London: Strahan.

Duncan, Ian (2003), 'Supernatural narration: *A Glastonbury Romance*, modernity, and the novel', *Western Humanities Review*, vol. 57, no. 1, 78–93.

Dunkin E.H.W. (1871), 'Some account of the megalithic remains in south Dorset', *Reliquary*, vol. 11, 145–46.

Earle, John (1899) [1628], 'An antiquary', in *Micro-cosmographie; or, a Piece of the World Discovered in Essayes and Characters*. London: J.M. Dent, 14–15.

Ebbatson, Roger (2006), *Heidegger's Bicycle: Interfering with Victorian Texts*. Brighton, England: Sussex Academic Press.

Edwards, Brian (2000), 'Avebury and other not-so-ancient places: the making of the English heritage landscape', in Hilda Kean (ed.), *Seeing History: Public History in Britain Now*. London: Francis Boutle, 65–103.

Eliot, George (1878), *Impressions of Theophrastus Such. Essays and Leaves from a Notebook*. Edinburgh: William Blackwood.

Epstein, Leonora (1987), 'Sale and sacrament: the wife auction in *The Mayor of Casterbridge*', *English Language Notes*, vol. 24, no. 4, 50–56.

Esty, Jed (2004), *A Shrinking Island: Modernism and National Culture in England*. Oxford: Princeton University Press.

Evans, Myfanwy (1937), 'Paul Nash, 1937', *Axis*, vol. 8, 12–13.

Evans-Wentz W.Y. (2002) [1911], *The Fairy-Faith in Celtic Countries*. Mineola, NY: Dover.

Farrer, James A. (1879), *Primitive Manners and Customs*. London: Chatto & Windus.

Forster, E.M. (1988) [1907], *The Longest Journey*. London: Penguin.

Fowles, John (1980), 'Introduction', to Richard Jefferies, *After London*. Oxford: World's Classics, vii–xxi.

Foy, Roslyn Reso (1998), '"Nothing but spiritual development": Mary Butts's *Ashe of Rings* and *Scenes from the Life of Cleopatra*', in Kristina K. Groover (ed.), *Things of the Spirit: Women Writers Constructing Spirituality*, Notre Dame, IN: University of Notre Dame Press, 183–91.

— (2000), *Ritual, Myth and Mysticism in the Work of Mary Butts: Between Feminism and Modernism*. Fayetteville, AR: University of Arkansas Press.

Franklin, Michael J. (2008), 'Market-Faces and Market Forces: [Corn-]Factors in the Moral Economy of Casterbridge', *Review of English Studies*, vol. 59, no. 240, 426–48.

Frazer, Sir James George (1994), *The Golden Bough: A New Abridgement*, ed. Robert Fraser. Oxford: The World's Classics.

— (1908), *The Scope of Social Anthropology. An Inaugural Lecture Delivered before the University of Liverpool*. London: Macmillan.

Freeland Natalka (2005), 'The dustbins of history: waste management in late-Victorian utopias', in William A. Cohen and Ryan Johnson (eds.), *Filth: Dirt, Disgust and Modern Life*. Minneapolis, MN: University of Minnesota Press, 225–49.

Gardiner, Rolf (1940–1941), 'AGENDA: The Vision and the Task', *North Sea and Baltic*, London: Storey, 169.

— (1943), *England Herself: Ventures in Rural Restoration*. London.

— (1972), *Water Springing from the Ground: An Anthology of the Writings of Rolf Gardiner*. Oxford: Alden Press.

Gariepy, Jennifer (1988), 'Mary Butts, 1890–1937', *Twentieth-Century Literary Criticism*, vol. 77, 69–109.

Garrity, Jane (2008), 'Found and lost: the politics of modernist recovery', *Modernism/Modernity*, vol. 15, no. 4, 803–12.

— (2006a), 'Mary Butts', in Faye Hammill, Esme Miskimmin and Ashlie Sponenberg (eds.), *Encyclopedia of British Women's Writing, 1900–1950*. London: Palgrave, 37–38.

— (2006b), 'Mary Butts's "fanatical pederasty": queer urban life in 1920s London and Paris', in Laura Doan and Jane Garrity (eds.), *Sapphic Modernities: Sexuality, Women and National Culture*. London: Palgrave, 233–51.

— (2003), *Step-Daughters of England: British Women Modernists and the National Imaginary*. Manchester: Manchester University Press.

Gatrell, Simon (2003), *Hardy's Vision of Wessex*. London: Palgrave.

Goldney, G. (1874), 'Archaeology', *The British Architect*, vol. 2, no. 38, 179.

Gomme, George Laurence (1914), 'Folk-lore', in *Hasting's Encyclopedia of Religion and Ethics*. London: Chapman, vol. 6, 59.

— (1908), *Folklore as an Historical Science*. London: Methuen.

— (1890), *The Handbook of Folklore*. London: Folklore Society.

— (1883), 'Primitive agricultural implements', *Antiquary*, vol. 8, 141.

— (1880), *Primitive Folk-Moots; or Open-Air Assemblies in Britain*. London: Sampson Low.

— (1890), *The Village Community, with Special Reference to the Origin and Form of its Survivals in Britain*. London: Walter Scott.

Goodway, David (1984/1985), 'The politics of John Cowper Powys', *The Powys Review*, vol. 15, 42–53.

Green, J.R. (1869), 'History', *Quarterly Review*, vol. 58, no. 34, xi.

Gribble, Jennifer (1996), 'The quiet women of Egdon Heath', *Essays in Criticism*, vol. 46, no. 3, 234–57.

Grimble, Simon (2004), *Landscape, Writing and 'The Condition of England' 1878–1917: Ruskin to Modernism*. Lampeter, Wales: Mellen.

Grinsell, L.V. (1940), 'The archaeological contribution of Richard Jefferies', *Transactions of the Newbury District Field Club*, vol. 8, no. 3, 216–26.

Guirand, Felix, ed. (1966), *The Larousse Encyclopedia of Mythology*, introd. Robert Graves. London: Paul Hamlyn.

Hapgood, Lynne (2003), *Margins of Desire*. Manchester: Manchester University Press.

Hardy, Thomas (1988a), *The Collected Letters of Thomas Hardy: Volume Seven 1926–27*, ed. R.L. Purdy and Michael Millgate. Oxford: Clarendon Press.

— (1987a), *Far from the Madding Crowd*, ed. Suzanne B. Falck-Yi. Oxford: World's Classics.

— (1986), *The Life and Work of Thomas Hardy*, ed. Michael Millgate. London: Macmillan.

— (1987b), *The Mayor of Casterbridge*, ed. Dale Kramer. Oxford: World's Classics.

— (1982), *The Personal Notebooks of Thomas Hardy*, ed. Richard H. Taylor. London: Macmillan.

— (1990), *The Return of the Native*, ed. Simon Gatrell. Oxford: World's Classics.

— (1988b), *Tess of the d'Urbervilles*, ed. Juliet Grindle and Simon Gatrell. Oxford: World's Classics.

— (1967), *Thomas Hardy's Personal Writings*, ed. Harold Orel. London: Macmillan.

— (2001), *Thomas Hardy's Public Voice: The Essays, Speeches, and Miscellaneous Prose*, ed. Michael Millgate. Oxford: Clarendon Press.

— (1987c), *The Trumpet-Major, and Robert his Brother*, ed. Roger Ebbatson. Harmondsworth, Middlesex: Penguin.

— (1914), 'A tryst at an ancient earthwork', in *A Changed Man and Other Tales*, London: Macmillan, 173–186.

Harrington, Ralph (2002), 'The cultural geographies of road and rail in inter-war England'. Location (stable URL): www.greycat.org/papers/roadrail.html

Harrison, Jane Ellen (1926), *Alpha and Omega*. London: Longman.

— (1962), *Epilegomena to the Study of Greek Religion and Themis: A Study of Social Origins of Greek Religion*. New York: University Books.

— (1924), *Mythology*. London: Longman, Green.

Hartley, L.P. (1925), 'Imagination and reality', *The Bookman*, vol. 69, no. 410, 123–24.

— (1928), 'Review of *The Strange Vanguard*', *Saturday Review*, vol. 145, no. 3770, 104–106.

Haslam, Sara (2009), 'Wessex, literary pilgrims, and Thomas Hardy', in Nicola J. Watson (ed.), *Literary Tourism and Nineteenth-Century Culture*. London: Palgrave, 165–74.

Hauser, Kitty (2007), *Shadow Sites: Photography, Archaeology and the British Landscape 1927–1955*. Oxford: Oxford University Press.

Hawkes, Jaquetta (1967), 'God in the machine', *Antiquity*, vol. 41, 174.

— (1982), *Mortimer Wheeler: Adventurer in Archaeology*. London: Weidenfeld.

Hawkins, Emma B. (2000), 'Chalk figures and scouring in Tolkien-land', *Extrapolation*, vol. 41, no. 4, 385–96.

Henderson, George (1911), *Survivals in Belief among the Celts*. Glasgow: James Maclehose and Sons.

Hodder, Ian (1996), *Reading the Past: Current Approaches to Interpretation in Archaeology*. Cambridge: Cambridge University Press.

Hodgen, Margaret T. (1936), *The Doctrine of Survivals: A Chapter in the History of Scientific Method in the Study of Man*. London: Allenson.

Hooker, Jeremy (1996), *Writers in a Landscape*. Cardiff: University of Wales Press.

Hoosen, David, ed. (1994), *Geography and National Identity*. Oxford: Blackwell.

Hoskins, W.G. (1949), *Midland England: A Survey of the Country between the Chilterns and the Trent*. London: Allen.

Hoste, M.R. (1900), 'Richard Jefferies', *The Argosy*, vol. 71, 227–33.

Hudson, W.H. (1910), *A Shepherd's Life*. London: Allen.

Hughes, Ian (1982/1983), 'A poor ragged maiden: the textual history of *Maiden Castle*', *The Powys Review*, vol. 12, 17–25.

— (1984/1985), 'A virgin with no name: the beginnings of *Maiden Castle*', *The Powys Review*, vol. 15, 14–21.

Hughes, Thomas (1857), *The Scouring of the White Horse; or the Long Vacation Ramble of a London Clerk*. Boston, MA: Ticknor and Fields.

— (2008), *Tom Brown's Schooldays*, ed. Andrew Sanders. Oxford: The World's Classics.

Humfrey, Belinda (1984/1985), 'Editorial', *The Powys Review*, vol. 15, 1–10.

Hunt, Robert (1865), *Popular Romances of the West of England; or, the Drolls, Traditions, and Superstitions of Old Cornwall: First Series*. London: J.C. Hotten.

Hunter, Michael, ed. (1996), *Preserving the Past: The Rise of Heritage*. Stroud: Allen Sutton.

Hutchins, John (1861), *The History and Antiquities of Dorset (interspersed with some remarkable particulars of natural history; and adorned with a correct map of the country, and view of antiquities, seats of the nobility and gentry)* 3rd edn., corrected by William Shipp and James Whitworth Hodson, 4 vols. Westminster: John Bowyer Nichols & Sons.

Huxley, T.H. (1901), *Science and Hebrew Tradition*. London: Macmillan.

Jackson-Houlston, C.M. (1999), *Ballads, Songs and Snatches: The Appropriation of Folk Song and Popular Culture in British Nineteenth-century Realist Prose*. Aldershot: Ashgate.

Jefferies, Richard (1980a), *After London*, ed. John Fowles. Oxford: World's Classics.

— (1889), *Field and Hedgerow*. London: Longman.

— (1978) [1879], *The Gamekeeper at Home, The Amateur Poacher*. Oxford: Oxford University Press.

— (1980b), *The Hills and the Vale*, ed. Edward Thomas. Oxford: Oxford University Press.

— (1896), *Jefferies' Land, A History of Swindon and its Environs*, ed. Grace Toplis. London: Simpkin.

— (1912), *The Life of the Fields*. London: Chatto.

— (1884), *Red Deer*. London: Eyre & Spottiswoode.

— (1880), *Round About a Great Estate*. London: Smith, Elder.

— (2002), *The Story of My Heart: My Autobiography*. Devon: Green.

— (1879), *Wild Life in a Southern County*. London: John Murray.

Johns, B.G. (1887), 'The literature of the streets', *Edinburgh Review*, vol. 165, 40–65.

Jones, Eric L. (2005), 'The land that Richard Jefferies inherited', *Rural History*, vol. 16, no. 1, 83–93.

Jones, Malcolm (2002), 'The English print', in Michael Hattaway (ed.), *A Companion to English Renaissance Literature and Culture*. Oxford: Blackwell, 56–69.

Jones, Sian (1997), *The Archaeology of Ethnicity: A Theoretical Perspective*. London: Routledge.

Kalnins, Mara (2004), 'Review of *The Journals of Mary Butts*', *Notes and Queries*, 331–32.

Keith, W.J. (1988), 'The archaeological background to *Maiden Castle*', *The Powys Review*, vol. 6, no. 2, 14–19.

— (1965), *Richard Jefferies: A Critical Study*. Toronto: University of Toronto Press.

— (1975), *The Rural Tradition: William Cobbett, Gilbert White, and Other Non-Fiction Writers of the English Countryside*. Sussex: Harvester.

Kendrick, Thomas (1927), *The Druids: A Study in Keltic Prehistory*. London: Allen.

Kidd, Alan J. (2000), 'Between antiquary and academic: local history in the nineteenth century', in R.C. Richardson (ed.), *The Changing Face of England*. Aldershot: Ashgate, 94–109.

Kipling, Rudyard (1937), *Something of Myself: For My Friends Known and Unknown*. London: John Lane.

Knoepflmacher U.C. and G.B. Tennyson, eds. (1977), *Nature and the Victorian Imagination*. Berkeley, CA: University of California Press.

Kort, Wesley A. (2004), *Place and Space in Modern Fiction*. Florida, FL: University Press of Florida.

Krissdöttir, Morine (1980), *John Cowper Powys and the Magical Quest*. London: Macdonald.

Krissdöttir, Morine and R. Peers, eds. (1998), *The Dorset Year: The Diary of John Cowper Powys, June 1934–July 1935*. Kilmersdon: The Powys Press.

Kroll, Allison Adler (2009), 'Hardy's Wessex, heritage culture, and the archaeology of rural England', *Nineteenth-Century Contexts*, vol. 31, no. 4, 335–52.

Kroll, Jennifer (1999), 'Mary Butts's "unrest cure" for the waste land', *Twentieth Century Literature*, vol. 45, 159–73.

Lane, Dennis (1980–1981), 'John Cowper Powys, Thomas Hardy and the faces of nature', *Powys Review*, vol. 2, no. 4, 48–57.

Lansing, Gerrit (1995), 'Foreword', in Christopher Wagstaff (ed.), *A Sacred Quest*. New York: McPherson & Co., xvii–xix.

Layard, Austen Henry (1853), *Discoveries of Nineveh and Babylon*. London: John Murray.

— (1897), *Nineveh and Babylon*. London: John Murray.

— (1848), *Nineveh and Its Remains*. 2 vols. London: John Murray.

Lee, Vernon (1904), *Hortus Vitae: Essays on the Gardening of Life*. London: Bodley Head.

Levine, Philippa (1986), *The Amateur and the Professional: Antiquarians, Historians, and Archaeologists in Victorian England, 1838–1886*. Cambridge: Cambridge University Press.

Linett, Maren Tova (2007), *Modernism, Feminism, and Jewishness*. Cambridge: Cambridge University Press.

Lock, Charles (1990), 'John Cowper Powys and James Joyce', in Denis Lane (ed.), *In the Spirit of Powys*, London and Toronto: Associated University Presses, 23–42.

Looker, Samuel J. and Porteus Crichton (1964), *Richard Jefferies: Man of the Fields: A Biography and Letters*. London: John Baker.

Lord Rosebery (1921), *Miscellanies: Literary and Historical*, 2 vols. London: Hodder & Stoughton.

Lothe, Jakob (2007), 'Space, time, narrative: from Thomas Hardy to Franz Kafka and J.M. Coetzee' in Attie de Lange, Gail Fincham, Jakob Lothe and Jeremy Hawthorn (eds.), *Literary Landscapes: From Modernism to Postcolonialism*. Basingstoke: Palgrave, 15–25.

Lowenthal, David (1994), 'European and English landscapes as symbols', in David Hoosen (ed.), *Geography and National Identity*. Oxford: Blackwells.

— (1997), *The Heritage Crusade and the Spoils of History*. London: Viking.

Lowenthal, David and Marcus Binney, eds. (1981), *Our Past Before Us: Why Do We Save It?* London: Temple Smith.

Lowerson, J. (1992), 'The mystical geography of the English', in B. Short (ed.), *The English Rural Community*. Cambridge: Cambridge University Press, 152–74.

Lubbock, Sir John (1870), *The Origin of Civilisation and the Primitive Condition of Man. Mental and Social Condition of Savages*, 2nd edn. London: Longmans, Green, & Co.

Lyall, A.C. (1873), 'The relation of witchcraft to non-Christian religions', *Fortnightly Review*, vol. 13, no. 76, 430.

Lyell, Charles (1997), *Principles of Geology*, ed. J.A. Secord. Harmondsworth, Middlesex: Penguin

Lymington (1887), 'Richard Jefferies, and the open air', *National Review*, vol. 10, no. 56, 249.

Makdisi, Saree (1998), *Romantic Imperialism*. Cambridge: Cambridge University Press.

Malcolmson Robert W. (1973), *Popular Recreations in English Society, 1700–1850*. Cambridge: Cambridge University Press.

Malinowski, Bronislaw (1984), *Argonauts of the Western Pacific*. Prospect Heights: Waveland.

Malley, Shawn (1996), 'Austen Henry Layard and the periodical press: Middle Eastern archaeology and the excavation of cultural identity in mid-nineteenth century Britain', *Victorian Review*, vol. 22, no. 2, 152–70.

Manning-Sanders, Ruth (1949), *The West of England*. London: Batsford.

Mantell, Gideon Algernon (1838), *The Wonders of Geology*. 2 vols. London: Henry G. Bohn.

Marett, R.R. (1917), 'The psychology of culture contact, presidential address to the folklore society', *Folklore,* vol. 28, 14.

Marzec Robert P. (2007), *An Ecological and Postcolonial Study of Literature: From Daniel Defoe to Salman Rushdie*. London: Palgrave.

Massingham, H.J. (1988), *A Mirror of England: An Anthology of the Writings of H. J. Massingham (1888–1952)*, ed. Edward Abelson. London: Green.

— (1924a), 'Cornish wilds', *English Review*, vol. 15, 902.

— (1926), *Downland Man*. London: Jonathan Cape.

— (1937), *Genius of England*. London: Methuen.

— (1924b), *In Praise of England*. London: Methuen.

— (1942), *Remembrance: An Autobiography*. London: B.T. Batsford.

Matless, David (2008), 'A geography of ghosts: the spectral landscapes of Mary Butts', *Cultural Geographies*, vol. 15, no. 2, 335–57.

Maxwell, Richard (1990), 'The lie of the land or, plot and autochthony in John Cowper Powys', in Denis Lane (ed.), *In the Spirit of Powys: New Essays*. London: Associated University Press, 193–213.

McDermott, John Francis and B. Taft Kendall, eds. (1932), *Sex in the Arts: A Symposium*. New York: Harper & Row.

McGann, Jerome (2006), *The Scholar's Art: Literary Studies in a Managed World*. Chicago, IL: University of Chicago Press.

McLennan, John Ferguson (1970) [1865], *Primitive Marriage*. Chicago, IL: University of Chicago Press.

— (1896), *Studies in Ancient History*. London: Macmillan.

Metcalfe, John (1998), *Nightmare Jack and Other Stories*, ed. Richard Dalby. Canada: Ash-Tree.

Millgate, Michael (1985), *Thomas Hardy: A Biography*. Oxford: Oxford University Press.

Milner, John (1886), 'Barrows in Dorsetshire', in George Laurence Gomme (ed.), *The Gentleman's Magazine Library: A Classified Collection of the Chief Contents of 'The Gentleman's Magazine' from 1731–1868. Archaeology: Part I*, London: Elliot Stock, 99–103.

Milton, John (1957), 'Areopagitica' in *John Milton: Complete Poems and Major Prose*, ed. Merritt Y. Hughes. London and New York: Odyssey.

Mitchell, Arthur (1881), *The Past in the Present. What is Civilization?* New York.

Mitchell, W.J.T., ed. (1994), *Landscape and Power*. Chicago, IL: University of Chicago Press.

Moore, Kevin Z. (1990), *The Descent of the Imagination: Post-Romantic Culture in the Later Novels of Thomas Hardy*. New York and London: New York University Press.

Moore-Colyer, R.J. (2002), 'A voice clamouring in the wilderness: H.J. Massingham (1888–1952) and rural England', *Rural History*, vol. 13, no. 2, 199–224.

— (1999), 'From great wen to toad hall; aspects of the urban rural divide in inter-war Britain', *Rural History*, vol. 10, no. 1, 91–105.

— (1999), 'Sir George Stapledon (1882–1960) and the landscape of Britain', *Environment of History*, vol. 5, no. 2, 221–36.

Moran, Margaret (1990), 'Animating fictions in *Maiden Castle*', in Denis Lane (ed.), *In the Spirit of Powys*, Bucknell: Bucknell University Press, 180–92.

Morgan, Lewis (1877), *Ancient Society*. Chicago, IL: Kerr.

Morris, Brian (2006), *Richard Jefferies and the Ecological Vision*. Oxford: Trafford.

Moses, Michael Valdez (1995), *The Novel and the Globalization of Culture*. Oxford: Oxford University Press.

Musselwhite, David (2003), *Social Transformations in Hardy's Tragic Novels: Megamachines and Phantasms*. London: Palgrave.

Myrone, Martin and Lucy Peltz, eds. (1999), *Producing the Past: Aspects of Antiquarian Culture and Practice 1700–1850*. Aldershot: Ashgate.

Nash, Paul (1936), *Shell Guide to Dorset*. London: Architectural Press.

— (1938), 'Unseen landscapes', *Country Life* (21 May), 526.

Nesbitt, Jennifer Poulos (2005), *Narrative Settlements: Geographies of British Women's Fiction between the Wars*. Toronto and London: University of Toronto Press.

Newton, Charles Thomas (1880), *Essays on Art and Archaeology*. London: Macmillan.

— (1850), 'On the study of archaeology', *Archaeological Journal*, vol. 8, 6.

Nicholson, N.C. (1951), 'The Shaping of Britain', *Times Literary Supplement*, 22nd June, 383.

Nord, Deborah Epstein (2006), *Gypsies and the British Imagination, 1807–1930*. New York: Columbia University Press.

Offer, Avner (1981), *Property and Politics 1870–1914: Landownership, Law, Ideology and Urban Development in England*. Cambridge: Cambridge University Press.

Paley, W.B. (1898), 'The roman roads of Britain', *Nineteenth Century*, vol. 44, no. 261, 840.

Palgrave, F.T. (1887), 'William Barnes and his *Poems of Rural Life in the Dorset Dialect'*, *National Review*, vol. 8, no. 48, 820.

Pamboukian, Sylvia A. (2008), 'What the traveller saw: evolution, romance and time-travel', in Steven McLean (ed.), *H.G. Wells: Interdisciplinary Essays*. Newcastle: Cambridge Scholars, 8–24.

Pater, Walter (1983), *Plato and Platonism: A Series of Lectures*. New York: Chelsea House.

— (1996), *The Renaissance*. Oxford: World's Classics.

Patterson, Ian (2001), 'Anarcho-imperialism, modernism, mystification and muddle', *Cambridge Quarterly*, vol. 30, no. 2, 183–90.

— (1998), 'The plan behind the plan: Russians, Jews, and mythologies of change', in Laura Marcus and Brian Cheyette (eds.), *Modernity, Culture and the 'Jew'*. Stanford, CA: Stanford University Press, 126–40.

Pearce, Susan M. and Alexandria Bounia, eds. (2000), *The Collector's Voice Volume 1: Ancient Voices*. Aldershot: Ashgate.

Pearsall, Ronald (1973), *Edwardian Life and Leisure*. Newton Abbot: David and Charles.

Pearson, Richard, ed. (2006a), 'Preface', *The Victorians and the Ancient World: Archaeology and Classicism in Nineteenth-Century Culture*. Newcastle, UK: Cambridge Scholars, ix–xx.

Pearson, Richard (2006b), 'A. H. Layard's *Nineveh and Its Remains*: The cultural material of Assyrian archaeology', in Pearson (ed.), *The Victorians and the Ancient World*. Newcastle: Cambridge Scholars, 41–60.

Peltz, Lucy and Martin Myrone (1999), '"Mine are the subjects rejected by the historian": antiquarianism, history and the making of modern culture', in Peltz and Myrone (eds.), *Producing the Past*. Aldershot, UK: Ashgate, 1–13.

Pick, Daniel (1989), *Faces of Degeneration*. Cambridge: Cambridge University Press.

Platt, Len (2001), *Aristocracies of Fiction: The Idea of Aristocracy in Late-Nineteenth-Century and Early-Twentieth-Century Literary Culture*. Westport, CT: Greenwood Press.

Poulson, Christine, ed. (1999), *The Quest for the Grail: Arthurian Legend in British Art 1840–1920*. Manchester: Manchester University Press.

Pound, Ezra (1914), 'The new sculpture', *The Egoist*, vol. 5, 67–68.

Pountney, Rob (2001), 'Hardy's Mai-Dun', *Thomas Hardy Journal*, vol. 17, no. 1, 69–72.

Powys, John Cowper (1932), '*Glastonbury*: Author's Review', originally printed in *The Modern Thinker* (March 1932); reprinted in *The Powys Review* (1981–1982), vol. 9, 7–9.

— (1933), *A Glastonbury Romance*. London: John Lane.

— (1966), *Maiden Castle*. London: Macdonald.

— (1985), 'D.H. Lawrence', *The Powys Review*, no. 16, 52–54.

Preston, Cathy Lynn, ed. (1995), *Folklore, Literature, and Cultural Theory*. New York: Garland.

Prins, Yopie (1999), 'Greek maenads, Victorian spinsters', in Richard Dellamora (ed.), *Victorian Sexual Dissidence*. Chicago, IL and London: University of Chicago Press, 43–81.

Pugin A.W.N. (1969), *Contrasts*, introd. H.R. Hitchcock. New York: Humanities Press.

Quiller-Couch, Arthur (1894), *Ancient and Holy Wells of Cornwall*. Penzance: Millers.

— (1893), 'Mr Quiller-Couch on Richard Jefferies', *The Critic*, vol. 20, 262.

Raine, Craig (1994), 'Conscious artistry in *The Mayor of Casterbridge*', in Charles P.C. Pettit (ed.), *New Perspectives on Thomas Hardy*. London: Macmillan, 156–71.

Rainey, Lawrence (1998), 'Good Things: Pederasty and Jazz and Opium and Research', *London Review of Books*, vol. 20, no. 14, 14–17.

Ramel, Annie (1998), 'The crevice in the canvas: a study of *The Mayor of Casterbridge*', *Victorian Literature and Culture*, vol. 26, no. 2, 259–72.

Randall, H.J. (1934), 'History in the open air', *Antiquity*, vol. 8, no. 29, 5–23.

Rands, Susan, (1984/1985), '*Maiden Castle*: symbol, theme, and personality', *The Powys Review*, no. 15, 22–31.

Read, Henry Darwin (1860), 'The reputed traces of primeval man', *Blackwood's Magazine*, vol. 88, 424.

Redding, Cyrus (1868), 'Public executions', *New Monthly Magazine*, vol. 143, no. 573, 329.

Rhys, John (1891), *Studies in the Arthurian Legend*. Oxford: Clarendon Press.

Richardson, Dorothy (1980), *Pilgrimage: Volume II*. London: Virago.

Richardson, Maurice (1937), 'Review of *Maiden Castle*', *The English Review*, vol. 64, no. 5, 631.

Rivers, W.H.R. (1913), 'Survival in sociology', *Sociological Review*, vol. 4, 295.

Rives, Rochelle (2005), 'Problem space: Mary Butts, modernism, and the etiquette of placement', *Modernism/Modernity*, vol. 12, no. 4, 607–27.

Rode, Scott (2006), *Reading and Mapping Hardy's Roads*. London: Routledge.

Rogers, Ken and Crowley, Douglas (1994), 'Wiltshire', in C. R. J. Currie and C. P. Lewis (eds.), *English County Histories: A Guide*. Dover: Alan Sutton, 410–22.

Rogers, Shannon L. (2001), '"The Historian of Wessex": Thomas Hardy's Contribution to History', *Rethinking History*, vol. 5, no. 2, 217–32.

Rose, Jacqueline (1999), 'Bizarre objects: Mary Butts and Elizabeth Bowen', *Critical Quarterly*, vol. 42, no. 1, 75–85

Rowley, Trevor (2006), 'Romanticism and recreation', in Barry Cunliffe (ed.), *England's Landscape: The West*. London: Collins, 230–44.

Ruskin, John (1985), *Unto This Last and Other Writings*, ed. Clive Wilmer. Harmondsworth, Middlesex: Penguin.

Rutherford, E. Havers (1926), 'The romance of King Arthur's country', *The Quiver*, vol. 22, 651.

Salt, H.S. (1898), 'The gospel according to Richard Jefferies', *The Pall Mall Gazette*, no. 7384, 13–19.

— (1888), 'The story of a heart', *To-Day*, vol. 55, 164–66.

Schwyzer, Philip (1999), 'The scouring of the white horse: archaeology, identity, and "heritage"', *Representations*, vol. 65, 42–62.

Scott, Bonnie Kime (2004), 'Review of *The Journals of Mary Butts*', *Modernism/Modernity*, vol. 11, no. 1, 188–90.

Scott-James, R.A. (1908), *Modernism and Romance*. London: John Lane.

Sharples, Niall M. (1991), *Maiden Castle*. London: Batsford.

Simmons, Jack, ed. (1978), *English County Historians*. Wakefield: Smith.

Sinnema, Peter W. (1998), *The Dynamics of the Pictured Page: Representing the Nation in the 'Illustrated London News', 1842–1892*. Aldershot: Ashgate.

Sir Cyril Fox (1932), *The Personality of Britain*. London: Holt.

Smith, Grafton Elliot (1934), *Human History*. London: Jonathan Cape.

Snell, K.D.M., ed. (1998), *The Regional Novel in Britain and Ireland, 1800–1900*. Cambridge: Cambridge University Press.

Snyder, Carey J. (2008), *British Fiction and Cross-Cultural Encounters: Ethnographic Modernism from Wells to Woolf*. London: Palgrave.

Stafford, Darby (1905), 'The home and haunts of Richard Jefferies', *The English Illustrated Magazine*, vol. 23, 431.

Stapledon, R.G. (1935), *The Land, Now and Tomorrow*. London: Faber & Faber.

Steedman, Carolyn (2002), *Dust*. Manchester: Manchester University Press.

Stevens, Hugh (2007), 'D.H. Lawrence: organicism and the modernist novel', in Morag Shiach (ed.), *The Cambridge Companion to the Modernist Novel*. Cambridge: Cambridge University Press, 137–50.

Stonier, G.W. (1933), 'Review of *Death of Felicity Taverner*', *Fortnightly Review*, vol. 133, 133–34.

Stout, Adam (2008), *Creating Prehistory: Druids, Ley Hunters and Archaeologists in Pre-war Britain*. Oxford: Blackwell.

Summers, Montague (1927), *The Geography of Witchcraft*. London, Routledge and Kegan Paul.

Swayne, G.C. (1880), 'The value and charm of antiquarian study', *The Antiquary*, vol. 1, 3–4.

Swift, Graham (1988), *Out of this World*. London: Poseidon.

Tandon, Bharat (2003), '"Among the ruins": narrative archaeology in *The Mayor of Casterbridge*', *Studies in the Novel*, vol. 35, no. 4, 471–89.

Theobald, J.R. (1932), 'John Cowper Powys', *The Bookman*, vol. 83, no. 493, 36.

Thomas Edward (1909), *Richard Jefferies: His Life and Work*. London: Hutchinson.

Thomas, Gilbert (1924), 'Review of *In Praise of England*', *The Bookman*, vol. 67, no. 397, 33.

Thomas, Julian (1996), *Time, Culture and Identity: An Interpretive Archaeology*. London: Routledge.

Thrift, Nigel (1996), *Spatial Formations*. London: Sage.

T. M. (1932), 'A Memorable Novel', *Manchester Guardian*, 9th December, 7.

Tobin, Thomas J. (1998), 'Women as others in *The Mayor of Casterbridge*', *McNeese Review*, vol. 36, 19–36.

Trentmann, Frank (1994), 'Civilization and its discontents: English neo-romanticism and the transformation of anti-modernism in twentieth-century western culture', *Journal of Contemporary History*, vol. 29, no. 4, 583–625.

Treves, Sir Frederick (1906), *Highways and Byways in Dorset*. London: Macmillan.

Trezise, Simon (2000), *The West Country as a Literary Invention: Putting Fiction in its Place*. Exeter: Exeter University Press.

Trigger, Bruce (1984), 'Alternative archaeologies: nationalist, colonialist, imperialist', *Man*, vol. 19, no. 3, 355–70.

Tylor, E.B. (1866), 'On traces of the early mental condition of man', *Proceedings of the Royal Institution of Great Britain*, vol. 5, 93.

— (1871), *Primitive Culture: Researches into the development of mythology, philosophy, religion, art, and custom*, 4th edn. 2 vols. London: John Murray.

— (1863), 'Wild men and beast children', *Anthropological Review*, vol. 1, 21–33.

Tyrrell, Robert (1888), 'The old school of classics and the new: a dialogue of the dead. Bentley, Madvig, Porson, Shakespeare, Euripides', *Fortnightly Review*, vol. 43, 48–59.

Udal, J.S. (1892), 'Witchcraft in Dorset', *Proceedings of the Dorset Natural History and Antiquarian Field Club*, vol. 13, 35–38.

Vaughan, W.H.T. (1998), 'Picturing the past: art and architecture in Victorian England', in Vanessa Brand (ed.), *The Study of the Past in the Victorian Age*. Oxford: Oxbow, 61–71.

Wagstaff, Barbara O'Brien (1995), 'The effectual angel in *Death of Felicity Taverner*', in Christopher Wagstaff (ed.), *A Sacred Quest*. New York: McPherson and Co., 224–42.

Wagstaff, Christopher, ed. (1995), *A Sacred Quest: The Life and Writings of Mary Butts*. New York: McPherson.

Wainwright, Valerie (2007), *Ethics and the English Novel from Austen to Forster*. Aldershot: Ashgate.

Walker, William H. and Michael Brian Schiffer (2006), 'The materiality of social power: the artefact-acquisition perspective', *Journal of Archaeological Method and Theory*, vol. 13, no. 2, 67–88.

Warne, Charles (1872), *Ancient Dorset: The Celtic, Roman, Saxon, and Danish Antiquities of the County, including the Early Coinage. Also an Introduction to the Ethnology of Dorset, and other Archaeological Notices of the County, by William Wake Smart*. Bournemouth: D. Sydenham.

— (1866), *Celtic Tumuli of Dorset: An Account of Personal and other Researches in the Sepulchral Mounds of the Durotriges*. London: T. Tegg.

Watts-Dunton, Theodore (1906), 'Introduction' to George Borrow, *Wild Wales*. London: J.M. Dent, i–xv.

Wescott, Glenway (1923), 'The first book of Mary Butts', *The Dial*, vol. 75, 282–84.

Wheeler, R.E.M. (1935), *The Excavation of Maiden Castle, Dorset: First and Second Interim Reports*. Oxford: Oxford University Press.

Widdowson, Peter (1989), *Hardy in History: A Study in Literary Sociology*. London: Routledge.

Wiener, Martin J. (1981), *English Culture and the Decline of the Industrial Spirit 1850–1980*. Cambridge: Cambridge University Press.

Wilde, Oscar (1994), *The Complete Works of Oscar Wilde*. London: Collins.

Williams, Raymond (1973), *The Country and the City*. London: Chatto.

— (1971), *The English Novel from Dickens to Lawrence*. London: Chatto.

Wilson, Angus (1973), 'The druid of Wessex', *Observer*, 2 December, 12.

Wilson, Daniel (1863), *Pre-historic Annals of Scotland*, 2nd edn. London: Chapman.

Wordsworth, William (1986), *The Prelude*, ed. J.C. Maxwell. Harmondsworth, Middlesex: Penguin.

Wright, Patrick (1985), *On Living in an Old Country*. London: Verso.

— (1996), *The Village that Died for England: The Strange Story of Tyneham*. London: Vintage.

Young, Robert J.C. (2008), *The Idea of English Ethnicity*. Oxford: Blackwell.

Young, Vernon (1986), 'The immense inane', *The American Scholar*, vol. 55, no. 2, 254–58.

Zeitler, Michael A. (2006), *Representations of Culture: Thomas Hardy's Wessex and Victorian Anthropology*. New York: Peter Lang.

Zimmerman, Virginia (2008), *Excavating Victorians*. Albany, NY: State University of New York Press.

Index

CPSIA information can be obtained at www.ICGtesting.com
Printed in the USA
LVOW072356110912

298438LV00003B/32/P